No Solitary Effort

No Solitary Effort

How the CIM Worked to Reach the Tribes of Southwest China

Neel Roberts

WILLIAM CAREY
LIBRARY

No Solitary Effort: How the CIM Worked to Reach the Tribes of Southwest China
Copyright © 2013 Neel Roberts

All rights reserved. No part of this book may be reproduced, stored in a retrieval system, or transmitted in any form or by any means—electronic, mechanical, photocopy, recording, or otherwise—without prior written permission of the publisher, except brief quotations used in connection with reviews in magazines or newspapers.

All Scripture quotations, unless otherwise indicated, are taken from the Holy Bible, New International Version®, NIV®. Copyright ©1973, 1978, 1984, 2011 by Biblica, Inc.™ Used by permission of Zondervan. All rights reserved worldwide. www.zondervan.com

The "NIV" and "New International Version" are trademarks registered in the United States Patent and Trademark Office by Biblica, Inc.™

Published by William Carey Library, an imprint of William Carey Publishing
10 W. Dry Creek Circle
Littleton, CO 80120 | www.missionbooks.org

Melissa Hicks, editor
Brad Koenig, copyeditor
Amanda Valloza, graphic design
Rose Lee-Norman, indexer

William Carey Library is a ministry of Frontier Ventures
Pasadena, CA 91104 | www.frontierventures.org

Cover photo is from North Thailand: Tribal background Christians harvesting rice at the J.O. Fraser Bible Training Center.

Library of Congress Cataloging-in-Publication Data

Roberts, Neel.

No Solitary Effort / by Neel Roberts.
   pages cm
Includes bibliographical references and index.
ISBN 978-0-87808-624-5
1. China Inland Mission—History. 2. Missions—Southeast Asia—History. I. Title.

23 22 21 20 19 Printed for Worldwide Distribution

Many books have been written on the successful stories of the China Inland Mission in the past. However, this book weaves together stories of successes and failures, struggles and triumphs of the China Inland Mission.

I appreciate the fact that much attention has been given to the post-Hudson Taylor period. The work among the tribal peoples, in particular the Miao and Lisu, has been carefully researched and analyzed. Two other key areas are explored in this book. Firstly, how modernity and liberal theology challenged the work and how the China Inland Mission responded to such challenge. Secondly, work has been devoted to a subject that remains extremely relevant in today's world, namely, the issue of indigenous principle, or indigenization.

The CIM, through different eras of leadership, from Hudson Taylor to Dixon Hoste and Bishop Houghton, strongly believed in the indigenous principle and emphasized working alongside the Chinese Church. According to Roberts, the missionaries evolved through stages, from being the primary evangelists, to becoming the motivators and finally the partners with the Chinese and tribal Christians.

There is much food for thought in this book for those who are grappling with critical issues in modern day missions. History informs us to critique our current practice and make wise decisions.

Rev. Dr. Patrick Fung
general director, OMF International

No Solitary Effort deserves a wider audience than just Christians interested in unreached people groups in China or SEAsia today. Suburban pastors engaged in global missions, short-term workers, Christians from tribal backgrounds, and others can all benefit. As an OMF missionary to tribes in SEAsia for over twenty-five years, Neel Roberts speaks with a wise, passionate voice as he describes the ups and downs of church planting among the Miao, Lisu, Nosu, and other tribes between 1865–1951. Christians today who partner with Majority World believers can see how a large mission organization like China Inland Mission/OMF needed to adapt from pioneer evangelism and leadership training to true partnerships between Western, Chinese, and tribal believers. Jesus said he would build his church and the gates of hell would not prevail against it (Matt 16:18). Roberts provides a historical perspective to show how many of the joint efforts produced biblical foundations that over sixty years of communism have failed to destroy. May God alone get the glory!

Julian D. Linnell, PhD
executive director, Anglican Frontier Missions

In a day and age where much is considered when discussing effective strategies in Christian mission and many churches have developed their own programs for putting those into practice, it is refreshing to read Neel Roberts pages on *No Solitary Effort*. Capturing seventy-five years of CIM history in a short book like this, and not simply touching the surface but pointing out significant details, is what this manuscript has accomplished. With his God-given ability to tell a story well in conjunction with his scholarly interest and knowledge of history, Neel Roberts has produced a piece of writing that is well worth reading for anybody interested in cross-cultural mission or responsible for anything that has to do with the mission enterprise. While the research done stays clear of promoting certain methods as "the only right approach," it shows that looking at and reflecting on what others have done in the past can render helpful insights. Some might see aspects of the work in the past in a new light. Moreover, features, possibly not even noticed before, might be recognized as what they really are: critical for eventually seeing the mission accomplished.

It is unique in the sense that I know of no other manuscript that has made a similar effort to combine the many lessons that can be learned from CIM's work, particularly in the upper Mekong region, in such a short and comprehensive way. It is the kind of book a new generation involved in missions should read!

Sam Wunderli
field director, OMF Mekong

Contents

Preface ix
Introduction xi

Chapter 1—Foundations: How the CIM Got to the Upper
Mekong Region 1
Chapter 2—First Period: 1865–1895 13
Chapter 3—The Upper Mekong Region at Last 27
Chapter 4—J. O. Fraser, the Lisu, and the CIM 71
Chapter 5—The 1940s and the Houghton Era 117
Chapter 6—In Summary 143

Appendix 153
Bibliography 157
Index 165

Preface

On occasion I have been invited by Christian missionaries in Southeast Asia to present lectures on the history of the China Inland Mission (CIM) and its successor, the Overseas Missionary Fellowship (OMF), in the Upper Mekong Region of Southeast Asia. Out of these lectures proceeded a request to put the material into written form. After reviewing the wealth of information available from primary sources, I first considered creating a compendium of stories written by the missionaries themselves with brief explanatory notes inserted as necessary. As I delved deeper into the topic, I realized that I was not in a position to make such explanatory comments. There were too many questions that I could not answer myself. Most of these questions related to how the Mission functioned as a corporate entity. Until these questions were adequately answered, the work of individual missionaries could at best be only partially understood or at worst be completely misunderstood. Therefore I decided that my focus must be on the work of the China Inland Mission and the Overseas Missionary Fellowship[1] among the peoples of the Upper Mekong Region from 1875 to 1975. After months of research and writing I discovered that I had bitten off much more than I could chew. Due to time and size constraints I have narrowed my sights for this book to the work of the CIM in Southwest China and bordering regions. This brings this story neatly to a close around 1951.

The title of this book came to me from a quote written by Robert Morrison (1782–1834) who was at one time the solitary representative of the Protestant missions in China.

> It is true, that, since health is uncertain, and life is short, the efforts of an individual being soon intermitted, produce but little effect, and therefore it becomes desirable in our plans of usefulness to unite

---

1   The China Inland Mission (CIM), which was founded in 1865, was forced to begin to withdraw from China in 1950. In 1951 it was agreed that the missionaries who withdrew from China would be given the opportunity to work in other parts of East Asia with a re-reorganized CIM. To reflect this change the name was changed to the Overseas Missionary Fellowship of the China Inland Mission (CIM/OMF) in 1951. By 1965 it was clear that reentry into China was not likely in the foreseeable future, and the CIM was dropped from the name. Therefore we will at various times refer to CIM, CIM/OMF, and OMF, based on the time periods we are discussing.

many persons who shall assist each other, and gradually attach more friends to succeed them, when they shall be required, by the great Sovereign of the universe, to remove to other worlds.[2]

I take it as axiomatic that the work of the individual missionary is of account to the degree that it builds on the labors of others and leads to the building up of a new generation of believers who will carry the work on to perfection. Therefore I seek to set the activities of individuals within the frame of the Mission's corporate efforts to evangelize the peoples of the Upper Mekong Region. Relationships with other mission agencies and with native believers are also considered. Furthermore I aim to show how the Mission interacted with the evangelical Christian communities that supported missions as well as the various governments, both Western and Asian, which for the most part barely tolerated, and in some cases actively opposed, the work.

As farmers in the Mekong Region long ago learned to work together in times of planting and reaping in order to obtain the greatest harvest so it should one day become obvious that Christians must join in cooperative efforts to reach the ends of the earth with the gospel. At the same time, I do not wish to hide in any way the reality of how hard it can actually be to labor together effectively on the mission field. It is essential to record the issues that mission leaders wrestled with in their attempts to accomplish a seemingly impossible task. Often times their greatest challenges revolved around the missionaries themselves, and not the emerging churches or the non-Christian populations they were seeking to evangelize. This reality must be acknowledged and properly dealt with if we hope to see the work, begun so long ago, brought to a successful conclusion.

While this book includes numerous historical facts, it is perhaps more of a historical study of the development of applied missiology than a history of missions. More attention will be given to why certain things were done than to comprehensively recording all that was done.

In all of this I write as a fellow Christian to friends of the cause of Jesus Christ in the non-Christian world. I hope that by sharing my findings with you it might in some way assist you to more effectively fulfill your calling in making known the glories of our God until the Day of Christ.

Maranatha!
Neel Roberts, Septemeber 10, 2012

---

2   Eliza Morrison, *Memoirs of the Life and Labours of Robert Morrison, D.D.*, vol. 2 (London: Longman, Orme, Brown, Green, & Longmans, 1839), 188. From a speech at the formation of the Singapore Institution, 1823.

Introduction

As noted in the preface, there are several ways the story of the China Inland Mission in the Upper Mekong Region can be told. One is to focus on the work of individual missionaries. Another is to attempt to record the history of the churches that were established from the local Christians' perspective. The goal here is to tell the story of the Mission as an organization. The CIM is especially suited for such a study because it claimed as one of its distinctives:

> That all the operations of the Mission are systematic and methodical; and in accordance with, and integral parts of one general and comprehensive plan for the evangelization of the whole of China; the aim of the Mission being, not to secure in a short time the largest number of converts for the C.I.M. from a limited area, but to bring about in the shortest time the evangelization of the whole Empire, regarding it of secondary importance by whom the sheaves may be gathered.[3]

What was the plan? How did it come into being, and how did it evolve over the decades? How was it applied to the unique environment of Southwest China and the bordering countries with their numerous minority groups? In what ways did the missionaries who worked in this particular region develop their own distinct methods, and to what extent did their experiences in turn affect the development of the Mission as a whole? These are the questions that will be addressed in this book.

This should be relevant to those who labor in the twenty-first century. Many Christians today question the need for organized missionary structures. With all the power of the Holy Spirit available to every believer, and every believer called to be a "missionary" to his neighbor, why should some people be set apart for a special work under the direction of human leaders? With modern transportation, global communication, and large, affluent churches that can fully support a team of missionaries themselves, are mission boards still needed? These are valid questions. A close look at how one mission agency operated in one area over a period of many years

---

3   J. Hudson Taylor, *After Thirty Years: Three Decades of the China Inland Mission* (London: Morgan & Scott, 1895), 3.

can help in the search for answers. My hope is that this book will help those who are engaged in missions as supporters, field workers, and as leaders to consider just what exactly are the benefits and the negative aspects of structured missionary endeavors. When we look at real missionaries working in cooperation, or in conflict, with others in real work situations, we can ask concrete questions and get concrete answers.

The story covers a period of approximately a century from the time Hudson Taylor first arrived in China in 1854 until 1951 when the CIM found it necessary to withdraw its workers from the country. From 1875 until 1951 the CIM maintained an almost continual working presence in the Upper Mekong Region. This stirs up questions of its own. When is a missionary endeavor considered complete? If the work was carried out properly, should it have taken so long? How do missionaries know that it is time to move on? These are difficult questions, even when working among a fairly homogeneous ethnic group, but when working in an area with numerous ethnic groups, divided by several political boundaries, the subject becomes much more complex. The CIM experience in the Upper Mekong Region provides a wonderful opportunity to delve into these questions, even if the answers are not always apparent.

Can we see God at work through human instruments and human organizations to fulfill His purposes to redeem a people for himself from out of all the nations on the earth? Skeptics have long mocked or criticized the missionary movement, first of all for claiming that there is a God who can be known by humans, and secondly for assuming that anyone has a right to claim that they represent Him here on earth. This book is not written as an apologetic aimed at skeptics. It is my conviction and assumption in writing this book that God is at work through His people in this world. The corollary is that as Christians we need to review our own actions continually to see if our works are truly His works. By looking at a work that has been going on for many decades we have ample opportunity to determine what good work, if any, has stood the test of time, and therefore, what, by implication, has shown itself to truly be a work of God.

Before entering into our story we need to briefly consider (1) the region, (2) its various peoples, (3) the mission organization, and (4) the era we will be covering.

The Upper Mekong Region

It is best to begin with the Upper Mekong Region. Geographic terms can be difficult to define. The Mekong River begins in Tibet, flows through Southwest China, forms the boundary first between Burma and Laos, then, in some places between Laos and Thailand. From there the Mekong passes through Cambodia and Southern Vietnam before at last reaching the sea. The Greater Mekong Region may be said to be the basin that empties into the South China Sea via the Mekong River. It is also used to define the conceptual area promoted by merchants and politicians of an economic/political sphere made up of the countries along the river; namely Yunnan Province in China, Burma, Laos, Thailand, Cambodia, and Vietnam. The term "Upper Mekong Region" serves the purpose of describing an area that flows over political boundaries and is defined more by topography than by any dominant race or nation that has ruled in the area. The borders that presently exist have all come into existence in the past 120 years. The region was quite unsettled until the late 1800s, and in some cases CIM missionaries were actually connected with the first Western surveys of the area. Mountains, jungles, rivers, local rulers, and bandits all tended to impede rather than promote clear borders, modernization, and uniformity.

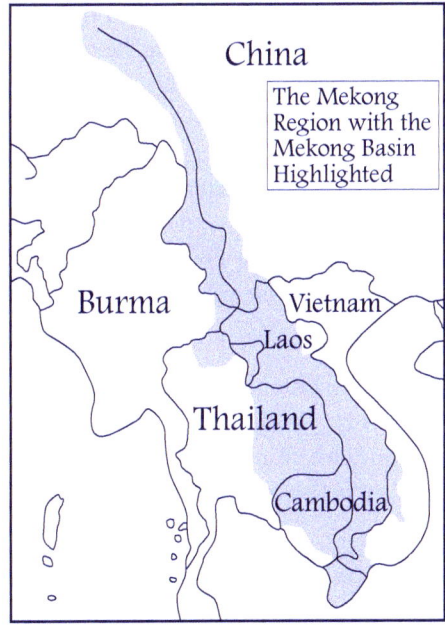

The Mekong Region with the Mekong Basin Highlighted

This book will use the geographical terms that were used by missionaries in their own writings. While it might seem simpler to only use modern place names, the reality is that it simplifies almost nothing. As recently as 2002 the Burmese military government ran newspaper headlines which referred to Thailand as Yodaya, which hearkens back to the days many centuries ago when Yodaya (Ayutthaya—the early capital of Siam, which is currently known as Thailand) was a vassal state of Burma. Meanwhile the rulers call their own country Myanmar, while most of the opposition groups still use the name Burma. The Mekong River itself has a variety of spellings and is called the Lancang Jiang by the Chinese, at least where it flows within their borders. The city of Jinghong in Xishuangpanna of Southern Yunnan is known by those who have a Thai perspective as Chiang Rung in Sipsongpanna. Therefore those who wish to learn about this part of the world will need to learn multiple names for numerous locations. Some maps along with occasional modern names in parentheses should aid that process.

While the Mekong River has long been viewed as a commercial corridor from Indochina to Southwest China, its real potential is only now being exploited in the twenty-first century with the blasting away of the rapids along the river between China and North Thailand. Climate and topography mold societies. Mountains and monsoons produced the sort of rivers that more often hindered rather than aided travel. Mosquitoes found safe havens in the valleys that were full of stagnant water for seven months of the year. These kept human population growth in check through malaria and dengue. Natural resources were present, but the great cost of seeking them out, and the even greater cost of hauling them out, meant that most fortune hunters found greener pastures elsewhere.[4]

Those who visit the region now may be easily deceived into thinking that travel is easy on the four-lane paved "highways" in Thailand or the newly paved roads in parts of Laos and Burma. In China the biggest delay to one's travel is often construction teams widening and paving rural roads. The drive from Chiang Mai to Lampang, which now takes just about an hour, was a four-day journey in the 1890s.[5] By using that simple time scale, one can readily understand how a trip that now takes a modern trekker a week could scarcely be accomplished in an entire dry season prior to the advent of asphalt roads along with stone or concrete bridges.

The People

In such an environment tribal groups maintained their independent existence long after they would have been assimilated or decimated in other parts of the world. All those who wish to discuss these groups are challenged by what to call them. This is a problem whether we are talking

---

4   Gems could be carried in one's pocket, and teak logs could be floated through rapids with minimal damage, but other resources required modern technology and modern roads to be harvested in any large quantities.

5   Lillian Johnson Curtis, *The Laos of North Siam* (Bangkok: White Lotus Books, 1998), 311–17. First published 1903 by Revell. Incidentally, Lampang was called Lakorn at that time.

about broad categories or specific ethnic groups. A popular term for some groups in Thailand is "Hill Tribes." But some groups have lived on the plains for centuries, and others were forcibly relocated to the plains during the past few decades. If we speak simply of "tribes," then what does the word "tribe" conjure up in our minds? While some groups were migratory—illiterate animists even a few decades ago—many groups are no longer so. Furthermore groups like the Nosu owned serfs and had a written language when the first white people arrived in Southwest China. Other groups like the Shan had palaces, princes, Buddhist clergy, and an ancient literature long before Chinese or Burmese rulers ever thought to lay claim to their lands. While each of these groups would be considered minorities when compared to all the Han Chinese in China, they often made up a majority of the population in their homelands. Thus the term "minority group" can stir up images in the reader's imagination which might never have entered the thoughts of the peoples being discussed in these pages.

The term "indigenous peoples" has been popularized recently in the United Nations, but it is incorrect to use it when almost all the groups currently in the region originally came from somewhere else and supplanted others upon their arrival. The terms "native" or "local," as opposed to those who are more recent immigrants, in some cases are useful, but it takes considerable historical research to be certain of who arrived at a particular place at a particular time. So for instance *some but not all* Karen and Lahu were found in the hills of what is now North Thailand long before Thailand had formal political boundaries, but groups like the Akha and Lisu for the most part arrived uninvited long after the Thai government staked its claim to the hills these tribes now occupy. In China the Hmong and Miao might be considered the native population in some of the hill regions where they now live. But their own history shows that they only moved into the hills after being supplanted in the lowlands by the Han Chinese. The CIM used the phrase "Aboriginal Tribes" in their monthly magazine, *China's Millions*, but this term has become archaic. "Ethnolinguistic group" is a fine technical phrase but has too many syllables. Moreover it assumes that one ethnic group will have one language. In reality, members of ethnic groups may change their primary language of communication within a period of one or two generations without losing their cultural or ethnic identity.

Another problem is what to call specific tribes or ethnic groups. The Hmong in China were referred to as Miao for many decades in all the official literature. One group that was first evangelized with much difficulty in the 1890s was the Heh Miao or Black Miao. But they are an altogether different group from the Black Hmong who are also known Hmong Sa. It would be anachronistic to use modern terms when quoting the reports of the early missionaries, but it would be inappropriate to refer to groups in the modern era according to obsolete terms as well.

Most groups have several names, one of which is usually the name they would call themselves in their own dialect when talking among themselves. But missionaries invariably come from the outside and first learn about an ethnic group from the lips of a neighboring ethnic group in a language that is foreign to both the missionary and the ethnic group which is being discussed. While most missionaries do make the effort to call an ethnic group by the name that they call themselves, it often takes several years of linguistic and cultural study before that term can be identified. If that name is then found to be difficult to pronounce or to transliterate into English, the chances are it won't take hold in the outside world. In the meantime a less accurate term will have gained currency, and even if it is not the best name it will be difficult to replace. For the purpose of this book we will generally refer to various groups according to the terms used by the missionaries who were writing about them and alert the reader when new terms became popular. In cases where there might be confusion, a more modern name will be found in parentheses.[6]

In concluding a discussion on names, it is worth seeking help from the Bible. Revelation 5:9, referring to Jesus Christ, states: "You were slain, And have redeemed us to God by Your blood Out of every tribe and tongue [language] and people and nation (NKJV)."[7] Such a string shows that one term is not sufficient to categorize all the different ways by which people have been dividing and grouping themselves ever since the Tower of Babel. At the same time it points out that some classifications are necessary because people are in fact divided into a variety of groups and grouping systems.

How did these various groups come to the Upper Mekong Region? Each came by a separate path over the centuries. Tribes from the east like the Hmong and Mien became hill tribes rather than be absorbed into the bottom layer of Han Chinese society. Other groups from the

---

6   I myself have been an American, a white, a WASP, an Anglo, a Shema (by members of one American Indian tribe), and a Farang (by the Thai). At times I have been mistaken for a Khaek (a Thai term which covers just about everyone from Bangladesh to Morocco), or an Indi, or a Paki (by Indian or Pakistani Muslims in Thailand). It is wise to seek to label others with a name that they approve of, without being offended or overly sensitive if a less appealing term is used by them about us.

7   Tribe (φυλη *phule*); tongue (γλωσσα, *glossa*); people (λαος, *laos*); nation (ἔθνος, *ethnos*).

Tibetan plateau, such as the Kachin and Lisu, never became lowlanders. By the time they arrived in the Upper Mekong Region, the hillsides were all that was available to them. The Tai groups, who probably originated in the area of Guangxi Province just north of Vietnam, were among the first to claim the river valleys. From the Red River north of Hanoi to the Brahmaputra Valley in Assam, the Tai became the dominant ethnic group.[8] While they established some large kingdoms in the thirteenth century, these tended to fragment into smaller principalities rather than coalesce into anything resembling nation states.

The region was no Peaceable Kingdom. Wars and rumors of wars were common, but the terrain was such that no one could hope, nor would anyone in their right mind particularly desire, to rule the whole land himself. The Shan in the valleys might try to expand their influence over other lowland communities but were generally content to leave the tribal peoples in the hills alone if they gave them a nominal tribute in due season. Great campaigns did sweep through the region periodically, as when the Burmese Konbaung Dynasty sought to bring the Sawbwas[9] in Southern Yunnan under their influence in the 1760s. This then led to the major invasion of Burma by the Manchurian Qing Dynasty from 1765 to 1769. This invasion did little to check the growing power of the Burmese who conquered Ayuthaya, the capital of Siam, in 1767. However, over the next few decades a resurgent Siam not only freed itself from Burma's yoke but also became the dominant power along most of the Mekong Basin from Cambodia to the border of Yunnan. In fact, in 1805 King Kawila of Chiang Mai, in his role as a vassal of the king of Siam, invaded the Eastern Shan State and marched as far as Chiang Rung in Sipsongpanna, taking numerous captives on the way, whom he then resettled in Lanna, which is now primarily within the confines of North Thailand.

There is evidence that some assimilation of groups has occurred in the past and that much more is occurring in the present.[10] Some of this assimilation was forced upon weaker groups by the more dominant powers in the region, but there are numerous examples of cultural transfer that

---

8   In the late 1920s Dr. Gordon Seagrave, a Baptist missionary, after treating thousands of Shan and tribal patients in Upper Burma, suggested that the Shan multiplied in the valleys because they were resistant to malaria. Gordon S. Seagrave, *Waste-Basket Surgery* (Philadelphia: Judson Press, 1930).

9   These princes were referred to in English literature as Sawbwas or Chaufas. This comes from the Shan term *Jao Pha*, which could be literally translated as "Lord of the Sky."

10   Sawaeng Malasaem, ประวัติศาสตร์ท้องถิ่น คนยองย้ายแผ่นดิน [Local history: The relocation of the Yong] (Bangkok: Thammasart University Press, 2001).

was freely entered into by both parties. When Christianity appeared on the scene and some groups responded positively to the message—along with the social and cultural implications of that message—it is important to realize that there were precedents for this behavior.[11]

When the nineteenth century arrived, there was a meeting of the Qing Dynasty of China which was ruled by Manchus, the Burmese Empire under the Konbaung Dynasty, and the Chakri Dynasty of Siam, all seeking to stake claims to the lands and peoples of the Upper Mekong Region. The arrival of the French in Indochina and the English in Northeast India and later in lower Burma added a sense of urgency to these Asian kingdoms who recognized that the Europeans would be swift to seize anything that was not nailed down by the Asian rulers themselves. The conflicts that ensued do not concern us here except insofar as they determined where missionaries could and could not travel at various times, and whose permission and favor they needed to curry if they wished to establish churches among the various peoples in the region. In actuality, missionaries and their converts could not avoid the political upheavals that would shape and reshape the region for well over a century, and for that reason wars and politics will be a concern of ours as well.

The Mission

Syrian or Nestorian Christians brought the gospel into China by the sixth century AD.[12] Details are sketchy at best but it seems that some Christian influence may have touched the Upper Mekong Region during the Middle Ages.[13] In the seventeenth and eighteenth centuries some Roman Catholic activities were carried out in Yunnan Province. This was primarily among the Han Chinese.

The first major Protestant penetration of the Upper Mekong Region began in the 1860s and 1870s. In 1861 Moses Homan Bixby of the American Baptist Mission made his first attempts to reach the Shan (Tai Long) of the Shan State in Upper Burma. They may have numbered about a million at that time. His efforts against great odds paved the way

---

11   Buddhism first reached the Tai Mau in the first century AD and has continued to spread ever since. Most but not all of the Tai peoples became Buddhist. Meanwhile, in the surrounding hills most tribal groups remained animists, but some became Buddhists and in several cases took on the Tai language as well.

12   Samuel Wells Williams, *The Middle Kingdom*, vol. 2 (New York: Charles Scribner's Sons, 1914), 275–86. First published 1882.

13   John C. England, *The Hidden History of Christianity: The Churches of the East before the Year 1500* (Hong Kong: CCA, 1998), 95.

for future workers who spread out in the Shan and Kachin States where they were to see significant ingatherings among the tribes and to a lesser extent among the Shan themselves.

In 1867, in what is now known as Thailand, another American, Daniel McGilvary, a Presbyterian, and his wife, Sarah, who had grown up as the daughter of a missionary in Bangkok, moved north from Siam to the tributary kingdom of Lanna. They settled in Chiang Mai (which was often spelled Zimme at that time) and established the Lao Mission in order to reach a number of Tai Buddhist groups who were found north of Siam and who used a script that was distinct from both that of the Shan to the west and the Siamese to the south. From that base he and his wife along with later recruits to the Lao Mission pioneered throughout what is now North Thailand, the Eastern Shan State of Burma, and even into Northern Laos and Southern Yunnan, making converts from among the various Tai Buddhist and animist groups they met with.

The CIM did not reach the Mekong Region until 1875, a decade after the Mission was founded with the goal of reaching all the interior of China. In early years there was considerable contact and cooperation with the American Baptist missionaries in Upper Burma. In later years when the CIM had to leave Southwest China, some of their work was to be transferred to the area that the Lao Presbyterian Mission had pioneered many decades before.

The China Inland Mission was founded by James Hudson Taylor with the goal of bringing the gospel to those parts of China which were not being reached or even targeted by existing Protestant missions. At the time that the Mission was inaugurated Taylor had written, "Our great desire and aim . . . are to plant the standard of the Cross in the eleven provinces of China hitherto unoccupied, and in Chinese Tartary."[14] As such the work in the Southwest of China was to be a part of the whole. Most of the work among the tribes was to occur in the two provinces of Yunnan and Kweichow (Guizhou). Even in these provinces the majority of the missionaries were engaged in work among Han Chinese in the larger towns and cities. This meant that the work among the tribes was to always compose, at most, a small portion of the overall work of the Mission. This needs to be borne in mind because it meant

---

14 Geraldine Guinness Taylor, *Hudson Taylor and the China Inland Mission*, vol. 2, *The Growth of a Work of God* (London: China Inland Mission, 1955), 69. First published 1918. The complete two-volume book can be downloaded from http://www.worldinvisible.com/library/bookcat.htm.

that many decisions which affected the work were to be made thousands of kilometers away in Shanghai by men who had never personally been engaged in tribal work themselves.

Superficial readings of some of Taylor's writings have led to extremely superficial statements about Hudson Taylor and the CIM. Even the great historian of Christian missions Kenneth Scott Latourette wrote:

> The main purpose of the China Inland Mission was not to win converts or to build a Chinese Church, but to spread a knowledge of the Christian Gospel throughout the empire as quickly as might be. To this end, when a province was entered, stations were opened in prefectural cities and, later, in subordinate ones. Preliminary exploration would, as a rule, precede these steps. The purpose was to cover the entire empire, so far as that was untouched by other Protestant agencies. Once the Christian message had been proclaimed, the fruits in conversion might be gathered by others. The aim was the presentation of the Christian message throughout the empire in the shortest possible time, not the winning of the largest possible number of conversions. In accord with this programme, the China Inland Mission did not seek primarily to build churches, although these were gathered. Nor, although Chinese assistants were employed, did it stress the recruiting and training of a Chinese ministry.[15]

Nothing that Latourette wrote was strictly incorrect, but taken together as a whole it painted the wrong picture, especially when others then quoted Latourette without studying Taylor's own writings and actions. A. J. Broomhall in his seven-volume set, *Hudson Taylor and China's Open Century*, does an excellent job of showing that Taylor did have a method, and that planting churches and working closely with native evangelists was always a major part of that plan. How that plan developed and was eventually put into practice among various people groups of the Upper Mekong Region will provide a common thread that binds this book together.

The Era

For those who want to know the end of a story before they invest the time in reading it, I provide the following outline of the era and the key events that will be covered.

Foundations

Our story begins with the opening of China to Western missionaries in the mid-nineteenth century, as a result of the clash of two empires, the

---

15   Kenneth Scott Latourette, *A History of the Expansion of Christianity*, vol. 6, *The Great Century in Northern Africa and Asia* (New York: Harper & Brothers, 1944), 329.

British and the Manchu. In between two of their wars, James Hudson Taylor came to China and learned how missions in China were being done. When he left temporarily in 1860, he took with him the seminal ideas that were to lead to the creation of the China Inland Mission.

First Period: 1865–95

The efforts to reach Southwest China took a decade to materialize and then got off to a slow start. From the very start of the work, the trading town of Bhamo in Upper Burma was established as a mission base because it was perceived as the easiest point of entry into the area. The pioneers tried to steer through a labyrinth of obstacles that were often the product of the British and Chinese government officials, who had their own agendas which they feared would be disturbed by missionary activities. As the work became more settled, the missionaries first worked among both the Chinese and the tribal people through the medium of the Chinese language. Only towards the end of the nineteenth century were some missionaries designated specifically to engage in full-time tribal work.

Second Period: The Tribes Begin to Respond 1895–1915

Tribal work began in earnest in the late 1890s as a wave of antiforeign unrest swept China. The early twentieth century saw the unprecedented turning of thousands of Miao to Christ at the time when CIM was experiencing its first major organizational change with the retirement of Hudson Taylor and the installation of D. E. Hoste as general director. The Miao themselves took the initiative not only in evangelizing their own people but also in beginning to reach out to other ethnic groups in the area. A comity agreement emerged as some of the Miao lived in areas ceded to another mission agency. Very friendly relations gradually became frayed as the work of both groups developed. The Revolution of 1911, which brought down the Manchus and brought in a weak Nationalist government, affected the work as well. The era ended with the deaths in 1915 of the leading missionaries, J. R. Adam and Samuel Pollard, who had given direction to the work among the Miao from its inception.

Third Period: The Emergence of Indigenous Methods 1916–38

This next stage saw the continued turning of the Miao to Christ and the development of work among other tribes, especially the Lisu and Nosu. As the years passed, the work became more settled with missionaries primarily engaged in training leaders in Short Term Bible Schools. J. O.

Fraser emerged with a model of what a missionary can and should seek to accomplish. He became the promoter of indigenous methods which were further developed by Allyn Cooke and John Kuhn. His methods were, depending on one's perspective, a great departure, or a logical step forward from earlier methods which Hudson Taylor had established for the Mission as a whole.

Meanwhile, as antiforeign nationalism swept through China, the Christians became first victims and then protagonists of the movement to rid China of foreign control. Indigenous methods became not merely an optional method but a necessity if the church was going to be able to stand against the accusations that believers were merely rice Christians. The 1930s was a decade of revival and advance in the midst of the growing threat of communism and Japanese aggression.

The Final Period: The Mission Is Succeeded by the Church 1938–51

The Second Sino-Japanese War, which began with the Japanese seizure of Manchuria in 1931, gradually expanded to affect the whole country by the end of the decade. On December 7–8, 1941, it merged into the Second World War. It brought great trials to China which were fully shared by the CIM missionaries. The work continued with the CIM general director Frank Houghton eloquently calling for close partnership between missionaries and the church that had emerged in China. With the war ending, a new, thorough survey of Yunnan was carried out and one hundred tribes were listed as needing the gospel. Plans were made to work with existing Christian tribal believers to reach the other tribal groups. At this time the Communists came to power and put an end to formal missionary work throughout China. Before being forced to depart, some missionaries were granted a chance to observe how the churches were being treated by the Communists and what their prospects were for the future without missionaries among them.

To contact the author please write to: prestegan@gmail.com.

Chapter 1
Foundations: How the CIM Got to the Upper Mekong Region

Why the CIM Came to Be

While it is our desire to study the work of the China Inland Mission (CIM) in the Upper Mekong Region, we must first consider why and how CIM missionaries became pioneer missionaries in the region. In our day there are very few places on earth that are truly inaccessible to evangelical Christians. That situation was quite different in the mid-nineteenth century. The Chinese Empire with its several hundred million inhabitants was for the most part off-limits to Westerners, with the exception of some Roman Catholic missionaries who lived secretly among their disciples at great risk to themselves and their flocks. The force that was to pry China open was the British army and navy; the immediate incentive was the right of British merchants to sell opium to the Chinese. While missionaries for the most part had very little interaction with opium merchants, they were lumped together with them as a foreign evil that came uninvited to China.[16] Some missionaries helped as interpreters for the British before, during, and after their military campaigns. While they were seeking to fulfill the role of peacemakers, their presence at the negotiating tables did not help improve their public image with the Chinese. That the vast majority of missionaries campaigned heavily against the opium trade did not earn them the love of the British merchants involved, nor did it get much if any favorable publicity among the Chinese in China. The average Chinese who did not know any foreigners personally was not likely to make distinctions between certain classes of foreigners who had come to their land.

---

16   It is interesting to note that for a century opium spread virtually unchecked while the gospel faced continuous opposition. It was not until the Communists came to power in 1949 and dealt severely with both opium and Christianity that at last the number of Christians began to increase until they vastly outnumbered opium addicts.

The First Opium War lasted from 1839 to 1842. When it ended, Hong Kong was ceded to the British. The five port cities of Shanghai, Ningpo, Foochow, Amoy, and Canton were opened to foreign trade. These cities quickly absorbed the existing missionaries to China. It did not exactly matter that most of China was still closed to the gospel if the opportunities presented by these newly opened cities fully occupied the attention of all the missionaries that were sent by the United States, Great Britain, and the mission societies of continental Europe. There was a need to learn the various dialects of Chinese spoken along the coast, and to establish schools and printing houses, as these were considered part and parcel of the mission enterprise at that time. However, those veteran missionaries like Walter Medhurst of the London Missionary Society, who were already fluent in several dialects of Chinese and who chose to test the limits of Chinese tolerance, found that it was not overly difficult to make itinerant visits to towns and cities not listed in the treaties.

Charles Gutzlaff, a German missionary who worked for the British government at that time, was one of those who continually tested the limits, not only of the Chinese but of the entire Mission's movement of his day. He was not content with seeing how far he could travel into the interior of China. He sought to multiply the effect by sending out a large number of Chinese itinerant evangelists to carry the gospel to all parts of the empire.

The term "itinerant" refers to a style of ministry which was very common both in the Christian world and the mission fields of the nineteenth century. Where there was a large population that had little or no knowledge of Christianity, it was in some cases thought best to have a preacher or bookseller who would *itinerate* or travel along a circuit preaching and distributing Christian literature, in the hopes of gradually increasing the level of interest until eventually groups of inquirers and then believers would emerge. As these groups emerged and the number of trained Christian workers increased, the itinerant worker would begin to hand his responsibilities over to local pastors and then expand his circuit into new unevangelized areas.

Itinerant work was not novel, nor was the idea of hiring Chinese Christians to assist missionaries in carrying the gospel further than the missionaries could do so on their own. What was novel was the scale on which Charles Gutzlaff was to promote this method in the late 1840s. Much of what Gutzlaff carried out during this period is to be found in A. J. Broomhall's *Barbarians at the Gate*. The short version of the tale is that he made a good salary working as an interpreter for the British government, and used his office as a preaching point for the gospel. This led to the formation of the Chinese Union which was a society of zealous Chinese Christians who recognized that it was their duty to evangelize China and who were willing to suffer the loss of all things on the model of Charles Gutzlaff in order to fulfill the task. To encourage them he began to solicit contributions on their behalf so they could spread the gospel to all the corners of the empire. They would return with glorious stories which he would translate into English (and his native German tongue), and thus he extracted considerable funds from Europe which made further outreach possible. Here is one sample in the curious spelling of the day:

> Funds—Besides the money collected by members, which was appropriated for local purposes, and which has lately increased, Dr. Barth, at Calw, in Wirtemberg, proved an unwearied friend of the institution, and sent from time to time his collections. Subsequently a society under the name of "Deutch Chinesische Stiftung," was purposely formed at Cassel in Germany, to aid the efforts of the "Chinese Union." The British and Foreign Bible Society like wise sent at the commencement of this year 100, to aid in the circulation of the Scriptures, whilst various private gentlemen forwarded their contributions. They proved however inadequate to the wants, which monthly increased, and now amount to above 400 dollars per month, and will likely be at the end of the year from 5 to 600. When your communication therefore reached us, we were more than 2000 dollars in debt, with the prospect of increasing our liabilities. We could, however, not bestow your generous gift to clear off old ones, but resolved to expend the same instantly for the furtherance of the Gospel, in the following manner: —Si ti guan was sent to Pekin for eight months, and received 45 dollars. Chin ze mei to Shoonking, in Che Keang, five months, 25 dollars; Wang tae chang to Tae ping foo, in Kwang se, on the borders of Tun kin, for five months, 30 dollars. He was accompanied by two assistants, each of whom received 14 dollars, total 28 dollars. [And so on and so on ...][17]

It would appear that Gutzlaff had almost single-handedly engineered a revolution in Chinese missions. But just as in the political world where most revolutions are soon crushed, so also in the world of missionary realities this revolutionary method of converting the multitudes was to prove a failure. In 1849, while Gutzlaff was in Europe, some members of the London Missionary Society began to make some detailed inquiries into the activities of the Chinese Union. This led some to cast doubts on

---

17   *The Christian Guardian and Church of England Magazine* (London: Seeleys, 1849).

the veracity of their claims. But long before the claims and counterclaims were sorted out, Gutzlaff was able to contribute materially to the long-term cause of missions in China by inspiring several dedicated Germans and Englishmen to go out to China, to live among the Chinese, to dress like the Chinese, to work closely with Chinese evangelists, and to thus cause the gospel to penetrate into the interior of China. One of those men (whose heart was already China bound) was Hudson Taylor. Taylor was stirred by Gutzlaff and joined the Chinese Evangelisation Society, which itself was formed under the inspiration of Gutzlaff.

There are many mysteries that need to be solved by some suitably qualified historian, but perhaps Gutzlaff was not as duped by his band of evangelists as some would claim. It appears that some actually did carry the gospel into the interior of China; if others simply made up stories, Gutzlaff was willing to let the stories pass uncontested in order to keep the work moving forward. It is worthy of note that at the very time when his evangelists were making their converts, the first-generation followers of Hong Siu-chuan were also emerging. These, in the early 1850s, were to become known as the Taiping rebels, who came close to toppling the Manchu Empire. In those later years they were to claim some connection with Gutzlaff, use his Bible translation, and call God by the name *Shang-ti*, which was the name that Gutzlaff was fond of promoting. This led to some speculation about Gutzlaff's involvement with the beginnings of the movement, as is noted in the comments of Captain Edmund Gardiner Fishbourne, who visited the rebels after they had captured Nanking in 1853:

> Even Gutzlaff's Chinese Union, though it was not satisfactory in all its members, or thorough in its teaching, deserves its praise.
>
> There can be no question but that it is Gutzlaff's translation of the Bible that they have; and it is more than probable that he circulated Bibles in Kwang-tong and in Kwang-se in 1848, in which province the rebellion commenced.
>
> And the Anglo-Chinese papers stated from time to time, that members of the Chinese Union were amongst the insurgents, and even that the movement had been originated by them. This was given the readier credence to, because Gutzlaff had stated that there would be a revolution soon, though others to whom he had stated this, understood him to mean that it would have its origin in secular motives. It is equally true, however, that Gutzlaff often said when people questioned the utility of his Chinese Union, or the fact that the missionaries were making any progress,—Well, wait a little, and you will see the contrary.[18]

---

18   Edmund Gardiner Fishbourne, *Impressions of China, and the Present Revolution: Its Progress and Prospects* (London: Seeley, Jackson & Halliday, 1855), 32–33.

Possibly Gutzlaff knew more about some of the early stages of the Taiping Rebellion than he chose to make public. As he died in 1851, he was not in a position to show what, if any connection there was between his work with the Chinese Union and the rebels' activities. For our purposes the big question is, to what degree did the gospel message actually take hold among the Han Chinese and the Miao of Kwangsi Province in the late 1840s? According to their own reports, the Chinese Union did send out their own evangelists to Kwangsi and to Kweichow.[19] It is evident that the Taiping Rebellion got its start with the loyal support of the Miao of Kwangsi Province.[20] The rebel leaders never went back to this recruiting ground after they marched north to Nanking. They probably had little knowledge or interest in the beliefs of the Miao or the implications of those beliefs in terms of launching a mass movement among them. Hong Siu-chuan was a disappointed Chinese office seeker and he never showed any interest in anyone besides the Chinese. The Miao in Kweichow on their part organized their own rebellion against the Manchus about the same time, but it never became anything more than a local revolt which the Manchus were able to contain until they had the time and resources to deal with it. Knowing the support that the Miao gave to the Taiping Rebellion at its earliest stages, and their warm response to the gospel in the early 1900s, we may wonder what stimulus they might have received from the evangelists of the Chinese Union, but to discover the truth of what actually happened in those early days is probably impossible in ours.

From just about any perspective, the Taiping Rebellion went very wrong. The little good that might be claimed of a war that lasted fourteen years (1850–64) and cost 20 million lives is that it stimulated Christian interest for China and led to twenty-one-year-old James Hudson Taylor being sent out from England as a missionary in 1853. By the time he was getting established in the environs of Shanghai in the mid-1850s, most foreigners saw that the Taiping rebels, for all their monotheism and use of some Christian terms, would not be the key that opened China to the gospel.

Indirectly the Taiping rebels did provide part of the key. Because of the threat they posed to the Manchu Empire at the very time that the French and British Empires were at war with her as well, it became evident to the Chinese Confucian gentry that the least of all evils was to keep the

---

19   *Christianity in China: State and Progress of the Work of the Native Evangelists Contained in a Series of Tracts* (London: Partridge & Oakey, 1850), 5, 9.

20   Thomas Taylor Meadows, *The Chinese and Their Rebellions* (London: Smith, Elder & Co., 1856), 84–88.

Manchus on the throne. The English and French were more than willing to do this once they got the political and trade agreements which they sought. These included opening Peking to foreign embassies, allowing merchants access to all of China, creation of several inland trading ports along the Yellow and Yangtze Rivers, and religious toleration. This last point was especially desired by the French who clearly foresaw that as long as they supported the Catholic Church and as long as Catholics got into conflicts of various sorts with the Chinese they could profit greatly in their role of patron and protector of the church. Years later Archibald R. Colquhoun was to write:

> The blood of the martyrs is in China the seed of French aggrandizement. France uses the missionaries and the native Christians as agents-provocateurs; and outrages and martyrdoms are her political harvest.[21]

Colquhoun was a model British imperialist and was probably biased, but he was correct nonetheless.

The official British attitude was slightly different. Government's duty was to promote and protect business. The work of missionaries was an unwanted complication which could best be dealt with by having missionaries avoid unnecessary risks. Some in the British government would later take it one step further and claim that all risks were unnecessary and missionaries should let the merchants open up the country themselves without interference.

Neither the British nor the French attitude was what an enlightened twenty-first-century Christian might consider an enlightened view, but by the mid-nineteenth century some evangelical Christians were coming to have a mature view of the relationship between church and state which recognized that the church could not and need not lean on the state for its support. From Geneva at this period the historian Merle D'Aubigné, referring specifically to the current situation in Europe, wrote:

> It is my own conviction, that at the present important period on which we have entered, evangelical truth can no longer be maintained, as formerly, by a human arm, and by the support of the State, by fortifications and cannon—but by means of the truth; by the power of the Word, and of the Holy Spirit; by the holiness and activity of Christians, and by the arm of the Lord. We must say now, as David did to Goliath, "I come not against thee with the sword, but in the name of the Most High God."...
>
> Our ramparts may be demolished, but let the standard of Christ be elevated more and more courageously amongst us, that souls may be converted, and

---

21 Archibald R. Colquhoun, *Overland to China* (New York: Harper & Brothers, 1900), 329.

baptized again with the baptism of the Holy Spirit—that Christian life may be revived in us, and Geneva become to future ages what she has been during those which are past.[22]

To evangelical Christians in the twenty-first century these words may appear to be obvious, but it was not always so. It might actually be said that it was the spread of infidelity among the ruling classes of Europe in the eighteenth and nineteenth centuries which freed evangelical Christians from the illusion that the state might be an ally of the church in the forward march of Christianity. On one hand, British evangelicals sought to put pressure on the British government to act in ways that were in line with Christian morals. On the other hand, they did not pretend that actual government policy was always an expression of God's will for his church on earth. As a result, many Protestant missionaries in China and their supporters in the West did not seek to have the church in China protected by foreign gunboats. They did however claim that the rights of a missionary who was a citizen of a Western nation was equal to the rights of the merchant. If the merchant had the right to travel, lease land, and advertise and sell his wares throughout the empire, then missionaries should share such rights in propagating their message. The Manchus wanted neither the merchant nor the missionary, and for most of their remaining years as the rulers of China they did what they could to hinder the efforts of both groups.[23]

As far as the mission agencies were concerned, there was little incentive to expand rapidly into the interior of China. First of all, the ports that were opened to missionaries after the First Opium War had already given missionaries full access to a population of 2–3 million Chinese.[24] With itineration in to surrounding towns and villages, several million more became accessible. At the 1860 Liverpool Missionary Conference, Dr. William Lockhart gave a detailed explanation of the method of itineration that the London Missionary Society had developed during those years

---

22 *Evangelical Christendom: Its State and Prospects*, vol. 3 (London: Partridge & Oakey, and Paternoster Row, 1849), 338. "A Monthly Journal Established and Conducted by Members of the British Organization in Connexion with The Evangelical Alliance."

23 Williams, *The Middle Kingdom*, 656–57. Williams was personally involved with the negotiations between the Americans and the Manchu rulers of China which led to the Treaty of Tientsin in 1858. He states that "he who is unwilling to acknowledge the overruling hand of God in this remarkable meeting of nations [involved in signing the peace treaty], would find it very difficult to acknowledge it anywhere in human history." However, in the very next paragraph he writes regarding clauses that legalized the opium trade, "The inherent wrong of the principle of exterritoriality was never more unjustly applied than in breaking down the moral sense of a people by forcing them to legalize this drug."

24 Meadows, *The Chinese*, 57.

when China was partially opened up to missions. The summary of his presentation is worth quoting in full, because in many ways it was quite similar to the model that the CIM was to use in the later 1860s and 1870s.

With regard to itinerating, it is one of those plans which has been most blest of God in China, and has been productive of greatest success. In the station where he [Dr. Lockhart] was employed they had carried out a succession of itinerancies, which had been commenced in the first instance by Dr. Medhurst and himself in 1843, and had been continued to the present time. They had adopted the plan . . . in having one large station where there were several missionaries; and he pressed upon the secretaries and officers of Missionary Societies the great advantage of having large and efficient establishments in certain localities, with a sufficient force of itinerants to go into the surrounding districts. It was essential to observe, in regard to itinerating, that single visits were almost useless. It was by keeping up a steady succession of efforts through a district of country that the real good was done. At Shanghai they had repeated instances of the good effects which followed these itinerating labours. The missionary remained a week in one place; then went to another and another, and returned to Shanghai in the course of a few weeks; from whence he began the same circuit again. The impression was thus kept up, and at all the missionary stations of the London Missionary Society near Shanghai little churches were springing up. He had been informed by recent letters from his colleagues, that many little places and villages, with which he was well acquainted, were being brought to a knowledge of the truth; and that within a circuit of fifty to eighty miles round Shanghai little churches had been formed, which had been in the first instance gathered together by this practice of itinerating, and which were now under the care of the various native agencies.[25]

It was during these years when China was being slowly pried open that Hudson Taylor was learning the art of evangelism and church planting from veteran missionaries from other societies. He did develop his own techniques and did become an "expert" through his own personal experience among the Chinese during those years. We will give attention to Taylor's own distinctive methodology and how at some stages his methods differed from others, but it must be emphasized that he was not a revolutionary or a critic. He appreciated what he saw other mission societies doing. In later years he could wholeheartedly promote their efforts and encourage Christians to support their work and go out as members with them to China. Taylor did not find fault with what most missionaries were doing in China. What he was critical of was the

---

25 Dr. Lockhart, *Conference on Missions Held in Liverpool*, edited by the secretaries to the conference (London: Nisbet, 1860), 38–39.

tragically small interest shown by Christians in the homelands to the plight of several hundred million Chinese who were without God and without hope in the world. He was critical of what was being left undone due to too few laborers.

Ning-po, to the south of Shanghai, was to become the primary sphere of Hudson Taylor's ministry from 1856 to 1860. Here he and fellow missionaries established a small church, which in a short time began to reach out to neighboring towns and villages. Through medical work, preaching in the hospital, and evangelistic outreach, the congregation grew to sixteen baptized believers with twelve more preparing for baptism by early 1860. This was Hudson Taylor's apprenticeship in the art of church planting among the Chinese. He saw that prayer and labors properly executed resulted in Chinese coming to faith and churches emerging. This was in line with his faith and expectation. If the gospel was preached, God would bless the work and Chinese would come to faith.

After six years in China, in 1860 Hudson Taylor, at the age of twenty-eight, returned to England with his wife, Maria, and daughter, Gracie. His health was broken and he needed time to recover. He also longed to stir up Christians in Great Britain to go forth as missionaries to China. He had been in China long enough to know what sort of workers were needed. He had ended his formal ties with the Chinese Evangelisation Society (CES) several years earlier, primarily due to the fact that he was committed to honoring God by not going into debt and the Society was not equally committed to that principle. But he was able to leave in such a graceful manner that the key individuals who supported him when he first went out with the CES continued to do so afterwards.[26]

On his return to England, as he slowly regained his health, he devoted considerable time to working on the translation of the New Testament in the Ning-po dialect in a romanized script. He was in regular communication with not only his co-laborers in Ning-po, but missionary associates involved in work throughout China as well. He also was regularly engaged in inner-city ministry in London where he befriended like-minded and like-hearted Christians who shared his love for Jesus Christ and concern for the lost. This meant that while he was in England he was actively engaged in a China-related ministry, but was not an agent of any mission agency which might circumscribe what he should or should not be involved with. He,

---

26 The fact that the CES ceased to exist in 1860 helped create a situation where Hudson Taylor and his co-laborers who eventually formed the CIM could be seen positively as successors to the CES rather that a splinter group from them.

unlike most furloughed missionaries of his day, was absolutely free to act in accordance with how he felt led by the Holy Spirit. The others were free to act in accordance with how the directors of their societies felt led by the Spirit. These societies were relatively few in number in that day and generally connected with particular denominations. They had numerous fields calling for their attention and a limited number of churches from which to draw workers and funds. The directors of the various societies had to balance the needs of various fields worldwide with the potential resources they could draw upon. They sought to do what they could, based on the means they had available. They were eager to contribute to the evangelization of China but did not feel they had the mandate to attempt to evangelize all of China. While they desired that missionaries on furlough would give rousing speeches, they had no intention of allowing those missionaries to set the agenda in terms of allocating where laborers would be sent. Taylor, on the other hand, became an advocate for China throughout all of Great Britain, and he was not simply representing a single mission society. When Hudson Taylor could not convince these societies to give special attention to China in line with the needs and opportunities that Taylor saw there he set out to accomplish that which no society would dare attempt: the evangelization of the whole Chinese Empire.

Had his health been better, it is more than likely that he would have recruited five new workers to join the work that was growing out of Ning-po. He would have been back in China by 1862, or 1863 at the latest. Had that been the case, the history of the church in China and in the Upper Mekong Region would have taken on a vastly different complexion. It was his enforced stay in Great Britain for half a decade that made him realize that the key to China was in the hands of the church in the West and that he was called of God to change the heart of that church. On June 25, 1865, Hudson Taylor submitted to God's will for his life and took the step to pray "for twenty-four willing skilful labourers" for the unevangelized provinces of China. That prayer was the beginning of the China Inland Mission. While several workers had gone to China while Taylor was still in Great Britain, the visible beginning of the CIM began when Taylor brought out seventeen new workers to China on the clipper ship *Lammermuir* in 1866.

Comparing Charles Gutzlaff and Hudson Taylor

Here we must pause to see the similarities and differences between Charles Gutzlaff and Hudson Taylor. Both were focused on China's millions. Both saw that the key to reaching China was through Chinese

Christians under the supervision of, or side by side with foreign missionaries. Both saw, even as Robert Morrison foresaw decades earlier, that a mission agency was needed to accomplish the task. Morrison could only write letters to encourage others to make it happen. Gutzlaff could rouse Christians in England and the continent to form agencies and send workers out to do it to the best of their abilities. Taylor would actually make the direction of such a mission his primary responsibility for over three decades. Gutzlaff did all things with haste.[27] Taylor was a man who paid attention to detail. Gutzlaff, in brief speaking engagements, inspired others to serve God among the Chinese; Taylor made relationships that in many cases lasted a lifetime, whereby he saw those he personally trained becoming leaders of the movement he set in motion.

More research needs to go into this point, but it does seem that Gutzlaff was theologically, temperamentally, or financially tied to the British government. He apparently believed that God was going to use "Christian" governments to open China. At a time when he did not need to work for the British in order to live in China (the 1830s and 1840s), he made the choice to give up his evangelistic tours of the coast because it was incompatible with his employment as an interpreter for the British.[28] Without being judgmental (but with a few suspicions), it does seem that Gutzlaff was committed to serving two masters. Taylor was distinctly different. A. J. Broomhall notes that Taylor did provide interpreting services to Thomas Meadows, the British consul at Ning-po during his early years there, but did so free of charge.[29] Taylor was willing to be of service to Her Majesty's government but would not compromise his first call to be a minister of Jesus Christ.

---

27 William Dean, *The China Mission* (New York: Sheldon, 1859), 149. William Dean was a contemporary of Gutzlaff who knew well of his works. This personal knowledge of the man adds weight to his words, "In all his writings, as well as his instructions to the people, there are marks of, what was true in fact, great haste."

28 Robert Morrison had no option but to be an employee of the British East India Company if he wished to live in Macao or Canton.

29 A. J. Broomhall, *Hudson Taylor and China's Open Century*, vol. 3, *If I Had a Thousand Lives* (London: Hodder & Stoughton, and Overseas Missionary Fellowship, 1982), 127–28. Presumably Meadows had a good command of Mandarin but needed help with the Ning-po dialect.

Chapter 2
First Period: 1865–1895

Hudson Taylor and Nineteenth-century Evangelicalism

I will not try to show the step-by-step development of Hudson Taylor's missionary principles and practices, which are traced in great detail in *Hudson Taylor and China's Open Century*, but rather consider the model that he was practicing and promoting as the CIM thrust out workers into the interior of China from the 1860s through the 1890s.

Hudson Taylor was very much a product and proponent of mid-nineteenth-century evangelicalism, which was closely connected with the modern missionary movement. William Carey was known as the father of that missionary movement. He was born in 1764, went out to India in 1793, and died in 1835 when Hudson Taylor was three years old. Carey, the first missionary sent out by the Baptist Missionary Society of England, believed that denominational mission societies should each pick out their sphere of ministry. They should pray for other groups to be blessed in their own vineyards, but he did not envision much closer interaction except in such matters as producing tracts or translating and printing Bibles. Then there was the Missionary Society founded in 1795. It later became known as the London Missionary Society (LMS). It aimed to unite all paedo-baptist groups (those which practiced infant baptism) but, with the notable exception of some Presbyterians including Robert Morrison, the LMS soon became a primarily Congregationalist mission society. The missionary movement did draw Christians from various backgrounds closer together. The enormity of the task and the recognition of the need to pray for all Christian mission work throughout the world brought Christians together who might otherwise have been divided by theological differences. It does appear that, as Christians became increasingly engaged in seeking to fulfill Christ's commands both at home and abroad, they were inevitably drawn closer to one another.[30]

---

30   Rose Dowsett, "Cooperation and the Promotion of Unity: An Evangelical Perspective," *Towards* 2010 (April 2007), http://www.towards2010.org/downloads/t2010paper08dowsett.pdf.

When Taylor created the CIM, it was as interdenominational as he was himself. His own background was Methodist, but his family had been part of a reform movement that broke away from the mother church when they felt it was veering away from the methods of John Wesley. When he went to China he was sometimes mistaken for a Brethren because he had close fellowship with them in England before going out to the field. Later he attached himself to a Baptist church but attended other churches regularly. This was not considered abnormal behavior, because in a sense he was a missionary at large for the cause of China and was actively helping various societies to select and prepare candidates to go to China. This was possible because of the positive effects of the revivals that swept through Great Britain in the late 1850s. A personal relationship with Jesus Christ, rather than denominational affiliation, was what drew hundreds of thousands of believers together. This new dynamic was what made it possible for Hudson Taylor to establish a *Mission* with the inland of China as its object, rather than a *Society* with a denomination as its subject.

For the evangelicals of the mid-nineteenth century, the one great essential for this life and eternity was to know Jesus Christ. Evangelicals rejoiced in the relationship that each person could have with Jesus. There were several missiological implications to this emphasis.

First of all, individuals needed to hear the gospel, even if they numbered in the hundreds of millions. The powerful story Taylor told of his Chinese friend Peter who drowned because of the callous indifference of nearby Chinese fishermen led to the following very practical application. In Hudson Taylor and the China Inland Mission the story is summarized in this fashion:

> In Scotland, with its population of four millions, several thousand ministers were needed to care for the spiritual interests of people already flooded with gospel light. China, with a hundred times as many precious, immortal souls, had not even one Protestant missionary, on an average, to every four millions. Moreover, its ninety-one missionaries of all societies were not by any means evenly distributed. They were gathered in a few—a very few—centres near the coast. Confined to the treaty ports, they were in touch with a mere fringe of the population of the provinces in which they were found; while beyond lay the vast interior, inhabited by two hundred million of our fellow creatures, amongst whom no voice was raised to tell of salvation, full and free, through the finished work of Christ. Yet we believe that the wicked shall be turned into hell, and all the nations that forget God. Amazing

inconsistency, appalling indifference to the revealed will of Him Whom we call Master and Lord, and to the deepest needs of the human soul![31]

This led Taylor to test whether his listeners had a living faith that led to service or a dead faith that would not work.

"Do you believe that each unit of these millions has an immortal soul," he questioned searchingly, "and that there is 'none other name under heaven given among men' save the precious name of Jesus 'whereby we must be saved'? Do you believe that He and He alone is 'the Way, the Truth, and the Life,' and that 'no man cometh unto the Father' but by Him? If so, think of the condition of these unsaved souls, and examine yourself in the sight of God to see whether you are doing your utmost to make Him known to them or not."[32]

The concept here that "each unit of these millions has an immortal soul" meant that all other issues must shrink to insignificance in the hearts and minds of those who believed that this was true. The task was enormous but it was very clear. The gospel had to be presented to each person. Some were critical, then as well as now, of this individualistic religion with its unabashedly spiritual focus, but the criticism stands or falls on the issue of whether or not each person, even if he is one of millions, has an immortal soul. There were many Christians in Europe and America at that time who firmly believed that this was true. That is why Taylor could and did draw thousands of Christians together with a common burden, which often motivated them for the rest of their lives to pray continually, to give sacrificially, and in many cases to go, without regard to personal well-being, to bring the gospel to those who had never heard.

Rev. James Hudson Taylor as a Strategist

Ralph D. Winter (1924–2009) was a missiologist well known for his interesting quotes. With regards to J. Hudson Taylor he wrote, "Even his early anti-church-planting missionary strategy was breathtakingly erroneous by today's church planting standards."[33] This is interesting because it suggests that missiologists had carefully studied Taylor's strategy at the time that Winter's quote was published in the 1990s. While Taylor was constantly making known both his strategy and the reasons for it, there does seem to be a lack of understanding about what he was trying to do. Perhaps part of the problem was that he became known

---

31 Taylor and Taylor, *Hudson Taylor*, 6–7.
32 Ibid., 7.
33 Ralph Winter and Steven Hawthorne, *Perspectives on the World Christian Movement: A Reader*, rev. ed. (Pasadena: William Carey Library, 1992), B-38.

as a man of faith, who emphasized our union with Christ as our source of strength for ministry. He emphasized trusting in God for finances, maintaining field-based leadership, dressing in Chinese clothing, and living close to the people. He not only worked with Christians from many denominations and countries, but also received applicants who had little formal training but a real heart for evangelism. While others have given much attention to the principles by which the CIM operated, the actual work they were trying to accomplish seems to have been often overlooked. Some of those who wrote about his ministry wanted to use the life of Taylor and the work of CIM as a model of how God should be trusted and obeyed. Perhaps universal spiritual truths were emphasized at the expense of missiological principles that might only be relevant to those who were doing pioneer missionary work in or near China. Be that as it may, it now needs to be recognized that Taylor did clearly express his views on what the CIM was to do. These views did mature and develop over the years, but he never departed from his original intent when he founded the Mission. Therefore it is necessary to let Taylor speak through his own words so that we can understand exactly what it was that he sent out hundreds of foreign and Chinese workers to accomplish.

In the third issue of *China's Millions* the CIM's Plan of Operations was clearly laid out:

Plan of the Operations of the China Inland Mission

In China, we might mass our Missionaries at the Free Ports; but such stations, while convenient for correspondence and European society, would have the disadvantages of all the evil influences of a large and nominally Christian community, among whom are many whose lives are less moral than those of the heathen around them. The early Missionaries, appear rather to have scattered themselves. They visited important centres, usually in twos or threes; stayed there long enough to commence a work, and then trusted much to the keeping of God, and to such help as could be afforded by epistles and occasional visits, for its further progress. They had advantages which we do not possess in China, in the godly Jews and proselytes, already acquainted with the Old Testament Scriptures, who were found everywhere; and who, when converted, soon became able to lead and instruct the converts from among the heathen. We may, therefore, anticipate the necessity of a somewhat prolonged residence in our districts, for the purpose of instructing in the Word of God those who may be converted. Still, the general principle, if a true one, should be kept in mind. Our desire, therefore, is:

First, to send two Missionaries, together with two native converts, to each unevangelized province of China, who may begin by itinerating through the province, and gather believers as the Lord enables them; locating themselves for a period of years in some important centre (say the capital of the province, if practicable), when He gives an open door.

Next, with the aid of converted natives of the province, to extend the work to the capitals of the circuits, then to prefectures, and subsequently to the county cities, from which it may easily be carried to the more important towns and villages of the county itself.

How Far Carried Out

But missionaries cannot go into distant provinces without knowledge of the language, customs, and habits of the people; and those who will become native assistants need, in the first instance, converting, and then instructing; and require time to show themselves possessed of gifts and of suitable spirit for such work.

Commencing from the basis of Ning-po, where God had already used us in gathering a Church, we began our operations as a Mission, by occupying the capital of the province, Hang-chau, for a few years. Thence we extended our work to the capitals of the four circuits into which the province is divided; and have since sought to occupy as many of the prefectural and county cities as we have been able. In other words, we have endeavoured to gain experience and suitable labourers, by carrying out among the thirty millions of Cheh-kiang (the province to which God first called us), the plan which we wish to see worked in each of the others.

From that province, again, we extended our operations by the Grand Canal to the northern part of Kiang-su, and by the Yang-tse-kiang to the (then) wholly unoccupied province of Gan-hwuy, and to stations in Kiang-si and Hu-peh, as bases for further operations in the regions beyond. We have gradually gathered around us a number of native Christians, and a staff of seventy-six native assistants, by whose instrumentality mainly, we are carrying on work in fifty-two stations—most of them important centres, and most of them occupied by our mission alone.[34]

This plan was fairly closely followed. Experience proved a good teacher and, with time, adjustments to the plan were made. In 1895 Hudson Taylor restated the distinctives of the CIM in such a way as to show that after thirty years their objectives had not changed, but he had become more precise in expressing why they were doing what they were doing.

That all the operations of the Mission are systematic and methodical; and in accordance with, and integral parts of, one general and comprehensive plan for the evangelization of the whole of China; the aim of the Mission being, not to secure in a short time the largest number of converts for the C.I.M.

---

34 China Inland Mission, "Plan of Operations of the China Inland Mission," *China's Millions*, September 1875, 31–32.

from a limited area, but to bring about in the shortest time the evangelization of the whole Empire, regarding it as of secondary importance by whom the sheaves may be garnered. Thus in occupying a new province, the first station, if practicable, is opened in the capital; though it is well known that this is the most difficult place in the province in which to gather a Church. The next step is, if possible, to open stations in the chief prefectures, then in the subordinate ones; leaving, as a rule, places of less importance to be occupied later on. If the staff thus needed were concentrated in a country district, a larger number of converts might be expected in a few years; but the influence of these country Christians would not be likely to extend beyond the boundary of their own villages. By the before-mentioned plan centres are opened from which the Gospel may be diffused throughout the whole extent of a province.[35]

It may be that this paragraph was misconstrued to imply that the establishment of churches was not a priority for Hudson Taylor and the CIM. These words may best be understood to mean that, in order to systematically reach all parts of the empire in the shortest possible time, it was necessary as a first step to establish mission centers and local congregations in each provincial capital as swiftly as possible. Then it would be possible to reach all the prefectures, counties, towns, and villages in each province simultaneously. This could only occur if an itinerant form of ministry was carried out in each province of the empire at the earliest possible date. The alternative would be a slow progressive march from the coast to the west, which would mean that in each successive province the work would need to be begun anew after the work in the more easterly provinces was considered complete.

Itineration as Preparation for a Great Ingathering

In the May 1877 Shanghai Missionary Conference, Hudson Taylor was granted an opportunity to explain his approach of using itineration near and far as a step toward the complete evangelization of all of China. There were some who tended to be critical of his approach or at least of what they had heard about his approach, so he was careful to explain the evangelistic methods of the CIM and the rationale behind them in great detail. He did not disparage the work of those who had a more localized, pastoral ministry, but showed why it was essential for the CIM missionaries to begin with itineration when entering new provinces.

> What is the place of itinerate work amongst the various agencies for spreading the gospel in populous and extensive countries?

---

35   Taylor, *After Thirty Years*, 3.

First Period   19

> The correct reply to this question will, I conceive, go far to remove some misconceptions which have existed about such work, and to correct mistakes which have sometimes been made in its prosecution. Here, as in every other part of our work, the Word of God must be our guide, and the example of our Lord and of His Apostles, as recorded there, our examples; while history shows the success of their efforts. Itinerate work should be looked on (1) as a most important *preliminary* to localized work, (2) as principally valuable as a *preparatory* agency, not being in any sense a final work, and (3) as necessary *so long* as there is any region without the stated preaching of the Gospel.

He recognized that both the message and the messengers were going to be completely new and foreign in each location they entered.

> The missionary who has frequently itinerated through a district is looked on by many with kindly feelings. His occasional presence has removed many misconceptions: he has made many friends. His character and object are becoming understood, and though he may not in *all* cases escape opposition, he will do so in *some*: and in others, the help he has secured will go far to carry him through it.

Not only did it take time for the messenger to become understood, it also took years for the message to be understood and considered desirable by the mass of the population. He considered it axiomatic that it generally took "five, ten or twenty years of labour, before any large ingatherings are made." Therefore the sooner the process began, even with a limited number of workers, the sooner a large number of people would become responsive to the gospel. Once again he qualified his statement.

> Some will be converted by the first promulgation of Christianity, others will be more gradually drawn into the fold; but many, many more will be prepared and preparing for the pastoral labours that *always should*, and in the providence of God *usually do*, follow the first itinerate efforts.[36]

Hudson Taylor expected some immediate results from itinerant ministry, but he expected more long-term results as well. He had a plan that would require hundreds and even thousands of workers and take decades to complete; but which would then result in great ingatherings of Chinese believers in every part of the Chinese Empire.

The Role of Chinese Workers

One area where we see an evolution of thought was with regard to the relative merits of using native as opposed to foreign workers. In 1873 Taylor wrote:

---

36   China Inland Mission, "Itineration Near and Far as an Evangelizing Agency: Delivered by the Editor at Shanghai before the Missionary Conference," May 12, 1877, *China's Millions*, September 1877, 123.

I am aiming at such organization of our forces as will enable us to do more work with fewer foreign missionaries. I think I may eventually attain to one superintendent and two assistant foreign missionaries in a province, with qualified Chinese helpers in each important city, and colporteurs in less important places. I hope I may be able, ere the year closes, to commence a college for the more thorough training of our Chinese helpers.[37]

This was written shortly before the CIM began to make its spectacular launch into the nine unevangelized provinces, and when highly effective recruits from Britain were still somewhat rare. He never followed up with this thought. He soon came to believe that foreign missionaries were needed in large numbers. A letter in *China's Millions* in 1878 by Arthur Douthwaite, who had only been on the field for four years at the time, showed the model that was developing in districts where work had become somewhat established already.

Among our converts in Kin-hwa there are two young men who are likely to prove very useful in spreading the Gospel, so I have invited them to come here for six month's study, and afterwards I will propose them to Mr. Taylor as preachers. They are very earnest, and have suffered no small amount of petty persecution for Christ's sake, and as far as I can see are just the sort of men we want.

The Prefecture of Kin-hwa contains seven district cities, in only one of which has the Gospel been preached; but I hope, if it be the Lord's will, to open a station in each of them next year.

The more I see of mission work here the more I feel convinced that if China is to be won for Christ, it will be by *Chinamen* and not by the hated foreigner, therefore I think the more *reliable* native helpers we can get the sooner our work will be accomplished . . .

A married missionary would find it hard to live on less than six hundred dollars a year, but *ten* native preachers could be supported at the same cost. A foreigner must have a better home than a native, and, moreover, must occasionally be sent home to recruit his health, etc. So you will see the great advantage of employing native agents when trustworthy men can be obtained.

I think that after a foreign missionary has "evangelized" for a few years, or by any means gathered a few converts about him, he should devote all his energies to *teaching* his converts, and to the special training of such as after careful consideration and prayer he may decide on employing. Then when he has got a number of out-stations opened and little churches formed in different parts of his circuit or "diocese" his time will be most profitably occupied in visiting, teaching, and encouraging those over whom he is

---

37　Marshall Broomhall, *The Jubilee Story of the China Inland Mission* (London: China Inland Mission, 1929), 90. First published 1915.

placed, who naturally look up to him for help and advice almost as a child looks up to its parent.[38]

A caution was evident in the matter of employing native workers, but when "reliable" and "trustworthy" ones had been trained after "careful consideration and prayer" and proposed to Mr. Taylor, presumably for his final decision, there was reason to hope for significant results.

Years later at the 1890 Shanghai Missionary Conference, Taylor was invited to give the opening sermon. In it he made a plea that an effort be made by all mission societies to raise up a thousand more missionaries for China. He stated:

> I do not know of any missionary work in China, and I have never heard of any, on which the LORD's blessing has not rested, or cannot rest, and in which we may not hope to see great enlargement....I do not think our present methods of work want to be materially modified, and certainly none of them should be weakened or abandoned, -they should all be strengthened,- but it does seem to me that we want to take this additional command of rapid evangelization to our hearts, (for I think it is additional) and say, what did the LORD mean, nay, what does the LORD mean to-day, by saying in his Holy Word, "Preach the Gospel to every creature. duty."[39]

Taylor was not calling for new methods. He sought a vast increase of workers who would follow the tested methods of the pioneers, along with an increased emphasis by new workers on widespread evangelism as a preparation establishing churhces and making disciples throughout the entire Empire.

Missionaries Needed

An area of controversy in 1890 continues to be one today. It had to do with whether or not it was a good policy to employ native workers with foreign funds in order to hasten the spread of the gospel in the early stages of the work. In this area Hudson Taylor held the middle-ground position between his old friend John Livingston Nevius and some of the more traditional missionaries. Nevius was an American Presbyterian who arrived in China about the same time as Hudson Taylor and devoted his life to what would now be known as a church planting ministry. His work in Shan-tung Province was highly effective. Nevius was committed to what he, in 1886, called "New Methods." Others called them "the

---

38 China Inland Mission, "The Work in Kin-chau: Native Preachers" [A. W. Douthwaite's letter of June 22, 1878], *China's Millions*, November 1878, 161.

39 *Records of the General Conference of the Protestant Missionaries of China held at Shanghai*, May 7-20 1890 (Shanghai: American Presbyterian Missionary Press, 1890), 1.

Nevius Method." These would later come to be called indigenous principles or three-self principles, which meant that missionaries would establish churches which were self-propagating, self-governing, and self-supporting. These concepts were not "discovered" by Nevius. Henry Venn of the Church Missionary Society and Rufus Anderson of the American Board of Commissioners for Foreign Missions had advocated these concepts for decades. Most missionaries on the field saw them as goals to be reached whereby missionaries would gradually hand over responsibilities to a church or a group of churches as they became mature enough to take on the responsibilities themselves. John Nevius was one field missionary who actually sought to apply them to pioneer work situations. He advocated that these principles should determine the method of the missionaries from the very beginning so that there would be very little or nothing to be turned over by the missionaries to the native church at some undefined time in the future.[40] Christians should continue in their previous occupations when they became Christians and serve God in the midst of their own community and without a salary. When churches grew and matured, it would be time enough for the local believers to choose those most suitable among them and provide them with financial assistance so that they could devote themselves to full-time service. As for meeting places, it was not necessary for foreigners to buy land and build a chapel; the homes and property of the church leaders would serve the purpose. Eventually chapels could be built by the Christians themselves on their own land with minimal support from the missionary.[41] As he promoted his views, it was natural that those who used the "silver method" as it was then referred to, and hired native workers would be somewhat critical. Hudson Taylor did not follow the Nevius Method, nor did he criticize it. Rather he used the topic to renew his plea for a united call for more missionaries.

> Rev. J. H. Taylor was asked why flood the country with foreign missionaries, who would be useless for three years, [while they learned Mandarin] when a few native evangelists are worth so much more? Mr. Taylor replied that there are no men fit to be used in this way as evangelists, who are not already used. Perhaps more are already used than is for the good of the church. If the missionaries are "useless for three years," they would be better out of China than in it.[42]

---

40 John Livingston Nevius, *Methods of Mission Work* (New York: Foreign Mission Library, 1895), http://www.newchurches.com/mediafiles/MethodsofMission-Nevius.pdf.

41 Ibid.

42 Report of the Missionary Conference, 33.

He recognized the value of hiring native workers (or supporting them with foreign funds) but felt that most were limited in what they could accomplish. Not being a mere armchair strategist, Taylor could see the strengths and weaknesses of using native workers as pioneer evangelists. One issue was that, while a congregation might benefit spiritually by sending out some of its best workers to start ministries elsewhere, there was a point of diminishing returns. The church in Ning-po, which Hudson Taylor helped to found in 1857, was a case in point. From this congregation a church planting movement had taken place which spread throughout Chekiang Province. In 1895 he was to write:

> The work here, commenced by Mr. Hudson Taylor and Mr. John Jones in 1857, was carried out by Mr. James Meadows from 1862 till the end of the year 1868. All of the first native helpers of the Mission were drawn from the membership of the Ning-po Church to the great benefit of the work generally, but to the serious loss of the Church itself. Nearly all the older members have passed away, many of them having been aged when baptized. The few who remain have been ministered to for some years by an unpaid native helper, more recently under the guidance of Mr. Warren.[43]

This helps to explain why Taylor made such a strong statement at the Shanghai Conference of 1890 "that there are no men fit to be used in this way as evangelists, who are not already used." It was not that the Chinese Christians were not good evangelists or church planters, but rather that their current numbers were so few that if too many were encouraged to engage in pioneer work, the churches that they came from would be left destitute.

A further issue was that even good Chinese workers were often unable to communicate in the vernacular once they departed from their home district. As early as 1877 he stated:

> The eighteen provinces of China in many respects more resemble eighteen kingdoms, or at least the provinces of some ancient empires, than the divisions of any modern dominion. The uniting bond is very slender, especially between those most remote. Viceroys of the different provinces are called by the Chinese "little kings," and are almost absolute in their own jurisdiction. Then the differences of dialects, and the clannish feelings of the Chinese, make natives of one province almost as much foreigners in another as we are. There is nothing more evident than that—

> The evangelisation of China must mainly be effected by native Christians. It is becoming almost as manifest that as a rule these natives can only effectively work in or near their own native districts.[44]

---

43 Taylor, *After Thirty Years*, 40.

44 China Inland Mission, "The Work of the China Inland Mission," *China's Millions*, April 1877, 46.

Taylor was not being patronizing here. He was stating what he had learned from experience. Most Chinese, at that time, were not highly educated, did not speak Mandarin as their first language, and had not learned to read and write sufficiently to read a Bible with any degree of comprehension upon first contact with the gospel. Of course the *literati* were well educated, but precious few of them were coming to faith in Christ, and the sort of education they had received would not necessarily have been beneficial in preparing them for the life of an itinerant evangelist in a distant province. So when all the factors had been duly considered, it still appeared that if several hundred million Chinese were going to hear the gospel, the messengers who would initiate evangelism in the unreached provinces, prefectures, and counties to a large extent would need to be recruited from Europe and America. Their converts would admittedly be relatively few in number, but those firstfruits in each center would form the nucleus of native workers who would evangelize the mass of the Chinese round about them.[45]

As for the question of how long it would take to make a missionary useful, Taylor did not believe it would take very long at all. Learning Chinese was a long process, but once a new worker had gained the essentials during his first year at language school, he could continue his studies in the field as he worked alongside senior missionaries and experienced Chinese evangelists. The missionaries who would engage in the evangelization of China did not need to master the Chinese classics or learn to run a mission station and school with all its Chinese staff in order to be "useful." They needed to be able to repeat the gospel story in a winning manner, in Mandarin and the local dialects, over and over again in tea shops and crowded streets, in city after city for months at a time. It would be hard work but not a whole lot harder than what an evangelist would be expected to experience in a city of England or on the frontier in America.

From the very start Hudson Taylor considered Chinese evangelists to be co-laborers with foreign missionaries. The failed experiment of the Chinese Union showed that the Western commitment had to go further than simply sending money. There was, however, no apology for sending money. Chinese co-workers were dependent on God to move the hearts of donors to contribute toward their needs just as were their foreign co-laborers. As churches grew and chose gifted individuals to pastor them, the congregations learned to support those workers. In many cases new churches would themselves contribute funds to support both their own pastors as well as evangelists who went to neighboring counties. (Baptist,

---

45   Ibid., 46–47.

Anglican, and Presbyterian missionaries along the coast of China had some examples of churches that were begun with paid workers and foreign-bought property, which eventually became significant contributors, to not only their own congregational needs but also to mission work elsewhere.) New missionaries would ideally be paired with Chinese evangelists during itinerant preaching journeys. The missionary would only have a minimal knowledge of Mandarin and perhaps little or no familiarity with local dialects, but his language would grow with use. He would not be as effective in drawing and keeping an audience as a Chinese evangelist. He was not there to attract a crowd by looking foreign. The whole idea of native dress and following Chinese customs in all things not sinful was expressly designed to keep the foreigner from standing out as foreign.

So what was the foreign missionary needed for? Taylor was convinced that the Chinese had to see godliness, and that meant that godly Christians needed to live among them and be seen by them. In 1886 Taylor gave a series of messages to missionaries in Shansi Province that were recorded in *Days of Blessing in Inland China*. All who set their hearts on missionary service would do well to read these words of wisdom. In these messages he revealed his views on what would in a later age be known as incarnational ministry.

> We tell this people the world is vain; let our lives *manifest* that it is so. We tell them that our home is above—that all these things are transitory—does our dwelling look like it? Oh, to live consistent lives! The life of the Apostle was thoroughly consistent. Everyone saw that he was a stranger and a sojourner; no one could feel that *his* home was here: all saw that it was up there ...
>
> Now do not you and I also want to live lives that will emphasize our teaching? But it is no use living lives such as *would* emphasise our teaching, if our lives are out of sight and our teaching only is in sight. Must we not seek to make our lives as public as our teaching? This is a grave difficulty. The man who lives two or three miles away from the chapel, and merely goes and preaches to his audience is often disappointed. I have known more than one who did not live among the people, who preached thousands of sermons, and yet left China having seen little result. I believe that if such men *could* have worked among the people all day, and have come into touch with them, their life might have told, and half the sermons produced greater results. What wisdom we need to live lives that do emphasize our teaching, and to see that our lives are so ordered that those who receive the teaching may catch the emphasis too ...
>
> It is not preaching only that will do what needs to be done ... Our life must be one of visible self-sacrifice. There is much sacrifice in our lives of which

the Chinese cannot know. God knows all about it, and we can well afford to wait His declaration of it and His award. There is much we have left for the sake of the Chinese which they have never seen. That will not suffice. They must see self-sacrifice in things they cannot but understand.[46]

Several hundred million Chinese urgently needed to see lives transformed by the gospel. There were simply not enough Chinese Christians to reveal the reality of the gospel to the masses of unreached Chinese. Therefore foreign missionaries were needed to fill the need until such time as the Chinese church was large enough and mature enough to do it unaided.

---

46   Montague Beauchamp, *Days of Blessing in Inland China: Being an Account of Meetings Held in the Province of Shan-si* (London: Morgan & Scott, 1877), 31–33, http://docs.google.com/View?docid=dd42sgj3_3dn2bsdb.

Chapter 3
The Upper Mekong Region at Last

Nearly nine years were to pass from the time the Lammermuir sailed in 1866 until CIM missionaries were able to enter into the Upper Mekong Region. Thus, for better or for worse, the methods for evangelism and gathering congregations had been well established in Eastern China before the first CIM missionaries began to work in the Southwest. There were several factors which caused this delay. As Taylor himself was later to write, "The Lammermuir party, consisting of seventeen adults and four children, sailed from London on May 26, 1866, and arrived in China after a voyage of a little more than four months, to find that, though inland China was open for purposes of travel, it was not so as to residence."[47] If Taylor was only interested in having his workers engage in itineration, he would have found freedom to do so, but his plans required residence as well.

Perhaps Taylor had been overly optimistic about the speed at which new workers could become pioneer evangelists. *Hudson Taylor and China's Open Century* documents the time and energy that Taylor devoted to supervising the *Lammermuir* party, especially a few disappointing individuals, and the lessons he learned about the need to more carefully screen candidates for the future. It might be said that Taylor carved a curious niche for the CIM. On one hand, he was aiming for the evangelization of the whole interior of China as his object. On the other hand, he was careful not to try to attract applicants who were being trained for the ministry who might be suitable candidates to go out with their own denominational mission societies. The class of men and women he gathered together would not have been deemed unsuitable by a William Carey, a Robert Morrison, or a David Livingstone, who themselves came from undistinguished backgrounds. But these were exceptional men who rose to prominence due to incredible willpower and perseverance. Not every man is exceptional and, not surprisingly, few of Taylor's early recruits proved to be. Therefore one difficulty that he

---

47   Taylor, *After Thirty Years*, 7.

encountered by recruiting largely from the tradesman class was that he did not end up with many individuals who had leadership experience or, as time was to prove, much leadership potential. Many responsibilities devolved upon him alone until he was able to help a few of the new workers to develop the qualities needed to lead others.

A further cause for delay was that the Chinese officials and the *literati* class were often opposed to the presence of foreign elements in China. These local rulers did all in their power to hinder the missionary efforts to settle in the interior of China, no matter what the Manchu rulers and the Western powers might have stated in a treaty.

Another reality that became increasingly apparent was that Chinese were not all alike. Just as the Christians in Ning-po needed the Bible to be translated into their own dialect, so too did other segments of the Han Chinese population. Missionaries were expected to pick up Mandarin and several other local dialects as they moved into new areas for ministry. Chinese co-workers had to be willing and able to adapt to dialects, foods, and customs as well. As mentioned above, not many Chinese evangelists were effective outside of the district where they were born and raised.[48]

In some cases Taylor may have tried too hard in the early years to gain a physical presence in each provincial capital. His rationale was sound. A residence there would both convince all prefectural rulers that Christianity was permitted in the province, and it would help persuade other foreign missionary societies that it was truly reasonable to contemplate sending their own workers to begin a work in that province as well. Here we see a tension between a zeal to rapidly preach the gospel to all the Chinese and a commitment to lay strong foundations in the major cities with a visible foreign presence. If the only goal was rapid evangelization of China so that all Chinese could hear the gospel, one might be content with establishing centers in any city where they could find a welcome. Riverboats would serve as well as rented compounds. In that case centers would simply be a place for rest and renewal of weary itinerant evangelists and a place where they could pick up supplies for their next evangelistic tour. However, Hudson Taylor expected that over time churches would emerge and need to be strengthened and equipped so that they could continue the process of evangelizing China. For that to occur, large mission stations which would lead to strong churches were considered essential in the provincial capitals. Taylor was committed to

---

48   CIM, "Work of the China Inland Mission," 47.

immediate obedience to the Great Commission in terms of preaching the gospel to every creature, *and* he was also committed to making disciples of all nations. In the understanding of nineteenth-century evangelical Christians, this implied the establishment of missionary centers that made it possible for a missionary to remain in one city and oversee the work in the surrounding district for years or even decades to come.

All of these factors contributed to the somewhat slow start that the CIM made to enter into Southwestern China. During those years there was never a loss of vision. By 1875 Taylor had the right sort of pioneers with the physical stamina for the exertions required to travel vast distances, the adaptability to live in a Chinese manner for months at a time, and the spiritual maturity to make the most of their opportunities when they were able to enter new provinces.

The Back Door through Burma

The CIM approached the region from two directions. One was from the south. John Stevenson was a veteran missionary who had gone to China in 1865, even before the *Lammermuir* party had set out from England. Returning from a furlough in England in 1875 with a young man named Henry Soltau, they sailed to Rangoon, where they were welcomed by American Baptists and other missionaries in British-ruled Lower Burma. One missionary, A. Taylor Rose, had been to Bhamo on the China border back in March of 1868. With his aid, they went to Mandalay and had an audience with the king of Burma. This was near the end of the reign of King Mindon (reigned 1853–78.) He was an enlightened ruler who made a gallant effort to save his country from being swallowed up by the British empire. He was not anti-Christian. His own children were educated by missionaries, but he was a committed Buddhist, and he was also politically astute enough to realize the risks entailed in having foreign missionaries crossing over his borders into neighboring lands.

At first the king and his ministers sought to discourage them from going to Bhamo. Among the reasons which they gave as to why such an effort was unwarranted was that the Kachin were savages and would never make good Christians.

> The Mingyee [governor] who spoke most said words to this effect: "the people have no language, no religion, no books. It is of no use trying to teach those people."

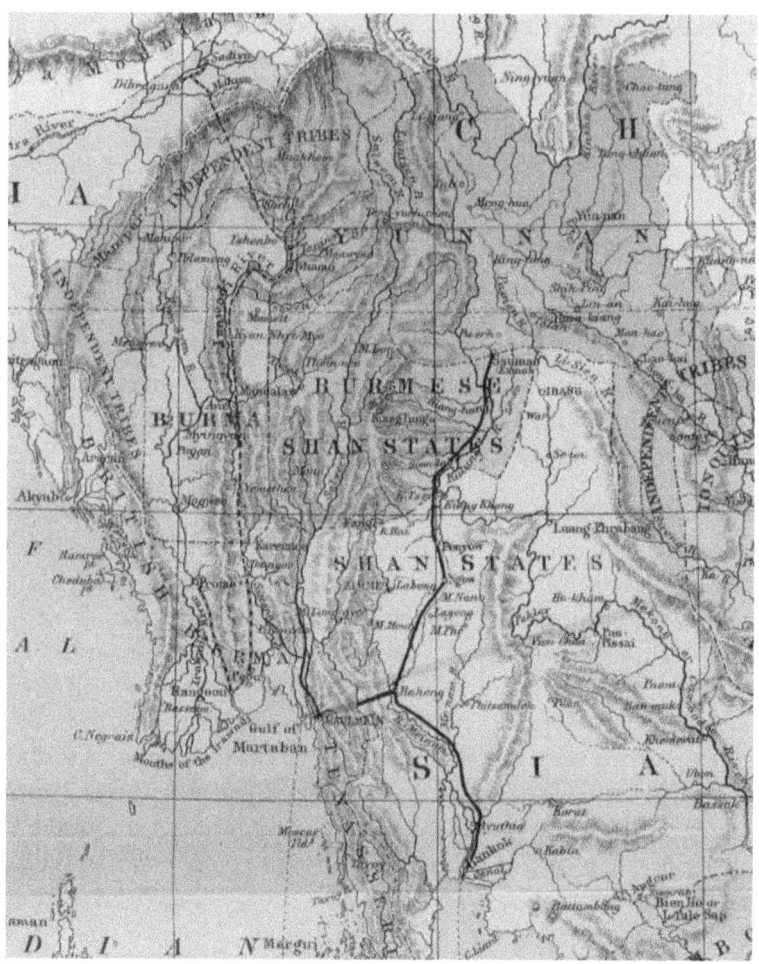

The Upper Mekong Region as it appeared in the 1880s.
http://www.lib.utexas.edu/maps/historical/indo_china_1886.jpg.

Mr. Rose replied that those are the very people who need teaching and teachers; we want to go to such. The Karens were once wild and uncivilized—they had no written language and no books ...

"Oh, they are very different," said the Mingyee; "the tribes around Bhamo are far more savage than they. These Karens had mixed more or less with the Burmans, and had become a little civilized."

Wild people around Bhamo are like wild birds. If you throw out paddy (i.e., unshelled rice) to the wild birds they will come and eat, but will not let you catch them. They want you to give, give, give, but will not let you tame or civilize them. You had much better stay here in the golden city: better for you and better for the king. If you go up there, though it is in the golden empire, the king cannot guarantee your security; yet if anything happens, he will be held responsible, as in the case of Mr. Margary.

We told him that nevertheless we wished to go: that Bhamo belongs to the golden empire, and we could not believe his Majesty was powerless even over those savage people.

He then criticised the idea of teachers coming over from foreign countries without first ascertaining the kind of religion taught here and filling themselves with the wisdom of this country. This he illustrated by saying, "If you have different vessels they can each only contain a certain amount. If teachers come out here they may be full of wisdom and learning, but they will find this people also full, and unable to take in any new religion. If a person has a pot of clean water what can there be better to drink? The Burmese are like vessels of pure water, and therefore all the efforts of foreign teachers will be altogether vain and useless."[49]

Augustus Margary, whom the Burmese official referred to, was a British consul who was sent with an expedition with permission from the Chinese government to explore the China-Burmese border with a view to developing a new trade route from India to Western China. He was murdered on February 21, 1875. Depending on which rumor one listened to, he was killed either at the command of the Chinese officials in Yunnan, or the king of Burma, or some bandits who were quite common in the area. The British used his death as one more excuse to place new demands on the Chinese government, which led to the Chefoo Convention on September 13, 1876. Some Chinese were probably guilty of his murder, but the king of Burma knew that if another incident occurred in that area his kingdom might well pay the price. Margary's family was Christian and he himself had made a personal commitment to follow Christ. John Stevenson was later to record that "the relatives of the gallant young officer who had lost his life in the service of his country, were longing and praying amidst their grief that his death might be the means of opening up those parts to the Gospel, and that even his murderers might hear the glad tidings of peace."[50]

This sort of interaction is a good sample of how missionaries sought to get permission to do their work throughout the Upper Mekong Region. The missionaries were welcomed in Mandalay. They were discouraged from going to Bhamo. They were assured their efforts would be wasted on savages and reminded that the Burmese already were full of the pure truth and needed

---

49   China Inland Mission, *China's Millions*, October 1876, 208.
50   China Inland Mission, *China's Millions*, July–August 1878, 94.

no foreign teaching. They were assured that the king could not guarantee their protection within his own borders where he held absolute sway. But in the end the missionaries got all they asked for and were allowed not only to reside in Bhamo, but also were granted land to build on.

Without Mr. Rose, it is very questionable if the CIM could have gotten to the China border. Mr. Stevenson was to write from Mandalay after their interview, "Mr. Rose has endeared himself very much to us, and has been of great service. In fact, his help in Mandalay has been invaluable; I don't see how we could have got on at all without him."[51]

Rose, Stevenson, and Soltau reached Bhamo on October 3, 1875. Land was granted to them to set up a clinic, as the king had promised. In May 1876 Dr. and Mrs. Thomas Harvey were to join them along with a single man, Joseph Adams. Their focus was to be the Chinese merchants from Yunnan who passed through Bhamo with their caravans. Stevenson, however, was also greatly drawn to the Kachin. As the Kachin have become one of the largest Christian groups in the Upper Mekong, it is worthwhile to note the beginnings of the work among them. The story of the Kachin church is admirably told by Herman G. Tegenfeldt in *A Century of Growth: The Kachin Baptist Church of Burma*.

The first Protestant missionary to meet the Kachin was the adventurous American Baptist, Eugenio Kincaid, in 1837. At first they were assumed to be Shan, perhaps because there was a tendency in those early days to assume that the Shan race was dominant throughout the region. Also, Kincaid most likely had an interpreter who used Shan as the medium to communicate with the Kachin whom they met. For the next few decades, follow-up was impossible, but the "new" view was that the Kachin were really a branch of the Karen. This was perhaps wishful thinking, but it did stimulate the Karen in Bassein and elsewhere to seek ways to reach the Kachin with the gospel. This burden for the salvation of the Kachin was retained even after it was determined that they were not Karenic after all.[52]

The CIM wanted to have a base in Bhamo as a station for missionaries who would pass from there into Southwest China. The permission from the Burmese was given, and following the Chefoo Convention of the same year,

---

51 China Inland Mission, *China's Millions*, December 1875, 66–67. During the 137 years since those words were written, the CIM and the American Baptists have had numerous occasions to work closely with each other in Burma, southern Yunnan, and northern Thailand. Christians from the Baptist churches that were established by the Baptists have also worked closely with CIM/OMF missionaries in efforts to evangelize new areas and unreached tribes.

52 Herman G. Tegenfeldt, *A Century of Growth: The Kachin Baptist Church of Burma* (Pasadena: William Carey Library, 1974), 86–87, 94.

the Chinese began to honor their agreements to allow foreigners to travel and reside at will throughout most parts of the empire. However, Bhamo did not prove to be the doorway that the missionaries hoped for. The obstacle was the British. Without going into great detail, it must be noted that the British Empire was growing rapidly in the second half of the nineteenth century. It did not happen accidentally. While not all British exploratory expeditions led to the growth of the British Empire, quite a few of them did have that effect. The expedition that Margary was part of may have only been a humble attempt to find an shorter route for Indian opium to reach potential future addicts in Southwest China. It is reasonable to assume that the British had no particular desire to rule over people whom they were seeking to turn into drug addicts. But whatever their ultimate goals, it was obvious that the presence of missionaries and the unanticipated incidents that might arise from their presence was unwanted. The British missionaries could therefore stay in Burma, but must not cross the border into China.

It took more than a year for the missionaries to be able to assume possession of land for a center in Bhamo, but on October 23, 1876, Soltau recorded in his diary:

OPENING AMONG THE HILL TRIBES

Bhamo, Monday, October 23rd, After a long period of waiting, arguing and treating, we have been able to-day to conclude the purchase of the site of land near the Zayat which we selected as the best spot for Mission purposes on our arrival in Bhamo. There is a frontage of 58 cubits on the main road, and the depth extends to about 125 cubits. On the ground are some fine trees. The whole piece is level, and affords a good view of the Kah-ch'en hills at the back, while the front is on the leading thoroughfare of Bhamo. Although the authorities cannot legally *sell* land, they considered themselves able to sell the right of possession, and the trees now standing upon it.[53]

With a base formally established, and Dr. Harvey available to maintain the station, Stevenson and Soltau were free to respond to a request from a Kachin chieftain to provide medical treatment for his sister-in-law in a village close to the China border.

Finding themselves on the edge of China with limited opportunities to minister to the Chinese, John Stevenson and Henry Soltau made a tour of the Kachin hills from November 3 to December 23. This was the beginning of the dry season. They found, as did Baptist missionaries before and after them, that the Kachin did not act savagely toward peaceful Western visitors. Their tour confirmed the view that the Kachin were a

---

53 China Inland Mission, "Good News from Burma," *China's Millions*, May 1877, 60.

people worthy of receiving focused missionary efforts. Stevenson had learned quite a bit of Kachin (Jingphaw) language during the previous year and was seriously considering working with the Kachin in Burma as a way to get the gospel into China. About this time he wrote, "Were it not for the restriction put upon us by our own Government, my firm conviction is that it would be as easy for us to go from Bhamô into China, as it is to pass from one county to another in England."[54] It would not be advantageous for the British to have their citizens crossing over the border from Burma to China. If they got into difficulties that would complicate the negotiations between Britain and China, but if they made the trip without incident that would weaken the case for the British who were still seeking Chinese concessions in the wake of the murder of Augustus Margary. Seeing that this obstacle might remain for quite some time, Stevenson looked for other ways to get the gospel into China.

> The Kah-chens I look upon as *our best allies*. A few days ago the native governor at Bhamo said publicly that we were at perfect liberty to go and come from the hills as we please, and when we please. We have no reason to doubt the sincerity of the statement. The Chinese have laid aside much of the suspicion and reserve that characterized them when we came here. Our constant intercourse, seeking to help the sick and dying, has brought us many "golden opinions." I am convinced that ere 1877 closes you will hear of greater progress yet—souls saved. We stayed 43 days upon the hills with the Kah-chens; they really were most friendly and cordial. We long to see them brought under the Gospel of Christ; they seem particularly ripe for it.
>
> I was delighted and thanked the Lord when I heard that a Christian Karen had arrived in Bhamo, sent by his brethren in Bassein to study the Kah-chen language and report as to the prospects of opening a mission among them. The Karens are likely to send up seven or eight young men next dry season, if the report is favourable. I am sure we will be glad to resign the Kah-chens to the care of our Karen brethren; but, as I said to Mr. Cushing, if no one else took them up now, we could no longer allow them to be without the Gospel. Of course the China Inland Mission has plenty and more than plenty to do with the thousands of Chinese, without commencing definite work among small scattered tribes. However, I am glad to find that we have stirred up others, introduced others to the work, and made it comparatively easy. We stayed at See-kaw (so called), the terminus of caravans from Yunnan. We were kept very busy giving medicine, as eight-tenths of the Chinese population were down with fever. We had a most hearty reception. They fed us well and loaded us with good things to bring away. If we saw our way to

---

54 Guinness, Geraldine. *The Story of the China Inland Mission* (London: Morgan and Scott, 1900) Vol. 2, p. 145.

advance at present, the Kah-chens and Chinese would take us into China free of expense, and receive us warmly.⁵⁵

All the evidence suggests that Stevenson loved the Kachin and would gladly have become CIM's first missionary to the aboriginal tribes of the region. But it is also likely that he was intentionally forcing the hand of the American Baptist Mission Board back in Boston. The implied "threat" that CIM would begin tribal work in Upper Burma was just what men like the American Baptist missionary Josiah Cushing needed to repeat to his board to convince them of the necessity of sending workers to the Kachin. Cushing himself was a bold Baptist pioneer missionary to the Shan. He came to Bhamo after Stevenson and Soltau in order to work among the large Shan population there. Faced with the challenge that Stevenson placed before him, he temporarily laid aside his duties to the Shan to formally engage the Kachin on behalf of the Baptists. One aspect of that was that he could not return to his base in Toungoo in the lower part of Burma, so for a year or more he worked in Bhamo while his wife covered the Toungoo station herself. Meanwhile, the American Baptists and the Karen Baptists began to send forth workers to engage the Kachin. The CIM workers were thus freed to focus solely on the Chinese population. The CIM missionaries made every effort to help the Baptists to establish their work in Bhamo just as the Baptists had so helped them in their efforts to gain access to the town in the first place. When Cushing first arrived in 1876, it was the CIM that provided him with accommodation until he could obtain property for himself. When Albert J. Lyon, one of the new Baptist workers, became sick, it was Henry Soltau who provided medical care for him until his death. When Soltau received a financial gift for "mission work in Burmah," he turned it over to Jacob A. Freiday, a new Baptist missionary, to use for his ministry to the Shan and Kachin.⁵⁶ It may be seen that close cooperation and fellowship could be maintained over the years by clearly separating responsibilities, with the CIM seeking to reach the Chinese from Yunnan while the Baptists focused on the Shan and Kachin.

Sending forth workers and keeping them on the field are two different matters. By mid-1877, with no hint of when the British Resident might allow the CIM missionaries to enter Yunnan, John Stevenson chose to return to his family whom he had left behind in Scotland two years before. Dr. and Mrs. Harvey first lost their baby to disease and then the doctor

---

55   China Inland Mission, "Letter from Burma," *China's Millions*, July 1877, 87.

56   Mr. and Mrs. Jacob A. Freiday, "Report from Shan Department, Bhamo," in 65th Annual Report, ed. American Baptist Missionary Union (1879).

himself became quite ill. So they tried to sail to East China, where he hoped better climate might aid his recovery. But he and his wife were shipwrecked in the Andaman Sea and after much suffering at last got back to Rangoon, where Baptist missionaries cared for them until they were able to take a steamer back to England.[57] Thus, by 1878, of the CIM team, only Henry Soltau and Mr. Adams (whose fiancée was sailing out to meet him) were left at Bhamo. In such situations loneliness was to be expected. Soltau recorded the joy of meeting with two Karen evangelists who were coming up to reach the Kachin. Fellowship was a multilingual experience.

> Mr. Soltau accompanied Mr. Stevenson as far as Mandalay. On his return journey he found two Christian Karens, native pastors, going up on the steamer to work among the Kahchens. Mr. Soltau writes: "In the evening I invited the Karens into my little cabin for prayer. They can speak Burmese, and my Chinese boy can do likewise, so he acted as interpreter. I told them that we were brothers in Jesus, and though unable to understand each other, we could unitedly pray to our Heavenly Father, who understands all four languages. I then mentioned what we would pray for. They were greatly pleased. First I prayed in Chinese, and Ah-sz (the boy) followed in Chinese very nicely. One of the Karens then prayed in Burmese, and the other in Karen. I have no doubt that our Heavenly Father's ear was open to our feeble trembling cries. The one name of Jesus drew us together, and there was great joy in the little prayer-meeting notwithstanding the prayers were in an unknown tongue."[58]

The Way West

While the plans of the CIM were being held in check in Upper Burma, more progress was being made by the missionaries who were working their way west from the occupied provinces of China. Charles Judd, who had been in China for nearly a decade, traveled with a new missionary, James Broumton, who happened to be his wife's younger brother. They worked their way through antiforeign Hunan where a plot was brewing against foreigners, had their boat hit a rock while traveling up a river, and were nearly caught in an out-of-control brush fire. In the end they were able to peacefully set up a center in Kweiyang (Guiyang) in Kweichow Province. Broumton

---

57 China Inland Mission, "History of the Bhamo Branch of the China Inland Mission," *China's Millions*, May 1879, 56. "Friday, August 3rd, found us once more safe in the port of Rangoon. Kind sympathizing missionaries of the American Baptist Society paid us every possible attention. Whilst some gave us a home in their house, others supplied us with clothes and money. One dear aged brother took me to a tailor's and paid for a suit of new clothes. The ladies of the mission turned out from their wardrobes articles for my dear wife. From far and near help came from nearly all parts of their mission. They seemed to vie with each other in their attention and liberality. May God ever remember them for it, and supply all their need."

58 China Inland Mission, "Missionary Correspondence," *China's Millions*, September 1877, 118.

remained there while Judd went on to Szechwan (Sichuan) Province. He was to spend several relatively peaceful and profitable years in Kweiyang and received visits from other itinerant missionaries and evangelists who passed through on their way to or from more western provinces. One reason for his good reception was that General William Mesny, who had fought for the Manchus against the Taiping rebels, was now a high-ranking military officer in Kweiyang and was a warm friend of the CIM. Furthermore, an influential local official, a Mr. Fan, helped them to get settled in. His case was interesting in that he was once a "Christian" Taiping rebel leader who chose to join the Manchus at the right time when he got rewarded with an official position rather than with decapitation. In that capacity he and a compatriot "had gone back to some degree of idolatry, having no Christian teacher to help them, and with but little knowledge of the Word of God."[59] Mr. Fan was delighted to have missionaries come, and as he had oversight of the local Miao (Hmong) population, he gave them access to that tribe as well. In those days misclassifying tribes was not uncommon. Judd wrote:

> One interesting point we have learned is that the language of the Miao tribes is largely understood by the Burmese; and hence probably related. The Burmese embassy passing through here some time ago, were surprised to find that they understood much of what the Miao-tsi said, while the Chinese could not understand a word. Many of them can now speak Chinese, so interpreters for the Gospel will not be difficult to find.[60]

It may seem hard to understand how Miao was thought to be related to Burmese, but as mentioned previously, only a few decades earlier the Kachin were thought to speak a dialect of Shan until it became obvious (to some) that their language must certainly be a dialect of Karen. The confusion can best be cleared up by assuming that whoever recited the story to Judd had lumped one of the Yi groups (which actually do speak a language similar to Burmese) with the Miao groups. Linguistics and classifications of tribes were in their infancy in the late 1800s and is changing even now. It is one reason why we need to be very careful before jumping to any conclusions about the history of mission work among the tribes when reading the writings of missionaries from an earlier generation.

While Broumton was left in relative peace and had regular visits from itinerant missionaries and evangelists who certainly benefited by having a mission base in this city, the local population was not responsive to the gospel. In 1895 the statistics for the provinces were as follows:[61]

---

59   China Inland Mission, "Letter from Mr. Judd," *China's Millions*, August 1877, 92.
60   Ibid.
61   Taylor, *After Thirty Years*, 76.

Stations												
KWEICHOW	Rank	Work Begun	Outstations	Missionaries, Associates and Their Wives	Ordained Pastors	Assistant Preachers	School Teachers and Colporteurs	Bible Women	Unpaid Helpers	Communicants in Fellowship	Baptized from Commencement	Organized Churches
1 Kwei-yang	Cap.	1877	-	7	-	1	1	1	-	46	63	1
2 Gan-shun	Fu	1888	2	4	-	1	1	-	1	22	21	3
3 Tun-shan	Hien	1893	-	2	-	-	-	-	-	-	-	-
4 Hing-i	Fu	1891	-	1	-	1	-	-	-	2	-	-
			2	14	-	3	2	1	1	70	84	4
						Total, 6						

Statistical Table for Kweichow

Stations												
YUNNAN	Rank	Work Begun	Outstations	Missionaries, Associates and Their Wives	Ordained Pastors	Assistant Preachers	School Teachers and Colporteurs	Bible Women	Unpaid Helpers	Communicants in Fellowship	Baptized from Commencement	Organized Churches
1 Bhamo (Burmah)	-	1875	-	2	-	-	-	-	2	12	22	1
2 Ta-li	Fu	1881	-	3	-	-	1	-	-	2	3	1
3 Yun-nan	Cap.	1882	-	5	-	1	-	-	-	4	12	1
4 Küh-tsing	Fu	1889	-	5	-	-	-	-	-	2	2	1
5 Chau-t'ung	Fu	1887	-	5	-	-	1	-	-	2	2	1
6 Tung-ch'uan	Fu	1891	-	5	-	-	-	-	-	1	1	1
			-	25	-	1	2	-	2	23	42	6
						Total, 3						

Statistical Table for Yunnan

By any measure, the Chinese of Kweichow and Yunnan were not in any rush to enter the kingdom of God. Several causes might be said to have contributed to this cold response. One, quite possibly, was the presence of a large Roman Catholic population in the province. On his first Easter in Kweiyang, Broumton went to attend the service in the cathedral and saw hundreds at that particular service, which was one of four for the day. Broumton, along with other pioneer missionaries who had no particular attachment to Roman Catholic ceremonies or to various aspects of Catholic theology, nonetheless were convinced that some Chinese Catholics were true followers of Jesus Christ. The problem was that the Roman Catholic Church, under the protection of the French government, encouraged its missionary priests and bishops to dress in garb that portrayed them in the eyes of the populace as being government officials. When Chinese Catholics came to these priests for redress for various grievances, real or imagined, the priests would become advocates on their behalf. While this might have helped them to overcome a certain degree of persecution, it also led some (or many) to come into the church specifically to gain a friend in court. Naturally, those who did not need a friend in court or who lost cases due to the Catholic patrons of their adversaries developed a negative attitude toward Christianity as a whole and Chinese Christians in particular. Broumton recorded an incident in his journal which reflected the situation he faced.

> *May 29th* . . . In the evening, while Mr. M'Carthy [a visiting veteran missionary] and I were talking together, the inquirer Fan came in, and after a short time said he would like to ask our advice concerning a little difficulty he was in. He said that some twenty-four years ago his father (or grandfather) had lent some friend the sum of 30 taels, which he has never been repaid. He (Fan) is now anxious to obtain it; his father is dead and also the borrower, and the son of the debtor refuses to pay, as he says he knows nothing of the affair, he being but a child at the time. Before he had finished his story, however, others came in and he left off; but he afterwards made known his case to Yao, the native helper, who told him that we did not interfere in such matters. I very much fear that Fan's idea was that we would help him as the Romanists help their converts. If so, I am very disappointed in him, for I thought he was sincere. This shows we need to be very careful, and to wait much on God for guidance as to how to deal with candidates for baptism.[62]

So not only did the French-sponsored policy of the Roman Catholics alienate many Chinese, it also created a level of distrust of missionaries towards the motives of inquirers, which while perhaps necessary to some degree, could only hinder the creation of true fellowship between them.

From Kweiyang it was nearly a four-week-long walk over some very hilly and much deserted countryside to Yunnan Fu (Kunming). John McCarthy was the first CIM missionary to enter the city. He arrived there on July 2, 1877, as a part of his epoch journey, in large part on foot across China. One purpose of the trip was to show that an evangelist who was fluent in Chinese, was willing to sleep in Chinese inns, eat Chinese food, and be bitten by Chinese bedbugs could accomplish. From there he went on to Ta-li Fu and then headed south to Bhamo, which he reached on August 12. He was in no rush. He sought to meet with the people, get an

---

62   J. F. Broumton, "Work in Kwei-yang," *China's Millions*, January 1878, 12.

idea of where future missionaries might be located, and get a feeling for the reception which such workers might hope to expect. His reports were all very positive. Once again, the only opposition to continuing his journey by returning to China came from the representative of the Government of India in Bhamo, T. T. Cooper, who was simply following orders from the British Viceroy. They asked him for a report of his trip, for which they gave him their thanks, but then they would not let him go back to China. In the end he had to go to Rangoon, from whence he sailed back to England to pick up his family and speak on the open doors in China's interior.

The efforts of men like Soltau, Stevenson, Broumton, and McCarthy showed that Southwest China and the Upper Mekong Region were open to those who were willing to "suffer in order to save." Their efforts were of great value to Hudson Taylor in his propaganda campaign both in China and in Great Britain. In order to fulfill his calling he had to convince the Christian public, and the missionary societies as well, that China was truly open to foreigners and that they should therefore greatly expand their efforts in the country. To do this he needed the evidence that men like Broumton, as a lone missionary in Kweiyang, and McCarthy, on the highways and waterways of China, could provide. Taylor's friend Reginald Radcliffe, at the twelfth anniversary meeting of the CIM in Mildmay, England, in May 1878, rightly claimed that the pioneers of the CIM were not missionaries but spies.

> I cannot call Hudson Taylor and McCarthy or the late W. C. Burns "missionaries." I call them by a more honourable name. I say they are merely *the spies*, and they have gone out and *looked* at the land, and thank God, some of them have tarried there a long time, and they have brought of the fruit of the land. But you do not mean to tell me, after listening to what has taken place to-night in reference to these millions of China, that this is an institution for missioning China. It is simply sending out the men as spies, to come and bring us a report of the land, and to make us utterly and entirely inexcusable if we do not begin to mission China, but on a vastly wider scale. These beloved brethren and sisters are occupying the honourable position of Caleb and Joshua, who were sent out to look at the land, and they said, "The land is a good land." And McCarthy and others of them tell us, "If the Lord delighteth in us, He will give us the land."[63]

The CIM did not have a fraction of the workers that would be necessary to evangelize the Chinese. They did, by the late 1870s, have enough of the right sort of workers to show to the Christian world that the evangelization of China was now a real possibility. With this

---

63   China Inland Mission, "Reginald Radcliffe," *China's Millions*, July–August 1878, 110.

possibility came an obligation. The CIM's primary and oft-stated goal was to stir the Christian church to action on behalf of China. Therefore the pioneer efforts were extensive rather than intensive. They were not designed to stake out a territory for the CIM but to challenge Christians in many lands and from numerous denominations to enter into fields that were proven to be open to foreign workers.

The Bible Christian Church: An Associate Mission

When this early goal of the CIM is clearly perceived, then their methodology in provinces like Kweichow (Guizhou) and Yunnan becomes easily understandable. The main cities were occupied by foreign missionaries, and efforts to establish Chinese congregations were begun. There were not enough laborers to give special attention to the tribal populations in the hills, and for several decades little was done among them. While Taylor's philosophy and methods did have its detractors, it also achieved the objectives for which it was designed. Other denominations contacted the CIM, learned of where they might effectively engage in ministry in China, and then sent out workers to develop ministries in depth in those regions. This was to lead to several pioneer workers being sent out to China by means of the Bible Christian Church. This was a small denomination with Methodist roots. It was later to unite with several like-minded bodies and form the United Methodist Church in England. As the churches gained a clear sense of their responsibilities to take part in world evangelism, they invited Hudson Taylor and his brother-in-law, Benjamin Broomhall, to address them on missions. The event was recorded thus:

> The founder of the China Inland Mission, Dr. J. Hudson Taylor, was invited to visit the London Conference in 1885. He came with Mr. B. Broomhall, the Secretary of the C.I.M., and gave an address at Jubilee Chapel, Hoxton, which fanned the missionary enthusiasm of the Conference to white heat. As a result of his exhortation, two young ministers, Samuel Thomas Thorne and Thomas Grills Vanstone, were set apart for work in Yunnan as "associates" of the China Inland Mission. The reasons assigned for the choice of this district were that it was the largest and most needy unoccupied district in China, where Mission work could be freely carried on at that time; that it was one of the healthiest and most beautiful provinces of the Empire; that there were Methodists already working at Chungking, Kuei Yang, and Yunnan Fu, vast cities in direct communication with Yunnan, which might eventually become a great highway, through Siam, from Europe to China.[64]

---

64   W. A. Grist, *Samuel Pollard: Pioneer Missionary in China* (London: United Methodist Publishing House, [1920?]), 9.

The Bible Christian Church sent workers to China as an associate mission of the CIM. One of their most famous workers was to be Samuel Pollard, the son of an English evangelist. Samuel Pollard went out to China in 1887 at the age of 23. He attended the CIM-run language school in Gan-king for about eight months before moving on to Chao-tung in Yunnan where he continued his Chinese language study. He maintained cordial relations with CIM missionaries but took his directions from his own mission board in England and eventually became the superintendent of the Bible Christian Mission (BCM) in Yunnan. The strengths and weaknesses of CIM's commitment to working interdenominationally and in close partnership with other missions is reflected in the life and ministry of Samuel Pollard. While he benefited greatly from attending the CIM language school and was grateful for what he learned, he did not always find it easy to relate to those of other theological backgrounds. In one letter he wrote:

> They [the CIM missionaries] are very kind; but their rank Calvinism and persistent longing for our blessed Lord to come and do [i.e., play] the Emperor, I don't like. These ideas must necessarily influence all their methods of work. I don't want Christ to come down to reign as an Emperor. Let us have the meek and lowly Jesus as our King until the world is won, and when we leave here let us enter into the other Kingdom . . .
>
> Never mind, I'm happy in it all and eager for the work. But want our Mission to be carried on along our own lines.[65]

Once in Yunnan, Pollard and his Bible Christian Mission co-workers had plenty of room to develop their work along those lines, and it appears that the CIM itself tended to send their own Methodist members to work in neighboring districts, at least in the early years, so that good cooperative fellowship (with one notable exception) could be maintained.[66]

Beginnings of Tribal Work

While associate missions and the steadily increasing size of the CIM itself made it possible to establish numerous stations in Southwest China, the focus continued to be on reaching geographic locations rather than ethnic groups. While James Broumton was able to baptize three Miao believers in 1884,[67] there were no workers formally assigned to work among the aborigines (as they were then called) for another decade.

---

65 Ibid., 20.
66 Ibid., 317.
67 Marshall Broomhall, *Some a Hundredfold: The Life and Work of James R. Adam among the Tribes of South-West China* (London: China Inland Mission, [1915?]), 9–10.

In his book *Among the Tribes of South-West China*, Samuel R. Clarke described the development of the work.

> It was not until the year 1896 that definite efforts were made to reach these people. Naturally the missionaries who first settled in Kweichow had as much and more than they could do to reach the Chinese immediately around them. In the year 1895 there were four stations open in the province, namely, Kweiyang, Anshunfu, Singyifu, and Tushan, and these were occupied by nineteen missionaries. At all these places the time of the missionaries was entirely given up to work among the Chinese, so that neither in the province of Kweichow, nor elsewhere in the west of China, were any special efforts made to evangelise the non-Chinese races.[68]

James R. Adam became one of the first and most noted CIM missionaries to the Miao. A Scotsman from the Free Church of Scotland, like Pollard, he was born in 1863, came to China around 1887, and died in 1915. Adam was a gifted evangelist before he came to China. He was sent to Anshun in Kweichow, where he had contact with the Miao. As early as 1896 he asked Hudson Taylor if he might concentrate his energies on the Miao, but as there were no other workers available to maintain the Chinese ministry, he was told, "Go on, dear brother, and do the best you can for both."[69] It would appear that the concern expressed by Adam did have its desired effect, for within a few years new workers were sent to Anshun to carry the ministry to the Chinese so that Adam could be set apart for work among the Miao. It might be asked why the work among the Chinese took a priority when they had shown themselves so unresponsive to the gospel for well over a decade. One answer is that the Chinese were the rulers of the Miao, and the Miao had been in a state of rebellion until only a few years before the first CIM missionaries had arrived on the scene. Had the missionaries given their attention only to the Miao, the Chinese would have had every reason to assume that foreigners were plotting to stir up a new rebellion. As it was, many false charges were made against the Miao who showed interest in the gospel, as well as the missionaries who came to work among them. The only way that missionaries were able to allay these suspicions to some degree was to approach the government officials and explain what they were doing. This required that the missionaries speak excellent Mandarin,

---

68   Samuel R. Clarke, *Among the Tribes of South-West China* (London: China Inland Mission, 1911), 140.

69   *A Modern Pentecost Being the Story of the Revival Among the Aborigines of South-west China*. (London: China Inland Mission, Morgan & Scott, 1906), 2. This small book consists of numerous pictures of the Miao as well as the observations of the missionaries in Kweichow at the time that the revival among them occurred.

understand the protocol of contacting officials, and have existing positive relations with at least some government officials already.[70]

The early history of the spread of the gospel among the Miao has been well recorded.[71] Therefore only a brief outline of what happened is given here. Our concern is to consider how missionaries as individuals, and the Mission as a whole, contributed to and responded to the movement that occurred.

The first step was to survey the various tribes in the region and determine how much similarity existed between them. The three main groups that came to the attention of the missionaries were the Chung-chía, the Nosu, and the Miao. The Chung-chía, who numbered 6–7 million, were recognized as being related to the Shan, the Siamese, and the Lao. They consisted of several subgroups, and the American Presbyterians of the Lao Mission, which was centered in Chiang Mai, became the "experts" on these groups to the degree that anyone could be called an expert on the ethnic groups of the region at that time. They went by various local names a century ago, and go by new names now. The name Chung-chía has almost disappeared from the literature, and these various groups are generally now identified by the fact that they speak varieties of the Tai family of languages. It was noted that those in Southwest Yunnan and in the countries to the south were predominantly Buddhist, while those farther east were still animist. Some work was done among them, but the results among them were minimal. The Yi Nosu, sometimes referred to in the literature of that day as Lo-lo, were the native landowners. Many owned large estates which the Miao farmed. For this reason they were very interested in any movement that might occur among their tenants. In earlier years they had been independent and had a reputation for their warlike nature, but by the end of the nineteenth century all but those in Sichuan Province had been subjugated by the Chinese.

---

70   The annals of missions are filled with stories of those who refused to allow themselves to be distracted from their objectives of reaching a minority people group by devoting time to first developing relations with the local rulers. Invariably the missionaries and their converts experienced persecution which might have been avoided had they shown respect to those to whom respect was due. The beauty of working in a large mission like the CIM, with a geographic rather than merely an ethnic focus, was that in one location it was possible to have some workers focus on the ethnic Chinese while others gave their attention to the tribes. Thus corporately they could build good relations with the ruling class while giving specific attention to the tribes in their own languages. It is rarely the case that a single missionary has the time, the linguistic abilities, and the multicultural skills necessary to effectively engage both groups at once.

71   The following books along with the *China's Millions* from about 1904 to 1915 are good sources for history about the amazing growth of the Miao church: Grist, *Samuel Pollard*; Broomhall, *Some a Hundredfold*; and Clarke, *Among the Tribes of South-West China*.

The term "Miao" referred to a number of related tribes who are now better known as "Hmong." It was only as work was begun among them that the differences between the various Miao groups became recognized. Samuel Clarke noted:

> It was in 1895, while in charge of the Mission station at Kweiyang, that I was asked to commence work among the tribes-people, to find out all I could about them, learn their language, and reduce it to writing. There were at that time in the Church at Kweiyang a man named P'an Sheo-shan and his wife, who were Miao but had lived in the city for many years and passed among the people generally as Chinese. I asked this man if he would teach me his language, and found him not only willing to teach me, but anxious to assist in every way in preaching the Gospel to his own people.
>
> With P'an Sheo-shan as teacher, the writer began the study of the Miao language and dialects. We had previously known something of the names by which the various tribes were known to the Chinese, but it was only after some study of their language that the great differences there are in their dialects became evident. My teacher belonged to the *Heh* or Black Miao, who are found in great numbers four days east of Kweiyang, and from east and south to the borders of Hunan and Kwangsi. After studying my teacher's dialect for about three months we went to Anshunfu, three days west of Kweiyang, where there are a great many *Hua* or Flowery Miao, and found their dialect so different that my teacher could not understand anything said by the Hua Miao. However, in consequence of this visit, Mr. James R. Adam, who was in charge of the station at Anshunfu, began to study the language of the Hua Miao. We also visited the Ya-ch'io Miao, four days south of Kweiyang, and found their dialect quite different to both Heh Miao and Hua Miao. The Hung-tsang Miao and other Miao in the neighborhood of Kweiyang also speak another dialect, and one which the Heh and Hua Miao do not understand.[72]

It took the missionaries in Kweichow (Guizhou) twenty years to start sorting out who the tribal groups were in the hills around them. Moreover, men like Teacher P'an only became actively engaged in tribal outreach to their own people when the missionary first took the initiative by expressing interest in the Miao and their languages. Cross-cultural missionary work is rarely "spontaneous." It is axiomatic that culture determines one's view, and people who are not part of one's own culture rarely come into one's view as a potential recipient of the gospel. The missionaries had entered wholeheartedly into the Chinese culture as had Teacher P'an and his wife. So they could live for years without giving much attention to the Miao tribes round about them. Certainly there was an interest on the part of some like J. R. Adam to reach the tribes, but

---

72 Clarke, *Tribes of South-West China*, 140–42.

still it took time before the Mission leaders took a new initiative which led to gaining a new, more complete view of the tribes.

Early Efforts among the Miao and the Opposition It Engendered

The work began in several prefectures in the late 1890s. It was not an auspicious time to begin work. The Chinese had been humiliated in 1895 when they had been defeated in battle by the Japanese, whom they had long considered (rightly or wrongly) to be a tributary state. Attempts were made by the young emperor to initiate reforms, but these efforts were suppressed by the Dowager Empress, and that meant that those who supported antiforeign policies were encouraged to turn their attitudes into actions. At such a time, missionaries were naturally going to be on the receiving end of antiforeign agitation, and those who showed an interest in tribal communities would be considered a serious threat to the traditional-minded Chinese rulers.

Clarke relates in some detail how the work and the opposition developed in the market town of Panghai. It is a good example of what the early missionaries were up against as they sought to reach the tribes.

> By July 1896 such progress had been made in the study of the language of the Heh Miao that a primer was compiled for students of that dialect, also a commencement made with Miao-English and English-Miao dictionaries. We had also translated a catechism, some tracts, and several hymns. During this month Mr. and Mrs. F. B. Webb, who had recently come to Kweichow specially to work among the tribes, and who for some months had been studying the language of the Heh Miao in Kweichow, set out for the Heh Miao district. Earlier in the year, Mr. Webb had twice visited that part of the province and had engaged a Heh Miao man as servant. This man, together with P'an Sheo-shan, my teacher, accompanied Mr. and Mrs. Webb. For more than a month they wandered about, living in wretched inns and houses on the borders of the Miao district. It was a very trying experience for them, but at length they succeeded in renting from a relation of their servant, half a house in the middle of a Miao village of about eighty families. It was not a large house, and the half of it that they rented was merely a large, lofty, barn-like room, all open on one side to the wind and rain.
>
> At first, the Miao seemed friendly or indifferent, and the Chinese of the market village of Panghai on the other side of the river half a mile away, uttered no protest. Before a fortnight passed, however, the Chinese began to raise objections, and suggested to Mr. and Mrs. Webb that they should leave. Panghai is in the Tsingpinghsien district, and the magistrate sent runners from that city to escort them out of the district; but they declined to

The Upper Mekong Region at Last

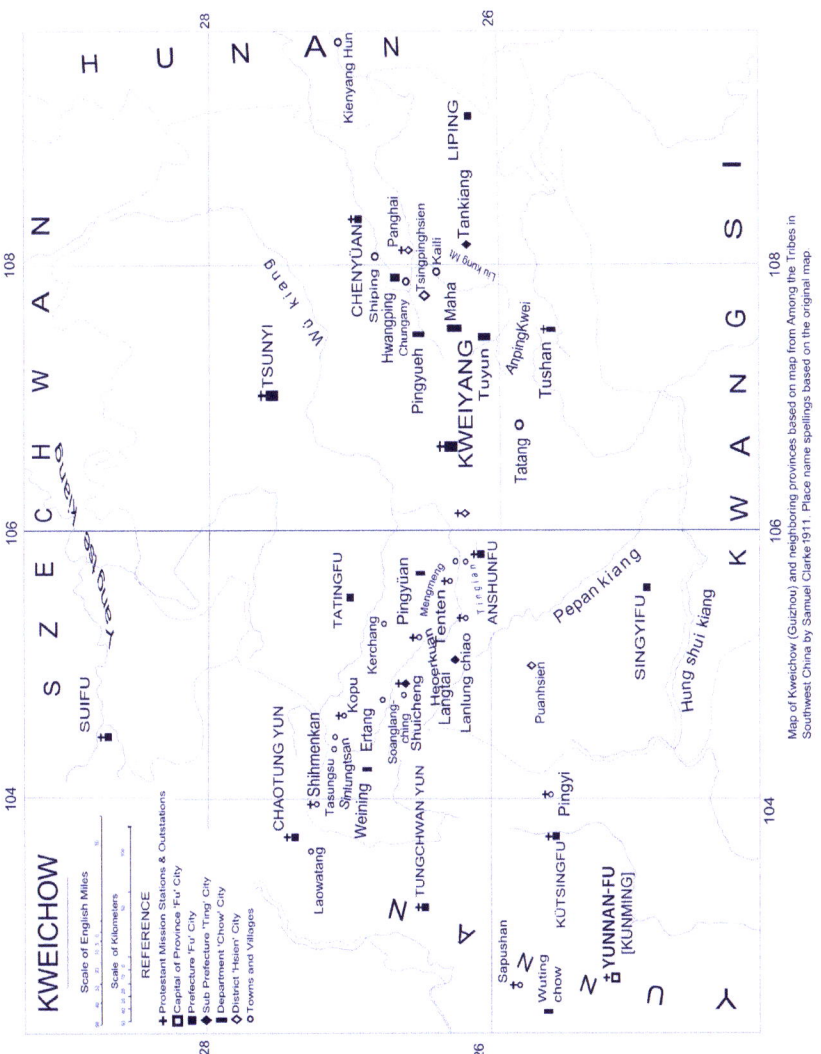

Map of Kweichow (Guizhou) and neighboring provinces based on map from Among the Tribes in Southwest China by Samuel Clarke 1911. Place name spellings based on the original map.

leave. Thereupon the leading men of Panghai very carefully tried to impress upon Mr. and Mrs. Webb that it was not safe for them to live among the Miao, who were a people of bad manners and ungovernable tempers. As Mr. and Mrs. Webb thought otherwise, the Chinese began to say plainly that if the missionaries did not go they would pull down the house about their ears, and carry off all their things. At the same time they threatened the Miao man who had let half his house to them, that if he did not get rid of his objectionable tenants they would make it a serious matter for him, and the poor man was very much alarmed.[73]

---

73 Ibid., 142.

A few points deserve to be noted. First of all, the missionaries were not invited by any local Miao to come and live among them but went because they were sent by their leaders. Some might argue that they should have waited for an invitation, but that might have been years in coming or might never have come at all if the missionaries did not first show their interest in the Heh Miao of that district. Secondly, the opposition, as far as they could ascertain, was not of local origin but almost certainly came from Chinese communities, either at the initiative of the district magistrate or due to his response to a request from other Chinese closer to the scene. What occurred locally in Panghai and in countless other towns and cities in the days and years to come was inevitably the result of human forces much larger and more complex than might be inferred by those who merely look at the actual local participants.

Because the missionaries did not have an invitation, they were forced to depend on a few helpers, Mr. Webb's servant, Teacher P'an, and the servant's relative from whom they rented half of a half-open house. While these individuals may have had some personal sympathy for what the Webb's were seeking to do, their actual involvement was the direct result of a financial arrangement. The net result was that suspicions arose which gave rise to lies and rumors. These in turn created fertile ground for agitators to exploit the situation for what they hoped would be to their benefit. But perhaps the lies led to the suspicions. What is obvious is that there was and still is a class of people who are ever on the lookout for situations to exploit, and when the first missionaries came to live among the Miao, these provocateurs had just such a situation to work with. The story as told by Samuel Clarke went like this:

> It was just at this time that the writer joined Mr. and Mrs. Webb at Panghai. The Chinese were threatening, the landlord and his friends were in great fear, but the rest of the Miao were indifferent. We thought we might be driven away with more or less violence at any time, but we hoped and prayed that we might be allowed to remain. Some days passed quietly, and we began to think that the trouble was over, when, about ten days after my arrival, the storm gathered again and seemed about to burst over us. The Chinese headman of Panghai and neighborhood called upon us with riff-raff of the village and the local robbers at their heels, to the number of about one hundred and fifty. They explained very elaborately that they personally had no objection to us, but the people were opposed to our remaining. They, the headmen, had done their best, but as a matter of fact if we did not go away, the people had decided to pull down our house and loot our things. Some of the rough fellows present, who had knives in their sleeves to emphasize

what the headmen had stated, said, with appropriate gesticulation, "If you don't go away, we are going to beat you, pull down the house, and carry off your things."[74]

It is a universal truth that the ties between robbers and rulers are generally much tighter than those who have little interaction with either party might imagine. Obviously Clarke had some experience with both, for he knew how to set the two against each other and reduce the threat that he and the Webbs were facing.

> We told them quietly that we were there by treaty right; we had our passports, the high provincial authorities knew we were there, as did the local magistrate at Tsingpinghsien, and we intended to stay. They might pull down the house if they wished, but if they did it would be rebuilt. Finally, we said to the headmen: "Look here, Mr. Chang, Mr. Wang, Mr. Lui, etc. you are all at the bottom of this trouble. These people off the street would not have dared to come and speak to us as they have done if you did not support them. But mark this, this trouble has been threatening for some time, and the names of every one of you headmen have been sent to Kweiyang, so if anything should happen to us you are the men who will have to answer for it. Even if you should kill us, it won't help you a bit, for your names and surnames are all known at Kweiyang."

> This placed the matter in quite a different light, so they withdrew for a consultation. We were told afterwards that as soon as they were outside the house, the riff-raff and robbers wanted to start pulling down the house and plundering it right away. "Only give the word," they said to the headmen; "and we shall do the work." "Quite so," replied the headmen; "It would be very nice for you to do the looting, but we are the men who would be asked about it."[75]

After this the crowd gradually dispersed, but only after several more weeks did the threat fully subside. Clarke later came to the conclusion "that the headmen had been advised by the Tsingpinghsien magistrate to use every possible means to frighten us away, but on no account to proceed to actual violence."[76]

In the episode we see clearly the value of having a deep understanding about how the Chinese operated at the village, town, prefecture, and even provincial level. Humanly speaking, a missionary who only sought to relate to and understand the workings of a Miao village would have been absolutely clueless about how to respond to such a situation; and thus in a nutshell we have the reason why effective tribal work could not have

---

74 Ibid., 143–44.
75 Ibid., 144–45.
76 Ibid., 143–46.

been carried out before the 1890s when the work among the Chinese in the capital and main cities of the province had been well established.

Mr. Webb was able to gain the favor of the local Miao population by providing basic medical care. For the most part, all he did was to help clean and bandage wounds which would otherwise have become seriously infected. Had he actually been a doctor, he might have accomplished much more but, in comparison to the Miao who knew nothing about modern hygiene, his methods worked wonders. By traveling to other villages and attending markets and festivals, he became known to many. At times hundreds would come to visit his mission station, which gradually emerged out of the half-open house he and his wife first dwelt in. His wife, however, suffered from malarial fevers, and in June 1897 they had to leave, first for Shanghai, and then later for her home in America in order to recover. Mr. Bolton, who had been engaged in strictly Chinese work in Panghai, then assumed responsibility for the emerging Miao work. He began a school for Heh Miao boys where they were taught to read both their own language and Chinese. His preference was for the scholars from distant villages who would have to live at the mission station. Partly this was due to the fact that local boys were always being called away from school to do errands for their parents, but it was also a means by which the missionary "made friends with their parents, and was able to visit them and gain a hearing for the Gospel in new places."[77]

On one hand, this step might lead to a methodology of missions which would extract boys from their communities in order to convert them. On the other hand, it was an attempt to overcome the indifference or fear that until then had kept the Miao from welcoming missionaries in their midst. Clarke himself tried a slightly different approach with the Chung- chía, where schools were opened in three villages, which then gave the missionary occasion to regularly spend the night at the villages so that he could interact with the parents in the evening. He noted that he only made three converts and they were "by no means satisfactory," for he noted that the Chung-chía were on the whole a people whose "thoughts were of the earth, earthy."[78]

In 1898 Clarke and his wife were working on translation-related work near the coast. Robber bands were active in Panghai district, and Mr. Bolton saw fit to go to Kweiyang for a break. It was agreed that a Mr. W. S. Fleming, who had been doing evangelistic work among the

---

77   Ibid., 150.
78   Ibid., 153.

Chinese, would go to cover Panghai with the help of Mr. P'an Sheo-shan, the Miao native helper. Because of increasingly troubled conditions, most of the Chinese and Miao in the area had taken refuge in the other cities or in the hills. It became evident to Fleming that it would be best for him to do likewise. So with P'an Sheo-shan and P'an Sï-yin, the local school teacher and only baptized Miao believer from Panghai, he began his several-day journey back to Kweiyang. In the town of Chung-ngan-kiang, Fleming and P'an Sheo-shan were destined to receive the martyr's crown. Without any discussion or accusation of any sort, a man with a sword first struck down P'an with a sword and then, when Fleming, after dismounting from his mule, rushed to the dying man's aid, he too was struck down and soon died with many wounds. P'an Sï-yin was able to flee and save his life. It took him about eight days to get to Kweiyang and tell the missionaries there what had happened. Meanwhile bandits and soldiers in Panghai took advantage of their deaths to ransack the mission station. At this same time J. R. Adam, who was beginning his work among the Miao in the Anshun Prefecture in western Kweichow, was in Kweiyang at the time, and he with a native preacher and an official escort went to retrieve the bodies and learn the details of what had happened.

> When they arrived at the scene of the murders, they found the bodies had been put in two cheap coffins and left unburied by the roadside. The bodies were, with as little delay as possible, put into decent coffins and conveyed to Panghai.
>
> After killing Mr. Fleming and P'an Sheo-shan, some of the Chung-ngan-kiang men went off at once to Panghai, and assisted by the soldiers there, thoroughly looted the Mission-house. Everything in the place was carried off or destroyed. While at Chung-ngan-kiang, Mr. Adam learned that the murders had been deliberately planned and carried out. The country round about Panghai was overrun with robbers, who since the burning of Panghai were called rebels, and in case of inquiry the headmen had thought to lay blame on them, or if this contention should be disproved, as the anti-foreign party were in power, they might still hope to escape all punishment for the crime.
>
> Some of the people of Chung-ngan-kiang, however, were already sorry for what had been done. One man said to Mr. Adam: "They were all saying that the foreigner was importing arms and ammunition among the Miao, but when they searched his luggage, and ransacked his house, they found no arms, nothing but good books; he was certainly a good man and it was a mistake to kill him."[79]

---

79 Ibid., 158–59.

Thus Fleming became the first martyr in the annals of the CIM, and P'an Sheo-shan became the first Protestant Miao believer in Kweichow to die for the cause of Christ. Their deaths occurred in the context of great unrest, with robber bands and soldiers creating distress for many. Some might have questioned their wisdom in having gone out to Panghai at such a time when the risks to life and limb were certainly evident. They might perhaps have waited until the land was peaceful, but that would have required a wait of fifty years, for Kweichow remained in an unsettled state until the 1950s, and then missionaries were no longer permitted to preach the gospel in China. The missionaries who brought the gospel to Southwest China and the Upper Mekong Region did so knowing the risks they were taking. As it was, their lives were often preserved in the midst of extreme trials. On occasion lives were laid down due to malaria, drownings (as was the case with a later missionary to Panghai, Mr. Charles Chenery in 1905) and, in rare cases, martyrdom. Those who died did not experience anything beyond what they had bargained for when they committed their lives to follow Jesus Christ as his ambassadors. While rewards are promised to all those who lay down their lives for the gospel, and it ought not to be considered an unbearable tragedy when some do die for the sake of the gospel, it is undeniable that their deaths often led to a grievous loss. Fleming's and P'an's deaths by sword, coupled with severe illnesses that caused the Webbs and Mr. Bolton to leave the field, followed the drowning of Mr. Chenery, certainly hindered the work. Learning the languages and cultures took time. Building relationships and learning how to do missionary work in a new setting without the help of an experienced senior missionary or native evangelist to look to for advice will generally take a minimum of several years. In Panghai the process had to be repeated from scratch several times. So it should not be considered a mystery that the work among the Heh Miao in that district did not bear the same results that were found in other places.

For a comparison, it is necessary to look again at the ministry of J. R. Adam in Anshun. Here was a man who was able to spend most of twenty-seven years (October 8, 1888, to August 9, 1915, with a few furloughs back in Scotland) in one prefecture, and to give nearly twenty of those years to the Flowery Miao. A long time in one general area with one ministry to focus on is no guarantee of success, but there is plenty of evidence to support the view that great accomplishments occur where gifted and dedicated workers spend a decade or more among responsive populations. Adam was granted the privilege of presiding over one of the great mass movements to Christ in the early twentieth century. He made the most of the opportunity which was granted to him.

Back in 1895, when Clark was beginning his survey of the Miao in Kweichow, Adam was still dividing his time between the Chinese and the Miao in the Anshun area. In the town of Anshun was a Chinese church of twenty-eight members, and good relationships were being developed with some of the bolder Miao. "Some of them were rather afraid, not of Mr. Adam, but of what the Chinese might say if they showed themselves friendly to a foreigner and received him in their houses."[80] After 1896 he became more fully engaged in work among the Hua or Flowery Miao as others came to take up responsibilities among the Chinese. In 1898 he first began to baptize Miao believers. It would seem that the first stages of a movement were becoming evident when in 1900 the Boxer Rebellion erupted. The Chinese sometimes this conflict the War of Eight Nations.[81] It may have begun originally as an anti-Manchu uprising, but it was quickly redirected by the Dowager Empress in Peking into an attempt to turn back the clock a century, force the foreign barbarians to depart from the empire, and leave her as its unrightful ruler. The attempt was futile and pathetic. The dowager and her chosen advisors were utterly ignorant of the true state of affairs, not only in foreign countries but within their own country as well. They actively encouraged an uprising which would only lead to disaster.

The antiforeign feeling certainly did exist and with just cause. The French, the Russians, the British, and the Japanese were busy dismembering the Manchu Empire. While the loss of Tongking (modern Northern Vietnam) may not have meant much to the average Chinese peasant, the construction of a railroad line into Yunnan would have. The presence of French officials and their Annamese soldiers, with weapons at Yunnan-fu (modern day Kunming), was one of many provocations to the Chinese.[82] One cannot suppose that the French were oblivious to the implications of their behavior. A violent response from the Chinese would have given them all the excuse they needed to enlarge their empire by consolidating Southwest China as their sphere of influence. The response was both greater and smaller than they might have anticipated. Catholic churches were burned down along

---

80   Ibid., 173.
81   Great Britain, France, Germany, Austria, Italy, Russia, the United States, and Japan.
82   Annam was the name of the French protectorate which now makes up the central part of Vietnam. Grist, *Samuel Pollard*, 114, 116–17.

with the homes of the CIM and Bible Christian Mission (BCM) in Yunnan-fu. The French commanded that all missionaries evacuate to the coast, and the British consul confirmed that the British subjects must do so also. The Chinese viceroys in South China would not obey the imperial edict to kill the foreigners, but the situation was very tense until the foreigners reached the European-controlled ports on the coast.

By the autumn of 1900 the uprising had run its course. The atrocities committed by the Boxers were excessively avenged by the foreign armies. The helpless condition of the Manchu rulers and their Chinese subjects became obvious to all from the greatest to least. The Boxer Uprising and its aftermath contributed to make Kweichow Province even more unsettled than it had been before.[83] As missionaries returned to their stations in late 1900 and 1901, they found that the Chinese who had previously opposed their work had been active during their departure to dissuade the Miao from showing interest in the foreigners or their message in the future. Robber bands had been active and had plundered the market of Kai-li, near Tsingpinghsien. The magistrates claimed that there was actually a rebel army that needed to be suppressed. Since there was no such army, some alternates had to be found to be caught and punished. Those Miao who had previously shown hospitality to the foreigners or interest in the gospel suffered greatly. The local Miao headmen decided that these Miao would be suitable scapegoats and accordingly rounded up and executed thirty-four heads of families. Others had their houses plundered, were fined, and were forced to sign documents renouncing Christianity. Thus the headmen hoped to both snuff out all interest in the foreigners' teachings and to be duly rewarded for putting down a rebellion.

In an earlier age their plans might have succeeded. But times had changed. Before the missionaries had returned, P'an Si-yin, who had been appointed to oversee the work, went to the British consul in far-distant Chungking (modern spelling: Chongqing) to seek help. Some might say that he should not have appealed to the foreigners, but the alternative was to leave the unjust officials free to claim that the Christians were murderous rebels who had to be put to death. At the same time that P'an had come with his appeal, "Mr. Wilton [the British consul] had also received a dispatch from the new governor of the province stating that the Christian Miao had attacked Lai-li, killed two military officers,

---

83   It might appear that the only thing that changed in this province for decades was the way the name was spelled: Kwei-chau, Kweichau, Kweichou, Kweichow, and finally Guizhou.

wounded the civil magistrate and his secretary, etc., etc."[84] Such an accusation required a formal response through official channels. The British consul arranged to have Adam and Clarke with a Chinese official appointed by the governor to visit the area, make an investigation, and report back the result of their findings. Then the governor sent his own official to determine if the first team had made an accurate report. Both investigations confirmed that the so-called Miao Christians had in no way been involved with any robberies or rebellion. Hence, some Chinese officials and Miao headmen were evidently guilty of a gross miscarriage of justice.

> But how was the affair to be settled? It was explained to us that the Governor was convinced that the Christians had no hand in attacking Kai-li, but if we demanded satisfaction for the death of thirty-two innocent people, they would be compelled to maintain that those men were guilty, for if they did otherwise, the Chinese magistrates, some of them of high rank, some of whom had been deceived by the Miao headmen, and were responsible for this miscarriage of justice would necessarily have to be degraded. If, however, we would not demand satisfaction for the thirty-two men executed, they were quite prepared to admit that the Christians had not been among the rebels, and would indemnify them for their pecuniary losses.
>
> As Christian missionaries, we had no desire to demand satisfaction for any man's death, but we certainly did wish that Christians who were altogether innocent should be cleared of the grave charge of killing and robbing in Kai-li. So we told them that we made no demand for the punishment of any one, and if they would put out a proclamation exonerating the Christians from all participation in the Kai-li affair and indemnify them for the pecuniary losses, we should be satisfied. We also suggested that those headmen who had so wickedly abused their positions should be removed from their positions as Justices of the Peace. And that was how the matter was settled. The Governor and local magistrate put out proclamations declaring that the Christians took no part in the attack on Kai-li; the headmen who had wrongly denounced them were named and removed from their positions; and the families who had been squeezed and plundered were partly indemnified.[85]

To Otto von Bismarck has been attributed the quote, "Politics is the art of the possible." Most Protestant missionaries lack the training in politics and diplomacy which marked the Jesuits of yesteryear. A few have learned the basic rules in the school of experience, and combining it with the ethics of the Sermon of the Mount, have applied it with good effect. This particular incident required the utmost wisdom to deal with. Those

---

84 Clarke, *Tribes of South-West China*, 165.

85 Ibid., 168–69.

who died had not been formally incorporated into the church through baptism. They were not offered the choice of recanting or being killed. Some had never even professed faith, but only been inquirers or hosts of foreigners. As such it is hard to see how the missionaries could truly be considered as the formal representatives of those who had been killed, fined, or plundered, except for the fact that no one else could or would represent their cause. The case had been brought to the attention of the British consul, not by the missionaries themselves after the missionaries knew the facts firsthand, but by the Chinese governor on one hand and the Miao teacher when the missionaries were absent on the other. Therefore they themselves were in no position to know the whole story until they carried out their investigation. Furthermore, the damage which had been done, as great as it was, could not compare to the harm that would have resulted if the accusation that Christians had led a rebellion and killed Chinese officials was maintained by the Chinese officials from the governor on down. That the missionaries came up with a response which was acceptable to those who had suffered, the British consul, and even the Chinese governor is a tribute to their Christian ethics and their many years of close interaction in Mandarin with Chinese officials.

After the Boxers

China was transformed by the Boxer Rebellion. While the eight nations had for the most part done nothing to gain the love of the Chinese, they had convinced them that Confucianism could not triumph over modern arms and armies. The largest contingent of the invasion force was sent by the Japanese, who only fifty years earlier would not have dreamed that their soldiers could have marched at will over Chinese soil. Japan had changed its form of government and thus had been able to modernize its military. The Chinese saw clearly that they needed to change their organizational structure if their nation and their civilization were to be saved. Reforming Confucianism would not be enough. New forms of education were needed and new subjects must be studied. Samuel Pollard's biographer, W. A. Grist, recorded:

> At that time China was in such a state of dissatisfaction with her old ways that she was almost, if not quite willing, to adopt Christianity if the Church did not insist upon rejecting the worship of ancestors, and the equation of Confucius with Jesus. Although Pollard would make no such compromises as these, he used every opportunity for establishing Christianity as an ideal and as an institution in North Yunnan. The following is his summary of the results of the tour he had just completed: "Hundreds of people gave in their

names as inquirers, representing a community of many thousands; three chapels were formally opened; three others are in course of preparation. Writing now six weeks after our return, and after hearing the report of Mr. Yen and Mr. Wang, who are also back, the whole movement seems marvelous. In this prefecture of Chaotong there are people from thirty-four places asking us to teach them. Most of them are Chinese; but some are Mohammedans, some are Miao, and some are I-ren. Nearly all are absolutely ignorant of what real Christianity is; some are moved by impure, selfish motives; but in the movement there is the hand of God plainly and lovingly seen."[86]

Missionaries in all parts of China were having almost the exact same experience as Pollard in the first few years of the new century.

There have been mass movements and people movements throughout history. Mass movements or people movements are the result of a large population, in a fairly short period of time, making a decision, often as a community, to change their religious allegiance. For example, the Anglo-Saxons entered the Christian church as part of a mass movement in the seventh century AD. The Burmans entered the Buddhist religion in mass when they entered the land now called Burma about one thousand years ago. Such movements are a sociological and historical fact. At certain times in history, communal and/or political leaders and their followers recognize that there would be benefits in changing their belief system. In some cases an entire ethnic or geopolitical group makes a change, and within a generation the religious beliefs and practices of its members are completely realigned. At other times the movement is checked by various forces and only a segment of a larger population makes the change. Then those who have made the change and those who remain unchanged become separate cultures, even though they may share the same language and general geographic location. Movements may occur peacefully or involve violent altercations. They may themselves lead to violent change.

The movement toward Christianity that was noticeable throughout China in the first decade of the twentieth century never became a large movement. Missionaries themselves responded cautiously to a movement which was typified, in their minds, by ignorance and impure and selfish motives. Furthermore, no Chinese national leaders emerged who could direct the movement. While the missionaries had raised up many evangelists and a fair number of ordained pastors, there had been no development of a truly national Chinese leadership at this time. The Chinese who were looking to

---

86 Grist, *Samuel Pollard*, 135.

the church in this time of crisis found a foreign-dominated institution which could not speak to their felt needs. Within a few years' time the movement passed away. Church membership had increased in some locations, often however with a lower standard of Christian commitment and morality than had existed before the Boxer Rebellion.

At roughly the same time, a movement of a completely different nature occurred among some groups of Miao which was to lead to thousands of converts being added to the church in a short period of time.

The Mass Movement among the Miao

When the the missionaries who had been designated to tribal work returned to Kweichow after the Boxer Rebellion, they found that their work had been set back considerably. Besides those new believers and inquirers who had been killed, there were many others who had been cowed by threats that they would experience a similar fate if they dared to show interest in the foreigner's religion. Meanwhile, in the Panghai area there was a dearth of missionaries to reach out to the Heh Miao after death and disease had taken its toll.

Dramatic change was coming. Near Anshun, J. R. Adam and his Chinese co-workers were able to baptize twenty Hua Miao in 1902. Then his attention was directed to the Shui or Water Miao twenty miles to the north near the village of Ten-ten. By 1904 a movement was underway.

> The gospel spread so rapidly that when Adam went to some villages he found them "already able to sing many Gospel hymns adapted to their own chants, and able to repeat the Lord's Prayer, the Ten Commandments and outlines of the Gospel story . . . Of their own accord they gathered together their sacrificial drums, the sorcerers' wands, their charms and 'spirit packets,' and cast them into the flames. In some villages all traces of idolatry were removed, the spirit trees were cut down and an anti-opium campaign begun." They were careful to observe the Sabbath.[87]

In 1903 J. R. Adam met some hunters from the Great Flowery (Ta-hwa) Miao tribe. He shared his food with them and then the gospel. An elderly man in the group said, "It is not good for us to keep such news to ourselves, let us go and tell our kinsmen." This old man proclaimed that Jesus "was 'Klang-meng,' i.e., the Miao King."[88] In this way many hundreds more came to hear and respond to the gospel.

In that year J. R. Adam saw six baptisms. By 1906 the number had

---

87 Broomhall, *Some a Hundredfold*, 17–18.
88 Clarke, *Tribes of South-West China*, 184.

risen to 1479. At one baptismal ceremony, applicants for baptism were examined by a missionary, B. Curtis Waters. Representatives from the various villages sat in on the examination to approve or declare anything wrong in the life or practice of the candidate. Questions included such subjects as "the person of God, the Trinity, the incarnation, . . . together with matters relating to life and practice: opium, wine, immoral practices, participation in idolatrous or superstitious rites etc." The questions were asked in such a way that the applicant could not give memorized responses. Curtis recorded a few examples of questions and answers that were given.

> Take an old man's testimony. "Why, you are more than seventy, what do you want to believe in Jesus for? Do you think He wants an old fellow like you? Ah, these younger men may believe on Jesus and be His disciples and serve Him: But you have only a few years to live. Will Jesus not say 'this old man has served the devil for over seventy years and now he comes to me! Do I want an old fellow like him?'"
>
> "Want! He longs after old people like us exceedingly." Or another old man in answer to the same proposition said, as if astonished at my putting it so, "Why, He died on the cross to save us."[89]

J. R. Adam tells the story of an old woman whom he interviewed after questioning her concerning all the major points of doctrine. He asked, "Where are your sins?" She answered, "Oh, I have not got any, my sins all passed over on to the body of Jesus and He took them away on the cross."[90]

The work spread into Yunnan Province through the evangelistic activities of the Miao themselves who went out to various villages near and far in pairs and taught far into the night. The Chinese, their Nosu landlords and even their own tribal leaders, often perscuted them by means of robberies, beatings, fines, and imprisonments. Eventually the Chinese magistrates put an end to the persecution by making it clear that the religious movement was not an act of rebellion. In 1907 only 3 of the over 1,400 who were baptized in 1906 had fallen away. By 1915 in Adam's district there were 5,590 communicants, 42 evangelists, 29 school teachers, 639 scholars, 2 colporteurs, 3 Bible women, and 323 unpaid helpers.[91]

How can this movement be explained or understood? As we have already noted, this was a period of great change throughout China. The antiforeign movement had clearly failed. Western arms had proved victorious and therefore Western ideology was worth considering. But

---

89   China Inland Mission, *China's Millions*, U.S. ed., 1907, 4.
90   *A Modern Pentecost*, 16.
91   Broomhall, *Some a Hundredfold*, 24.

most Miao were not literate and certainly were not reading the writings of Chinese reformers in Peking or Shanghai. They may well have sensed the uncertainty of local Chinese magistrates and felt the need of patrons who could help them through a time of troubles. They might have experienced a certain degree of increased freedom which emboldened them to respond to the message that the missionaries brought to them. This does not explain the extent of the movement. The majority of the Miao did not respond to the preaching of missionaries but to their own relatives and Miao evangelists. The missionaries often came to their communities long after they had responded to the message. The missionaries did in various ways act as patrons to the Miao believers, but their assistance was of the nature to decrease the oppression that Miao Christians faced. It was not the sort of patronage that would directly entice animists to become believers.

Furthermore, the movement had a very clear moral impact on the Miao who were influenced by it. Prior to the movement the Miao were notorious for their festivals where drunkenness and promiscuity were indulged in without any restraint. Where the movement occurred, these twin evils virtually disappeared almost overnight and did not reemerge for years to come. Equally significant was the fact that these Miao, unlike the mass of Chinese who were flocking to churches in other parts of China at roughly the same time, knew the gospel both as doctrine and in its application to their own lives. They rejoiced to know that Jesus had come to die on the cross to take away their sin. They wept for those who did not yet know the good news, and they sacrificed their time and wealth, and even risked their lives to carry the gospel to their brethren who did not know the Savior. In the early stages of the movement at least, they also were instrumental in sharing the gospel with other tribes as well. As such it represented one of many such movements which swept the globe in the first decade of the twentieth century and needs to be considered in that context. In order to understand what was happening among the Miao of Southwest China, it is essential to step back and get a grasp of what was occurring worldwide at that time.

The Worldwide Revival of 1904–7

The second half of the nineteenth century saw the height of British imperialism. This was the Victorian era and Queen Victoria did not merely give her name to the era, she also gave to it her moral stamp. While the British aristocracy was not transformed as with a magic wand from the amoral behavior that predominated during the reigns of the Georges and William IV, they did at the very least choose to practice a dignified hypocrisy out of respect to the queen and the middle class. For the Victorian era was a period when Christian morality was in vogue. Men like Charles Spurgeon knew that it was a temporary state. He took advantage of it but warned his listeners that it would not last.

By 1901 Queen Victoria was dead, as were men like Bishop Ryle, Spurgeon, George Mueller, and D. L. Moody from America. An era was ending. A new age of skepticism, socialism, and mocking unbelief was coming to dominate the scene. Intellectuals like T. H. Huxley, H. G. Wells, and Bertrand Russell were providing alternative views of progress that saw religion as a reactionary idea that hindered man's advance. Authors and playwrights such as Bernard Shaw and Jack London popularized alternative views on how man can get on without God. In America Samuel Clemens would mock the traditional view of God, but with a generally cynical view of human nature he could not imagine any utopian alternative. Skepticism and unbelief were not at all new, but with the development of the theory of evolution the atheists and agnostics at last found themselves with a somewhat convincing worldview which could effectively compete with Christianity for general acceptance. One of the finest qualities of such a worldview was that it did not require the studied hypocrisy which Christian morality demanded of all who did not wish to partake of Christian sanctification.

The result was mass apostasy, which happened so swiftly that it would amaze all but those who had read the Old Testament and found that it was a common tale in the history of the nation of Israel as well. It was this apostasy that woke many Christians out of their stupor and led to a prayer movement which resulted in a worldwide awakening. This awakening first became evident in Wales in 1904. A. T. Pierson, who was one of the last surviving evangelical leaders of the late nineteenth century, wrote about what had led to this awakening in *The Missionary Review of the World*.

> In 1902, Christians in Great Britain, deeply stirred by the rapid decline in evangelical faith and preaching, formed at Keswick, in July, "a circle of prayer for world-wide revival," the design of which was expressly stated to be, in the simplest possible way, to band together those who are willing to pray daily for a fulfillment of the Divine Word, "I will pour out my Spirit upon all flesh," and to go on praying until the answer is given. Not mere revival in our churches, but the Divine and gracious visitation of the millions outside all churches is what this prayer circle seeks.
>
> That prayer circle rapidly extended until its membership is counted by tens of thousands and is found in every part of the globe. There has been from the beginning a profound conviction and expectation that some remarkable results would come from this agreement—this symphony of praying souls.

And quite simultaneously with the formation of the praying band, revival fires began to kindle in widely separated places ...

Those who had thus banded themselves for definite prayer at Keswick in 1902, and asked others to join them, naturally began to act as if they expected blessing ...

Just before he died, Dean Howell, in 1903, wrote and published a paper on the "chief need of Wales." ... The "chief need" as he felt it was "a spiritual awakening." Not a reform but a revival; not a local agitation, as may be witnessed in connection with a "simultaneous mission," but a sort of spiritual high tide to flood the whole country, such as would saturate all classes with the baptism of the Holy Ghost. And as though he had written when the eternal world was already dawning on his consciousness, he closes his appeal with these significant words:

"Take Notice!" If it were known that this is my last message to my fellow countrymen before being summoned to judgment, and the light of eternity already breaking over me, the chief need of my country and my dear nation at present is a spiritual revival through the outpouring of the Holy Ghost.[92]

This in fact was what Wales received. J. Edwin Orr, the great historian of revivals, showed clearly in his various writings that more than eighty thousand new members were added to the churches of Wales through this movement, and the vast majority remained faithful Christians throughout their lives. Furthermore the revival was in no way confined to Wales. Many other parts of Great Britain experienced the revival, and similar movements occurred worldwide between 1904 and 1907.[93]

Terminology becomes important at this point because there are many definitions of revival and awakening. Orr's own definition is as good as any and perhaps better than most.

Outpourings of the Spirit are exclusively the work of God; but revivals are the work of God with the response of believers; awakenings are the work of God with the response of the people. The work of man, besides praying and preaching appropriate truths, lies in evangelising and in teaching, the former in the call for repentance and conversion, the latter in making known the commandments of the Lord in all respects of life. This is the great commission, truly the commanded mission of the Church which, if not accomplished by disciples of Christ, will not be done at all.[94]

---

92 A. T. Pierson, "The Welsh Revival and God's Signals," *The Missionary Review of the World* (March 1905): 167.

93 J. Edwin Orr, *The Outpouring of the Spirit in Revival and Awakening and Its Issue in Church Growth* (Pontypridd, UK: British Church Growth Association, 2000), http://www.churchmodel.org.uk/Orr%20HS%20BOOKLET%20A4.pdf, 10.

94 Ibid., 6.

Christian communities in Wales and elsewhere experienced revivals that led to awakenings of the previously unchurched populations of these Christianized lands. There were simultaneously numerous awakenings among totally pagan populations in Southeast Asia. Some of the groups that responded dramatically to the gospel at this time were the Garo and Mizo in Northeast India and the Lahu in Burma. In some cases the revival in Wales led Christians to pray more fervently for their mission fields, while Welsh missionaries dared to pray for greater outpourings of the Holy Spirit in their fields of ministry. In the Khassia (now written as Khasi) Hills of Northeast India, Welsh missionaries were active. There it was recorded:

> For two years some faithful men in Mawphlang had been praying for a blessing, and as they prayed on, eighty persons joined the church. The news of the Revival in Wales stimulated the prayer and the longing, not in Mawphlang only, but throughout the Khassia and Jantia Hills. In Wales also, Christians were praying for Khassia with deepened intensity, and on March 5, 1905, the first droppings of the shower fell.[95]

There was not always such a direct connection, but there was one common element that was evident worldwide. Revivals and awakenings occurred only where the Christian missionaries or local believers believed that God could pour out his Holy Spirit and suddenly transform lives, and where they in united prayer sought for him to do so. At about the same time, in Honan Province of China, Jonathan Goforth became instrumental in numerous local revivals where Christians confessed sins, made restitution for harm they had caused to others, sought reconciliation, and became actively engaged in evangelism which resulted in many converts added to the churches. In his book *By My Spirit*, he makes a direct connection to what he heard of the revival in Wales and what he saw of the revival in Korea. In his case he worked for revival for several years before it began to occur in the churches where he ministered.[96]

What Helen Dyer recorded in India was true in China and elsewhere as well.

> The leaven of unbelief and misbelief that is honeycombing some of our home Churches is not unrepresented on the mission field. The life there, spiritually, is affected by the life in the home Churches that sustains it. "If the light that is in thee be darkness, how great is that darkness." Possibly somewhere in this direction may be found the reason why the Revival has *passed through* some missions, and almost *passed by* others.[97]

---

95   Helen S. Dyer, *Revival in India* (London: Morgan & Scott, 1907), 30.
96   Jonathan Goforth, *By My Spirit* (Grand Rapids: Zondervan, 1942), 19–25.
97   Dyer, *Revival in India*, 25.

With the work among the Miao, there is no such record of specific efforts being taken to promote revival. The missionaries gave themselves wholeheartedly to support and follow up on the movement that was occurring among the several Miao groups, but the initiative to do evangelism came from the new converts themselves, and the desire to break from sinful and immoral practices likewise took shape without any special movement of prayer or preaching by the missionaries. It is hard however, from any perspective, to understand why some Miao groups responded wholeheartedly to the gospel while other groups were virtually untouched. Moreover, the neighboring Chung-chía showed almost no interest in the gospel whatsoever.

Getting back now to the Miao in Kweichow and Yunnan, we can see that what was happening among them, while it was remarkable, was by no means unique. The individual missionaries who worked among them had not previously seen great movements of unbelievers coming to a vital faith in Christ. In fact the CIM had never before experienced such a movement in its history, but the members believed that it was within the range of possibilities, and they did all they could to promote and not stifle the movement when it did begin.

The Miao, when they responded to the gospel, brought the gospel to other tribes also. Presumably they used Chinese as their medium of communication. By 1907, Lisu and Lakka congregations had formed. They also reached out to other Miao groups far from their own homes. As a result missionaries found themselves in the unusual position of having many more inquirers coming to them than they could ever hope to follow up. Miao traveled for several days from the west to meet J. R. Adam in Anshun in order to learn more about the gospel. Knowing that he could not give them the attention they demanded, he encouraged them to seek out Samuel Pollard in Chaotong in Yunnan, which was much closer to their homes. Thus Pollard was drawn into Miao work even though he was at the time giving his attention to the Chinese. While he was to become one of the great pioneer missionaries to the Miao, he remained active in Chinese work and also took on increasing responsibilities as a field leader of the United Methodist Mission, which had become the successor to the Christian Bible Mission. His output was prodigious, but it was not concentrated solely on the Miao. J. R. Adam in Anshun was likewise tied down at times with responsibilities for Chinese work even after the movement among the Great Flowery Miao had begun.

How much more might have been accomplished through this

movement if there were more veteran missionaries available to help with the work at that time? We have no way of knowing. Furthermore, this line of questioning may be defective in that it is based on the unproven assumption that an increase of foreign workers can have a direct correlation on the numbers gathered in during a movement and the quality of the churches that the movement produces. It may well be the case that there is an optimal amount of foreign involvement in a movement. Without that optimal amount the movement can become subverted by false teachers, but too much outside help might keep indigenous leadership from developing or maturing. For this reason it may very well have been the case that the Miao work made progress, in part, because the optimal number of veteran workers actually was on hand to assist the movement.

Issues of Unity

Issues between J. R. Adam and Samuel Pollard emerged over time. The several days' journey between their stations might have limited the harm caused by these differences, but it also made it difficult to resolve differences that did exist. The details of these differences need not concern us here. They were not unique at that time. Success in opening up Western China, success in getting more mission boards to send workers there, and success to some degree in planting numerous churches in some parts of Western China all contributed to new challenges that the earliest foreigners never had to deal with. In January 1908 a conference was held for all the Protestant missionaries in Southwest China. The location was Chen-t'u (Chengdu) in Sichuan Province. Approximately 170 missionaries from ten mission boards attended.

In the China Inland Mission *Monthly Notes* for March 1908 there was a report about the event. Considerable attention was given to the spiritual nature of the gathering of so many missionaries, and also as a sign of the new age that was beginning in China it was mentioned that English-speaking Chinese Christians were invited to the event. Of special note was the fact that the viceroy of Sichuan actually came to briefly address the gathering. The participants focused on a topic that would demand considerable attention from missionaries and Chinese Christians for decades to come.

> The subject of the Conference was "The Formation of one Christian Protestant Church for West China." Although it was found to be impossible at present to form such a church, yet it was unanimously agreed that such a union church was the ideal towards which we should work, and a standing Committee of representatives from each mission was appointed to keep this

matter in view and to report progress year by year to the West China Advisory Board. *Although* perhaps nothing very definite has been accomplished along these lines, and even if the ideal should never be attained, yet it was felt that the Conference has been the means of uniting the missionaries of West China in a closer bond than ever before, and that henceforward individual missions and missionaries will take greater and more sympathetic interest in each other's work, which will go far toward removing causes of possible friction and misunderstanding. A resolution to the effect that missionaries of different societies should recognize the converts of societies other than their own was carried unanimously by a standing vote.[98]

In theory, many if not most missionaries believe in cooperation and unity among Christians. In practice this is not always so simple. When a new region like Southwest China was entered, and the overwhelming needs were clearly apparent, it was natural that a variety of groups would be able to cooperate closely as long as such cooperation meant nothing more than dividing up areas that would take several days to walk across. But the commitment to unity is tested when work expands. As it is told by Pollard's biographer, W. A. Grist, the problems in the Miao work were brought on by J. R. Adam.

At this time Dymond and Mylne [both members of the United Methodist Missionary Society] came to Si-pang-tsing with Pollard to meet Messrs. Adam and Page of the China Inland Mission. The West China Conference had roughly marked out certain spheres for the various missions. But Mr. Adam had driven a wedge into the district assigned to the United Methodists. In most instances both Missions would have welcomed such proximity as an opportunity for co-operation; but owing to Mr. Adam's peculiar theological views an estrangement arose which affected the relations of the two Missions. Some of Mr. Adam's evangelists even refused Pollard's men admission to the Communion. Pollard and his colleagues deprecated such misunderstandings among the native Christians and offered to withdraw from Teh-Choh if they might retain Tu-kai-tsi where they had No-Su and Chinese adherents. Although unable to come to a satisfactory arrangement Pollard never forgot that Mr. Adam had sent the Miao to see him at Chaotong seven years before.[99]

It is often safe to assume when reading biographies of real Christians that details of painful disagreements have been intentionally shrouded in a mist.[100] There seems to be evidence to suggest that Pollard himself was

---

98 China Inland Mission, *Monthly Notes*, March 1908, 2.
99 Grist, *Samuel Pollard*, 273–74.
100 "And above all things have fervent charity among yourselves: for charity shall cover the multitude of sins" (1 Pet 4:8 KJV).

not the easiest man in the world to cooperate with. Moreover, his own Wesleyan beliefs, which he held in high regard, might not have made it easy for a non-Wesleyan like Adam to cooperate closely with him. Our concern here is that it is one thing for numerous delegates at a conference to agree that unity is a good idea; it is quite another thing for a few of them to work in a united fashion on the field in those places where the work of two veteran pioneer missionaries comes into direct contact.

One topic of concern that did emerge was over the use of the Miao language in teaching. The promotion of literacy was acknowledged by all as being essential. The use of Chinese alone would not meet the needs of the emerging Miao churches. Pollard developed his own script which was inspired by an article he read on a missionary who worked with American Indians. The choosing of a suitable script is not a simple matter, and decisions made at an early stage of any work must necessarily have implications that last centuries. Written languages can unite and can also divide people.[101] When other missionaries among the Miao sought to develop a unified Miao script using a romanized script, the existing Pollard script became a stumbling block to cooperative efforts. Perhaps with more time and effort in the earliest years of the movement more cooperation might have been possible, but time was ever in short supply. With thousands of new believers, and hundreds of villages, not only of Miao but of neighboring tribes as well showing responsiveness to the gospel, men like Pollard and Adam did not have free time to sit down and sort out the fine points of what might promote long-term unity. In fact it might actually be claimed that unity is not always necessary in a movement of God; if only at the very least, opposing parties will leave each other alone to get on with their work. This, for the most part, is what actually happened.

It should be noted that relations between the Australian CIM missionary Arthur Nicholls and Pollard were much more positive. Nicholls actually spent several months with Pollard and his disciples before beginning ministry among the Miao in Wuting (Wuding). These Miao had migrated from the area around Chaotung and spoke the same dialect.

> When the Christian Miao at Shih-men-kan understood that Mr. Nichols was returning to preach the Gospel to their own people in Wuting district four of Mr. Pollard's preachers volunteered to go with him. Later on the Church decided, with Mr. Pollard's hearty approbation, to recognize these

---

101 One of the symptoms or causes of the Balkanization of the Balkans was the use of Cyrillic and Latin scripts among the various ethnic groups as they were Christianized during the early Middle Ages.

four preachers as their own and to be responsible for their support. Moreover, it was suggested that they should continue this ministry until such time as Mr. Nicholls should, from among his own converts, have trained native preachers to help him.[102]

Nicholls was of the Wesleyan persuasion, which would help explain the degree of cooperation possible with Pollard who later wrote:

> Our China Inland Mission friends in Yunnan Fu and in the north and east among aborigines and Chinese are Methodists, English Wesleyans, Australian Methodists and Primitives…By and by in Yunnan we can get a great Methodist Church known, please God, for its purity and missionary fire.[103]

The gospel spread rapidly among the Miao and did not stop with them. In Yunnan they carried the gospel to the Na-su (Nosu), the Le-su (Lisu), and the Lakka. The missionaries did not initiate this cross-cultural outreach but helped to follow it up.

The missionaries also helped in the role of patrons to the Miao church by visiting with their Nosu landlords, who were often called *lairds* in the contemporary literature, because their position was in some ways similar to that of Scottish lords in a previous era. Issues such as the Christians' refusal to work on Sunday, to give alcoholic drinks to their *lairds*, or contribute to offerings for demonic ceremonies all contributed to tensions between the new believers and their earthly masters. Many Miao were tortured, beaten, and imprisoned for refusing to follow the traditions. In one case Pollard himself was beaten nearly to death by "vagabonds" who were incited to act against him by the Nosu.

Clarke describes the sufferings that the Miao suffered in some detail. On one occasion Adam, while traveling through an area between his district and that of Pollard's, heard of Christians who were suffering and went with his helpers to encourage them.

> The devil was at his old work, and God's children were undergoing great tribulation simply because they were Christians. One of Mr. Pollard's preachers told them how he had been strung up and put through cruel suffering. Another Miao Christian, with a happy face, told how that for a day and a night he had to wear a chain weighing one hundred and eighty pounds, and had been robbed of his horse. Another described how his body was first twisted into an unnatural position, then bound to a frame, where he was left all night and told to pray to his God to deliver him. Others had their spring crops gathered for them and their cattle and sheep stolen. Two of Mr. Pollard's preachers, happening to pass a place where one of

---

102 Clarke, *Tribes of South-West China*, 287.
103 Grist, *Samuel Pollard*, 317.

the No-su lairds and his crowd of heathen were sacrificing to demons and drinking blood-water, were seized and compelled to join the heathen rites. For resisting they were beaten and bound, and carried in front of the idol. But the whole tale of suffering cannot be told.[104]

Clearly the missionaries were only able to help lighten their afflictions to a degree. The movement was so vast, in both numbers of converts and in the area covered, that the missionaries could not directly intervene in most cases. Even in those cases where they did make the effort to beg the *lairds* to stop molesting the believers, the results were limited.[105]

The movement suffered a great setback in 1915. In a period of several months, J. R. Adam was struck dead by lightning in his home, and Samuel Pollard died after an illness induced by his exertions in caring for his co-worker who was suffering from typhoid. By this time the Methodist work that Pollard headed up had seen several thousand baptisms and about ten thousand adherents gained. In Adam's district, results were similar. Marshall Broomhall, the CIM historian of that era, summarized the scale of the work numerically.

> It is a wonderful record of blessing. Twenty years ago the number of baptized Miao could be numbered on the fingers of one hand. To-day, speaking of Mr. Adam's district alone, and including 308 baptized this year, there are 5,590 communicants, while 6,449 have been baptized from the commencement. When we think of 42 evangelists, 29 school teachers with 639 scholars, the two colporteurs and three Biblewomen, together with 323 additional unpaid helpers, one can realize a little the magnitude of the work.[106]

To measure any work qualitatively is always a challenge. Suffice it to state that now, nearly a century later, these churches for the most part remain a living testimony to the first great ingathering of souls among the tribes of Southwest China.

---

104 Clarke, *Tribes of South-West China*, 236.
105 Ibid., 238.
106 Broomhall, *Some a Hundredfold*, 24.

Chapter 4
J. O. Fraser, the Lisu, and the CIM

In the annals of CIM history, J. O. Fraser stands out as the preeminent field missionary among the tribal groups of China. There is no doubt that he is worthy of that place. While some missionaries may become famous because of the skill of their biographers, Fraser was one who was a worthy object of attention for skilled biographers. I commend *Behind the Ranges* by Mrs. Howard Taylor (nee Gertrude Guinness) and *Mountain Rain* by Eileen Crossman to all who are interested in the cause of Christ among the tribes. I will not seek to repeat or even summarize what they have so well recorded. Our purpose here is to learn what he contributed to the CIM in terms of missionary methods, both among the tribes as well as to the work in China as a whole. Before this subject can be explored, it is necessary to first glance at the wider picture of what was occurring both in China and in the Christian churches which were sending missionaries to China during the three decades (1908–38) that Fraser lived and served in China.

The China of Fraser's Age
China had been conquered and ruled by barbarians in the past, but the Mongols and the Manchus after them had been sinicized by their subject populations. When the Western Barbarians came, first with their opium and then with their manufactured goods, they took China's silver and caused the form of government which had endured for millenia to come to a hasty end. The sleeping dragon was awakened, but it would be many decades before a semblance of a lasting new order would be established. Forces were at work that missionaries could neither control nor hold in check, but had to deal with directly if they and their objectives were not to be swept away.

China: 1908–38
The year that Fraser arrived in China was the year that the last Qing emperor was placed upon the throne. As he was just a small boy, Ci Xi, the Dowager Empress, continued to rule the country. It is safe to assume that when evil, corrupt, and incompetent rulers retain power over

weak countries, they are either passively or actively maintained in that position by foreign powers who benefit by having them rule their country in their slovenly and incompetent manner. After the Boxer Rebellion the Manchu Dynasty by all rights should have been swept away, but the "foreign devils" from England to Japan all benefited immensely by the treaties and indemnities that they had forced upon the dowager's government. Therefore they were content to see her remain in power, even when she punished all those government officials who actually supported the Western powers during the rebellion by protecting the foreigners in their midst. There were, however, an increasing number of Chinese who were willing to fight for revolutionary change. Revolutions don't succeed without outside support, and in the case of China the outside support was actually the Chinese communities around the world whose coffers were tapped by a Christian named Sun Yat-sen. He was actually outside of China raising funds when the Revolution began on October 10, 1911.

After the Revolution many factions emerged to vie for power. Yuan Shih-kai, who is only worthy to be known as the man who betrayed every party that ever trusted him, rose to the presidency in 1912, but he could not keep the country together. Nor could anyone else. The Confucian model had proved itself incapable of responding to outside forces. The powerful viceroys of the wealthier provinces gave way to governors and generals who could not unite the country but were more than competent in their efforts to keep others from doing so either.

The Western powers had no desire to help China establish a strong central government, as that would only weaken their own spheres of influence. Gradually several forces emerged as highly influential in making a new China. One was the new intellectual class, the college graduates who had imbibed Western ideas, in many cases through the medium of Christian schools and colleges. Few had been effectively evangelized while attending those institutions, and all of them recognized that in the eyes of patriotic Chinese they must appear suspect. Therefore many of those who had some sort of a Christian connection led efforts to "save" China.[107] The language they used was often borrowed from Christianity and some would claim to be Christians, but their goal was to save China from foreign rule and internal decay. By the early 1920s

---

107 Lam Wing-hung, *Chinese Theology in Construction* (Pasadena: William Carey Library, 1983), 53. Also the interested reader should delve into the monthly issues of the *Chinese Recorder* from 1919 to the mid-1920s to get a valuable contemporary view and ongoing analysis of the changes that were occurring in China, and how they were affecting the church during a time of great social unrest and intellectual ferment.

they were actively opposing foreign domination of all aspects of Chinese life. Naturally mission schools, mission stations, and denominations that were financed and controlled by foreigners would be targets for their anger. The Kuo Min-tang, first under Sun Yat-sen, and later under his wife's brother-in-law, Chiang Kai-shek, made use of this antiforeign feeling to unite the country and work toward ending extraterritoriality[108] and other "unequal" treaty agreements. This process which began with the end of World War I was to reach its climax in 1927 when antiforeign riots became so violent that all foreigners in the interior of China were forced to exit to the coast or, in the case of those in Yunnan, to evacuate into Upper Burma.

At the same time communism was making rapid inroads into the heart of China. As a totally foreign ideology which was in opposition, much more than Christianity, to the traditions of the Chinese, and with considerable foreign funding from Russia, it was able to make great strides and become thoroughly indigenized within a matter of years. Some Christians would find this highly disturbing and wonder what Christian missions might learn from the Communists. Part of the answer is fairly simple. The gospel is founded on truth and Christians are required to speak and practice the truth no matter what the cost might be. Communists were free from all such constraints and therefore could promise the masses heaven on earth with no God to spoil the party.[109]

---

    108 Extraterritoriality was a legal agreement between the Chinese government and foreign powers that foreigners in China would be tried by foreign courts according to foreign laws.

    109 Some readers will find this answer too simplistic, but after spending years studying the works and writings of Communists I do not believe that the ideology could have ever made an inch of progress if its leaders from Karl Marx onward were not fully committed to mastering the art of deceit, which they applied at every level from their personal relationships to their international policies.

    Mikhail Bakunin, a contemporary of Marx and Engels seems to have held to this view as well. Regarding Marx he wrote, "There was never any frank intimacy between us—our temperaments did not permit it. He called me a sentimental idealist, and he was right; I called him vain, perfidious, and cunning, and I also was right."

    As for Engels he stated, "In 1845 Marx was the leader of the German communists. While his devoted friend Engels was just as intelligent as he was, he was not as erudite. Nevertheless, Engels was more practical, and no less adept at political calumny, lying, and intrigue. Together they founded a secret society of Germany communists or authoritarian socialists." The details can be found in *On Anarchism* by Mikhail Bakunin.

    Jumping ahead a mere century and a half, an article on Hungary includes the following quote: "The state ideology imposed by Moscow was hated in Hungary not only on account of the terror and restrictions to freedom but also due to its core that was felt to be a lie. This was, namely, the promise to make all people equal and happy. 'A communist always tells lies' is therefore the slogan of moderate and radical anti-communists alike in Eastern Europe, and it was also to be heard during the Budapest protest demonstrations on Parliament Square in autumn 2006." Kathrin Lauer, "A Communist Always Tells Lies," *Report: Magazine for Arts and Civil Society in*

At first the Communists were primarily active along the coast. Sun Yat-sen and the Kuo Min-tang (KMT) sought aid from the Soviet Union, and Chiang Kai-shek was sent to Russia for education. The Communists sought to use the KMT for their purposes, but in 1927 Chiang Kai-shek violently purged the party of Communists and set the stage for a twenty-two-year-long civil war, which was continually being complicated by the warlords who actually ruled much of China. The failure of the first-generation Communists to enlist the more westernized urban populations along the coast contributed to the rise of Mao Zedong, who understood how to harness the aspirations of the rural peasants to fulfill his goals.[110]

In 1931 the Japanese, having long profited from China's weakness, began to expand more aggressively than before. By their quick seizure of Manchuria they were enabled to extend their rule, first over Northeast China and, following 1937, over virtually all of the more populated eastern provinces. Wars, floods, and famines were common, and bandits were active throughout the land. Western dominance decreased and violent missionary deaths became more common than at any time since the Boxer Rebellion.

Western Christianity

Meanwhile, evangelical Christianity was meeting major reversals in the homelands. The evangelical propensity to be tolerant of others with differing beliefs laid them wide open to having their colleges, seminaries, denominations, and mission boards overrun by those who preached "another gospel," euphemistically known as the social gospel. In part this could be attributed to good-natured naiveté. The other explanation, which needs to be considered, is that in many cases evangelical Christians created more institutions than they could staff with qualified, like-minded Christians. Rather than close down the institutions, the tendency was to staff them with those who did not share their values. Along the same lines was the need for funds to support overambitious projects. Trustees were chosen based on their financial rather than their spiritual portfolios. The result was that what modernists and liberals would never have established on their own became theirs by default.[111] Groups like

---

Eastern- and Central Europe, January 2007, http://web.redaktionsbuero.at/output/?e=58&page=rb_ARTIKEL&a=fee95ea1&c=Eastern%20Europe&f=e.

110 John King Fairbank and Merle Goldman, "The Second Coming of the Chinese Communist Party," in *China: A New History*, 2nd enl. ed. (Cambridge, MA: Belknap Press of Harvard University Press, 2006), 294–311.

111 See Kenneth Scott Latourette, *Beyond the Ranges* (Grand Rapids: Eerdmans, 1967).

the YMCA, which shared many common values with the CIM at the beginning of the century, grew increasingly liberal, theologically and politically, as the years went on.

Around 1930 the Laymen's Inquiry began. It was an attempt by Western laymen funded by John Rockefeller to visit and evaluate the effectiveness of Christian missions. Since laymen were footing the bill for missions, it was logical that they should want a voice in what was being done on the mission field. But as the inquirers were in many cases modernists, it would be hardly likely that they would find evangelical missions, with a focus on the conversion of the heathen, to be fulfilling the objectives that the Laymen's Inquiry sought.[112] Here is a specimen of their conclusions, which is typical of the whole.

> It is clearly not the duty of the Christian missionary to attack the non-Christian systems of religion—it is his primary duty to present in positive form his conception of the way of life and let it speak for itself. The road is long, and a new patience is needed; but we can desire no variety of religious experience to perish until it has yielded up to the rest of its own ingredient of truth. The Christian will therefore regard himself as a co-worker with the forces within each religious system which are making for righteousness.[113]

The inquiry was more of a sign of the times than an actual blow to evangelical missions as a whole. Its results and recommendations were evidence that downgrading of Christian belief that had been evident to Bishop Ryle and Charles Spurgeon had reached its logical conclusion.

Missions in China experienced serious challenges on other fronts as well. The economic troubles that affected England from the mid-1920s and the Great Depression in the early 1930s only added to their problems. After over a century of expansion, the word in the late 1920s

---

112 William Ernest Hocking, *Re-Thinking Missions: A Laymen's Inquiry after One Hundred Years* (New York: Harper & Brothers, 1932).

For years John D. Rockefeller had bankrolled American Baptist Missions and he wished to reevaluate his contributions with the help of modern "scientific" methods of research. The research team represented the mainline denominations of the northern United States. (The Southern Baptists were not part of the study.) Many of the results were predetermined before the inquiry occurred by the theological persuasions of the participants. "To some of our members the enduring motive of Christian missions can only be adequately expressed as loyalty to Jesus Christ regarded as the perfect revelation of God and the only Way by which men can reach a satisfying experience of Him. To others this motive would best be called the spirit of altruistic service, the desire to share with all mankind the benefits and the ideals of a Christian community. To still others, it would best be named the desire for a deeper knowledge and love of God, seeking with men everywhere a more adequate fulfillment of the divine possibilities of personal and social life" (p. xiv). Their views would not have represented the views of those who advocated and engaged in foreign missions in the nineteenth century.

113 Ibid., 327.

and early 1930s was "retrenchment." Retrenchment meant the cutting back of workers and funding for foreign missionary activities. The total numbers of missionaries decreased dramatically in the 1930s as entire denominations lost the faith, the vision, and the will to donate for a cause that many of their leaders no longer believed in.

The CIM under D. E. Hoste

The CIM was protected at least temporarily from the ill winds that blew in the home countries. Its "no solicitation / no debt" policy meant that the Mission avoided financial liabilities that drove it to making pacts with Christians of dubious theological or moral standing in order to get funds. Their supporters came from many denominations and these individual supporters did not change their own theological views just because their denominations had new leaders with new ideas. In fact it is quite possible that as the denominations became more liberal the appeal of the CIM became greater.[114] At the very time when other mission boards were retrenching and in some cases actually removing their missionaries from the field, the CIM was recruiting new workers in order to advance into unreached places and people groups of China. The historian Kenneth Scott Latourette noted that by 1936 the CIM comprised 23 percent of all Protestant missionaries in China. The corollary was that the "shifting complexion of the missionary body altered the kind of Protestant Christianity propagated. It was more theologically conservative and less liberal than was true in the decade which immediately succeeded 1914."[115]

The fact that the CIM was not merely able to survive in China but to actually advance during the period of violent changes that were convulsing China, while still maintaining its focus, must in part be credited, under God, to the wise leadership of D. E. Hoste, who succeeded Hudson Taylor as the director of the Mission in 1900. He was to remain in that position until 1935. Thus he was to be Fraser's director for most of his missionary career. Fraser's life and ministry exemplified many of the core values that

---

114 Stuart Harverson, *Doctor in the Orient* (London: Hodder & Stoughton, 1976), 22. In his autobiography, Dr. Harverson records the following incident: "In 1931 I qualified as a doctor; the next year I asked my vicar about possible mission fields. He was non-committal. No doubt he felt this was a matter in which the Lord Himself must direct me. He mentioned that some missions no longer believed in the inspiration of the Scriptures, and that certain ones were not so much 'alive' as they used to be. 'What about the China Inland Mission?' I asked him. 'Oh, yes, of course the C.I.M. is all right,' he replied." Dr. Harverson was to become a medical missionary in Yunnan among the Lisu and other ethnic groups of the area.

115 Kenneth Scott Latourette, *A History of the Expansion of Christianity*, vol. 7, Advance through the Storm (New York: Harper & Brothers, 1945), 348.

Hoste wished to see promoted throughout the Mission. In fact it is possible to trace the relationship between the challenges that Hoste was facing as director of a Mission which had over one thousand workers throughout China, and Fraser's successful methods which provided a model for how other missionaries might work effectively at other stations. Our objective is to study the work of the CIM in Southwest China from the perspective of the issues that leaders faced. Thus it will be necessary to give more attention to Fraser's work as it developed when he emerged as a leader of missionaries in the 1920s and 1930s rather than in its initial stages which are already well documented in *Behind the Ranges* by Mrs. Howard Taylor and *Mountain Rain* by Eileen Crossman.

J. O. Fraser: The Pioneer

James Outram Fraser was born in England in 1886. His background was Methodist. He studied engineering but then was led to become a missionary and went to China with the CIM in 1908. By 1910 he had finished his basic Chinese language study and was sent to Paoshan in the southwest corner of Yunnan Province to consolidate his Chinese and assist in the Chinese work in that city in preparation for future tribal work. It was here and in neighboring Tengyueh that he first came in contact with the Lisu, who were as yet untouched by the gospel in that area. Other Lisu had been won to Christ farther to the north and east, originally through the witness of the Miao and later through the efforts of the CIM missionary George Edgar Metcalf, but in his area Fraser was a true pioneer. In this capacity he had a great opportunity to build a tribal church from the ground up on his own model. He also had the opportunity to train and lead other missionaries who would greatly impact not only the Lisu but the whole CIM/OMF in the area of missionary methods for decades to come.

Numerous dates are not readily found in *Behind the Ranges* or *Mountain Rain*. Both books give their primary attention to the work that was done from about 1911 to the early 1920s.[116] The former book tells the story of a single man in his twenties and thirties who was a primary human force in the turning of thousands of Lisu to Christ. The latter book, while covering the same period in detail also adds some valuable glimpses into his last decade of life when he married Roxie Dymond who shared in his ministry during his time as a superintinendent of the

---

116 Both books do have some dates, but if one would compare these books briefly with Morrison, *Memoirs*, one will readily see a difference between a detailed chronology and a more topical, biographical study.

CIM work in Yunnan. In these two books much attention is given to his prayer life and his use of indigenous methods to establish churches that would be dependent on God and not on the missionary for their finances, leadership, and evangelistic outreach to new communities. The universal principles commonly drawn from his work are naturally the value of prayer and indigenous methods, both of which the CIM/OMF leaders found extremely useful to promote. The emphasis on prayer had long been a "distinctive" of the CIM. The attention given to indigenous methods was something new and essential in the new China with its growing nationalism and desire to be free from all foreign dominance or dependency.

While it took several years before Fraser saw results from his preaching among the Lisu, it must be recognized that he was a young missionary with no previous experience in tribal work among animists. Until the end of 1913 his primary responsibility was to the Chinese of Paoshan and Tengyueh, and not the Lisu. He also had few if any aids to Lisu language study and no written materials which described Lisu beliefs and culture. All of these things he had to learn on his own directly from the Lisu. What is remarkable is not the slowness of the Lisu response to the gospel, but the speed with which Fraser methodically learned the language, developed an understanding of the culture, completed a survey on foot of a large portion of the territory where the Lisu lived, and began to make an impact on the lives of many of them with the gospel message.

J. O. Fraser was a remarkable man by all accounts. While he was able to meet with missionaries and Chinese believers when he traveled through various mission stations on the plains, much of his time was spent on the trails and in Lisu villages where Christian morality was completely unknown. For a single young man who was brought up in a cultured British society, it is easy to imagine the trials of privation, not simply in terms of physical comforts such as a clean bed and a well-tuned piano, but even more, the encouragement of fellowship with Christians who shared his purpose. On the other hand, the temptations to quit, or to compromise in his efforts to reach the Lisu, or in his standards of personal holiness must likewise be readily apparent. Jesus sent his disciples out two by two, and this has long been considered a model for missionaries, but in the cases of David Brainerd (who worked with American Indians in the 1740s), Robert Morrison, and J. O. Fraser the option simply did not present itself. When the choice was presented to go alone to a lost people or not to go at all, they each chose to go alone.

In his journal and letters he refers to the spiritual oppression that he experienced. One wonders if it was far different from that of Saint Anthony in the Egyptian desert over 1,600 years earlier. While Anthony was a hermit, Fraser was often equally deprived of the fellowship of understanding Christians. Moreover, he had the active presence of those who worshiped evil spirits round about him. Twenty-first-century mission agencies, ever being reminded of the need for good member care and ever fearful of the legal ramifications of having someone go off the deep end either literally or spiritually, would not likely send out a young man on the mission that Fraser engaged in. Certainly there were many who have attempted to walk in Fraser's footsteps and failed. Yet, that being said, the Lisu church must give thanks that the leaders of the CIM allowed Fraser to move out into a pioneer ministry in the way that they did.

Close Interaction between Missionaries and National Believers

J. O. Fraser made a serious effort to learn Chinese and was preaching in Tengyueh, in southwestern Yunnan, nine months after his arrival in China.[117] He was gifted musically and that does tend to be an advantage in learning tonal languages. More importantly, however, was the fact that he was committed to being able to communicate effectively and therefore devoted himself to language study, including practicing conversations with those he met on the streets and tea shops. While his heart was fixed on the tribes, he first gave his attention to Chinese, and had a good grasp of it before later going on to Lisu. After only fifteen months in China, he went to the city of Paoshan, where he established a mission station on his own. Mrs. Howard Taylor, in her biography of him, noted that he became "one of the best Chinese speakers in the mission."[118] His study of Lisu was by means of immersion, living in Lisu villages and Lisu homes for long stretches at a time, generally with no other foreigner beside him. While it is possible for someone to learn a language and not become attached to the people, it was certainly the case with Fraser that he learned in order to build relationships through which the gospel could be shared effectively. Fraser made strong relationships which caused the Lisu to love him. Allyn and Leila Cooke went to the Lisu in Muchengpo after Fraser moved out in the 1920s. In a letter of August 3, 1925, Leila wrote to Fraser:

---

117   Mrs. Howard Taylor, *Behind the Ranges: Biography of J. O. Fraser of Lisuland* (Chicago: Moody Press, 1964), 39.

118   Ibid., 36.

They (the Lisu) appreciate you sending them the toys. They serve to bind their hearts even closer to you. Their love for you is almost pathetic. I do not believe I have ever heard a Lisu pray in meeting without praying for you. But (as far as I know) not one has gone back to heathenism because you did not return.[119]

Fraser made lasting relationships which drew converts not simply to himself but to his Savior. Whether with Ba Thaw, the Karen missionary to the Lisu in Burma who helped Fraser in so much of his pioneer ministry, or with Ting Li-mei, the well-known Chinese preacher who spent three months with him among the tribal villages, or with the Lisu themselves, Fraser showed that he enjoyed the fellowship of his brothers in Christ. This attitude rubbed off on other missionaries. In the same letter quoted above, Leila, referring to the loneliness she sometimes experienced when her husband was away visiting other villages, wrote, "But I must say the Lisu make just as good friends as any white man and I love them every one." On the other hand, it must be noted that Fraser would not allow relationships to interfere with the mission itself, and at a later date actually told the Cookes that they needed to leave the village and go elsewhere so that the local believers would develop their own gifts and not become dependent on the missionary in their midst.[120]

Sharing in Suffering

As the brief quotes from the Laymen's Inquiry suggest, there were many who were involved with the missionary enterprise who conceived of religion as being little more than man's search for universal truths that gave added meaning to life. The CIM missionaries who risked bandits and typhus to preach the gospel to the people of China clearly had another agenda. They measured the progress of the gospel by the love and joy that converts experienced in fellowship with Jesus Christ. They could not hope to solve the mass of problems that China was facing, but they could rejoice when they saw converts shining with the hope of the gospel in the midst of their afflictions. In 1926 the following story was recorded in the China Inland Mission *Monthly Notes*, which was an in-house publication for Mission members.

> Miss Kidd writes of a new interest among the Min-Chia of the Tali plain. Since the earthquake, many of them have been existing in abject poverty amongst the piles of stones that once formed their houses. Miss Kidd continues:
> "One dear old lady of sixty-five years who can always be found at her flower

---

119 Allyn Cooke and Leila Cooke, *Correspondence: Cooke, Allyn and Leila*; 1919–1932. Microfilm from Billy Graham Archives, Wheaton, IL: Collection 215, Box 4, Folder 1.

120 Eileen Crossman, *Mountain Rain*, joint ed. (Robesonia, PA: OMF Books, 1985), 208.

stall in one of the city gates, is one of the many whom the Lord brought to himself through suffering. On the night of the earthquake, five of her family were suddenly swept into eternity. Her heart, breaking with its awful and hopeless grief, vaguely remembered and dwelt upon a sweet story of one called Jesus—a story she had heard some time before, and to which she had then paid little attention. The lonely, grief stricken mother began to attend the services and she found what she sought, a Saviour who satisfies.

"About two months ago she passed through the waters of baptism to a life of victory in Him. She cannot read or write but every week she comes regularly to the meetings. She eagerly takes in the message and never fails to ask for a text or the text of a hymn to be written out for her. This she takes with her to the flower stall and when a scholar pauses to admire her wares she asks of him a character she has forgotten; thus little by little, she learns it off by heart.

"Fourteen men and women were recently received into the church. Four of these are the trophies of a comparatively new believer, the blacksmith of a village about four miles from the city. This man came to know the Lord about four years ago, and although much persecuted by his fellow villagers, he made a bold stand for the Master. Upon hearing of the black-smith's confession of faith in the Lord Jesus, some of the gentry took him to the magistrate for judgment. The blacksmith quietly submitted to the indignity, but his persecutors released him before the yamen. He immediately began to win others, and in a short time he not only overcame serious opposition, but had aroused deep interest in many hearts."[121]

This article encapsulated what the CIM missionaries wanted to see as the result of their labors. The seed of the Word had been planted and had borne fruit in due time. People grasped the eternal reality of the temporal nature of this life and were willing to suffer, if need be, for their faith because of the joy that they received from knowing Christ's presence here and now. Their boldness to be known as Christians and to make him known to others showed that the missionaries had reproduced their ambition in the hearts of the converts. There was not a plan or even a plea to find ways to avoid suffering. The missionaries themselves knew much of it. Deaths to typhus and other diseases were common. With over a thousand workers on the field, there were few months when there was no report of the death of a missionary or the need to send one home due to an untreatable disease.

Attacks by bandits and local armies afflicted missionaries as well as it did the local populations. Often the people did not even know who it

---

121 China Inland Mission, "Yunnan," *Monthly Notes*, July 1926, 3. The Min-Chia are now known as Bai and are found near Dali (formerly Tali) in Northwest Yunnan where they have lived from before the Chinese arrived in the region many centuries ago.

was that was raiding their village, but sometimes there were clues. One missionary in Kopu, Kweichow, reported:

> After the visit of the arch brigand it was possible to keep the doors and windows locked, but the robbers returned and peered in at the windows and in some cases begged to be allowed to come in and look around! During the raid they killed fowls, goats and a cow, but did not molest the pigs, so it was rather evident that they were Moslems.[122]

Mr. Warren, one of the directors normally based in Shanghai, wrote the following comments during a visit to Kweichow during that same period:

> The Miao Christians, who know the hills and the paths so well, took every care of us as we passed through dangerous areas, scouting ahead and advising to routes and necessary detours to avoid meeting parties of lawless men. Little has been said in these letters as to the dangers of the roads, but they are very real, and it would not be just to our faithful missionaries in these out-of-the-way places to leave the impression that, after all they are not very serious and can with care be avoided. Unmistakably this is not so ... Our fellow workers are constantly facing these dangers with unflinching courage and with no thought of turning back in the day of strain, having put their hands to the plough, they are steadily working their furrows. Should the altar of sacrifice be their lot rather than the daily labour, well and good, it is as the Lord wills. They can truly realize the apostle Paul's feegling, that to depart and to be with Christ is far better; nevertheless to abide in the flesh is more needful for the Chinese and Tribes communities.
>
> A party is passing along a wooded road under official escort. Suddenly a gunshot rings out and a bullet whizzes over their heads. The escort closed around, ramming cartridges into their rifles but since nothing is seen and no more follows, the journey is resumed. "Surely he shall deliver thee from the snare of the fowler."
>
> At a bend in the road two bleeding men walk painfully along. What has happened? Just a short distance away in a copse, through which they were passing, they have been set upon by a few men armed with knives, robbed of all they had, and wantonly wounded. The escort scatter through the copse firing off their rifles in all directions, which brought out the local militia from a village close at hand, who promised to look after the wounded men and scour the neighborhood. "A thousand shall fall at thy side—but it shall not come nigh thee."
>
> A path down a deep gorge ending at a ferry, the bank beyond too high and steep to be scaled, the spot held by a dozen or so armed men, who detained the boatman and would allow none to cross the river. Information came that there was another armed band on the road behind, so there was a complete

---

122 China Inland Mission, "Kweichow," *Monthly Notes,* February 1929, 2.

trap. The Evangelist took the cards of the missionaries in the party to the leader of those holding the ferry, requesting permission for the boatman to resume his duties. He was asked who the foreigners were. "Preachers of religion exhorting men to forsake evil and turn to good." "Fetch me one of their books!" It was not advisable to open up loads with such hungry eyes looking on. A search in pockets produced a well printed attractive-looking tract on "Repentance." It filled the need exactly, was in the direct line of the evangelist's statement, and was the only suitable one available without unpacking. After a most uncomfortable half hour it was decided to let the party cross the river, and unmolested they went. Why? The men were restrained by a power they knew not. "The Lord shall preserve thy going out and thy coming in this time forth and forevermore."[123]

There was no hint that better days were around the corner, nor was there a suggestion that the work might be deferred until the situation improved. The expectation was that missionaries would share in the trials that all of China was experiencing, that they would experience divine protection in the midst of those trials, and that if and when it was God's will and time, they would lay down their lives for the cause of Christ. This reality was clearly expressed in a story recorded by Isobel Kuhn of an event that occurred late in J. O. Fraser's life.

> I have often wanted to quote an experience Aristarchus loves to tell. It was back in 1936 when he was acting as servant to Mr. and Mrs. Fraser, an association which meant much to him spiritually. He, Mr. Fraser, and some coolies were travelling toward Gospel Mt. when they met robbers who took just everything they had with them, except the mule and what they wore. Aristarchus, of course, lost all his goods too. When those evil men had left them and they were alone Mr. Fraser said to the young Lisu comrade, "What think you Aristarchus, that God was not able to help us?" Perhaps an unhappy "No-o" was the answer. "No indeed" said that dear Counsellor. "God is able and the fact that He did not deliver us shows that this is a trial permitted of Him. Now let's face it as He faced His trials. Let us pray for those robbers." And right there in the empty road a prayer meeting was held for those who had despoiled them ... Mr. Fraser never saw any result from that experience that I know, but it brought incalculable spiritual riches to Aristarchus, who never tires of telling it and pointing out a lesson.[124]

The vast majority of mankind could only "deride or pity" the missionaries who set their sights on living such lives with no greater objective than seeing blacksmiths, flower sellers, and bandits repent and

---

123   China Inland Mission, "Kweichow," *Monthly Notes*, July 1926, 3–4.
124   Isobel Kuhn, "Prayer Trust," August 1938. Microfilm from Billy Graham Archives, Wheaton, IL.

be saved. The missionaries and their converts themselves must certainly have found their own standards of Christian practice far beyond their earthly powers to meet. Either the standard must be lowered or the power must be increased. For many it was the latter. The 1920s and 1930s were times of spiritual renewal in all of China. God used both foreign and local instruments to bring that renewal. It is essential to understand that revival and renewal in order to comprehend how the missionaries could accept the hardships they faced for years on end with an amazing complacency and to grasp just how the church in China survived and grew during the decades of Communist persecution that followed.

Spiritual Power for Service

The movement of spiritual renewal began in lonely mission stations and preaching circuits where individual missionaries struggled against weakness and sin within, and indifference or opposition all around. J. O. Fraser experienced and found victory on both fronts during his first term on the field. It included recognition of the reality of Satan and satanic opposition, which could be fully defeated only by claiming the victory that was gained for all believers by Jesus Christ on the cross. It is no surprise that Mrs. Howard Taylor was able to write with such empathy about this phase of Fraser's life, for she herself had gone through a similar life-transforming experience during her early years as a missionary as well.[125] Fraser's own experience of defeat transformed into victory by faith in Jesus Christ was to enable him to impart the keys to victory, first to the Lisu church leaders, and then in later years to fellow missionaries.

A variety of religious experiences claimed the attention of missionaries and Chinese Christians in the early 1900s. One was the Pentecostal movement. During the worldwide awakening that occurred during the decade prior to World War I, Pentecostalism first became a recognized stream within or alongside of Protestantism. The literature of the day was quite cautious in making any judgments about the movement when it first appeared in various parts of the world some time after 1905. While few of the recognized evangelical leaders of the day took part in the activities of the first groups which claimed to speak in tongues, they were hesitant to deny that those who did so were led by the Holy Spirit. It

---

[125] Geraldine Guinness, who was to marry Howard Taylor, shared somewhat of her personal testimony at a missions conference in 1894. Geraldine Guinness, "The Spiritual Need and Claims of China," in *The Student Missionary Enterprise: Addresses and Discussions of the Second International Convention of the Student Volunteer Movement for Foreign Missions*, ed. Max Wood Moorhead (n.p.: T. O. Metcalf, 1894), 54–61.

would appear that some members of the CIM or its associate missions did claim Pentecostal experiences including speaking in tongues. It was not until 1914 that a clear stand on the subject was taken. One tribal worker in Yunnan, a Mr. Fullerton, wished to marry a Miss Ronager, connected with the Pentecostal Missionary Union. This required that the matter be reviewed by the China Council which generally met on a quarterly basis in Shanghai. The possibility that the gift of tongues might still be given in the present age was acknowledged. However the council noted:

> Whilst we recognize the value of meetings for special prayer and meditation on God's word, both in regard to the personal Christian life and to the extension of the Lord's work, and without denying that there is a blessing in some cases in what are termed "waiting" meetings in connection with the P. M. U., we feel that these latter meetings, generally speaking, are accompanied by proceedings which tend to consequences of a dangerous character. For one thing the strain upon the brain occasionally is such that in some cases insanity has ensued, etc.[126]

It would appear that reports received either from stations in China or elsewhere in the world strongly suggested that the so-called "waiting" meetings were unhealthy and not held along scriptural lines. As it was not possible to separate the Pentecostal movement from these "waiting" meetings, it was felt necessary to keep the CIM from close involvement with the movement as a whole.

> It is admitted even by those most favorable to the movement that there are dangers and difficulties connected with it, and we do not think that, from the point of view of Mission administration, it would be wise to add to our already heavy burdens by co-operating with the P. M. U. Further, the Council feels strongly that to identify ourselves with a movement which, whatever its merits or otherwise, would involve us in an important new departure of a highly controversial character, would be inconsistent with the moral obligations resting upon us to keep faith both with fellow-workers in the Mission and with supporters at home who have entered into fellowship with us on the basis of an understanding, alike as to doctrine and to methods, which does not include such new departure. In the light of this conclusion it was agreed that the application of Miss Ronager could not now be proceeded with.[127]

While the specific case was quickly dealt with, the larger issues of the relationship between the CIM and the Pentecostal movement required over a year of council meetings and correspondence with home councils

---

126 China Inland Mission, "China Council 1914-09-09," 7. Microfilm from Billy Graham Archives, Wheaton, IL.

127 Ibid., 8.

before it could be settled. In the end the home councils agreed with the China Council draft which stated in part:

> In view of the clearly established and frequent instances of unscriptural confusion and other abuses arising out of the teaching and practice of the "Pentecostal" or "Tongues" Movement, the Mission cannot have any connection with it. Nor can it allow within its fellowship a class of meetings characterized by disorder and by manifestations which in some cases have led to mental derangement and maniacal ravings. Further, in view of the growing feeling on this subject amongst members of the Mission, through contact with the propaganda of the "Pentecostal" or "Tongues" Movement, and also amongst our constituencies in the home countries, it is important that the position of the Mission in regard to it should be guarded from any ambiguity or inconsistency.[128]

This policy seems to have been specifically concerned with certain practices and beliefs that were deemed harmful to the work of the Mission. It would appear that some of the associate missions were free to hold to Pentecostal teaching. Also it is evident that CIM missionaries in Yunnan often had good working relationships with members of Pentecostal missionary agencies.

While rejecting Pentecostalism with its various manifestations, many members of the CIM very much sought for the power of the Holy Spirit to be evident in their lives and in the life of the church in China. There was a strong element of the revivalism and holiness movement of the late nineteenth century evident in some CIM circles. The belief in divine healing was one element of this stream of Christian belief. It appears that J. O. Fraser discouraged missionaries from providing free medicine to tribal people. The local people were expected to make some sort of a payment for treatment. The standard price for one pill was one egg, no matter what the pill was for. This simple payment system was a key tool in keeping the new Christians from slipping into dependency upon missionary patrons.[129] At the same time he believed that the prayer of faith could and should be applied to seek divine healing. Missionaries and church leaders were expected to take seriously their responsibility to pray for the sick.

In the early 1930s Ray Buker, an American Baptist missionary to the Lahu and Shan in Burma, made a trip to visit his distant CIM

---

128 China Inland Mission, "China Council 1915-04-15," 28. Microfilm from Billy Graham Archives, Wheaton, IL.

129 Isobel Kuhn, *Ascent to the Tribes: Pioneering in North Thailand*, rev. ed. (London: Overseas Missionary Fellowship, 1968), 118. First published 1956.

neighbors, Allyn and Leila Cooke, across the border in China. When he arrived he saw a Lahu man who had come down with what appeared to be cerebral malaria. As his twin brother, Richard, was a missionary doctor and Ray had learned much practical medicine from him, he was well equipped to diagnose and treat the man. He proceeded to give the patient an injection, but Allyn Cooke forbade him from doing so because the patient had no way to pay for the medication. Buker was informed that this was a policy established for the tribal work in that area by J. O. Fraser. This distressed Buker considerably, but as he was a guest he reluctantly obeyed. All he could do was join the Cookes in prayer for the sick man. The next morning, much to Mr. Buker's surprise and relief, he discovered that the patient was not only alive, but up and walking.[130]

Here is an example of how spiritual principles were intimately tied to indigenous church planting methods. The goal of the missionaries was to lead the local people to faith in such a way that the new believers would be able to lead others to faith when the missionary was no longer around. Free medicine could attract a crowd, and might even be the means by which some from that crowd would be converted. But poor tribal believers would not be in a position to distribute free medicine to their neighbors. If they saw that missionaries made converts by providing free medicine, then the logical conclusion would be that they could not make converts on their own because they could not distribute free medicine like the missionaries had done. However, while local believers could not be expected in normal situations to have access to a trained medic or to Western medicine, they could always offer prayer on behalf of the sick, and therefore they were expected to do so. This line of reasoning only made sense if one assumed that God heard and honored prayer and would work without the means of medications when such things were not available.

Revivals and Rainy Season Bible Schools

In many churches throughout China during the 1920s and 30s, there was a longing for spiritual revival. A number of Christian men and women came to the forefront who were used of God to bring revival to many thousands of believers. According to Leslie Lyall, who was an eyewitness to God's work in China in the 1930s and 1940s:

---

130   Eric S. Fife, *Against the Clock: The Story of Ray Buker, Sr., Olympic Runner and Missionary Statesman* (Grand Rapids: Zondervan, 1981), 17–21. This story is recorded in a biography about Ray Buker. Had this incident been recorded in a CIM related publication it might have appeared with a slightly different slant.

All exercised a more or less nation-wide ministry, and the message was essentially the same: the exposing of secret sin, a call to thorough repentance, the need for restitution, the sufficiency of the blood of Jesus Christ to cleanse and deliver from all sin and the possibility of a fullness of the Holy Spirit. The results too, were characteristic: nominal Christians were truly converted, many lives were changed, new life flooded into the churches, Christians began to witness spontaneously to others, while joy and love overflowed in Christian fellowship.[131]

Among the Chinese, such revivals generally occurred when a preacher or a team came to a town or city for a week or more of special meetings which would occur each evening. In some cases the preaching itself was fairly low-key. Often the attendees were told to go quietly to their homes to think about what they had heard. Quite a few testimonies were recorded concerning Christian workers who were convicted of the shallow pretensions of godliness which cloaked a carnal life. Many were truly revived and devoted the rest of their lives to faithful service and abundant soul winning.

Among the tribes in the hills, such revivals often were connected with the Rainy Season Bible Schools. Educational standards were low for all the Christians. Christian literature was rare and reading skills limited. Church leaders, like the ordinary church members, were generally hill farmers themselves. It was both necessary and possible during the rainy season to gather together for Bible training those Christians who had a teaching or leadership role in the church or who regularly went out to distant villages as evangelists. These Short Term Bible Schools were designed for those who had little or no formal education. The Lisu New Testament was not completed until 1938, so when the students and missionaries came together they had an opportunity to write down texts from newly translated but not-yet-printed portions of the Bible. It was also an opportunity to develop their singing abilities and learn new songs. Fraser was a gifted pianist. Leila Cooke brought a portable organ with her from Burma. Allyn played the violin. While they could not reproduce their musical instruments, they could teach the Lisu how to sing in four-part harmony.

Isobel Kuhn, whose husband, John, became a noted Bible teacher among the Lisu, wrote in one of her prayer letters:

> Our Cleverest (as far as exams are concerned) had desired to find him a private nook where he could practice the conducting of our newest musical attempt . . . He chose the corner between his cabin and the pig sty, quite

---

131 Leslie T. Lyall, *A Passion for the Impossible: The Continuing Story of the China Inland Mission* (London: OMF Books, 1975), 105. First published 1965.

unconscious that he was in view of Ma-ma's window. I happened to look out and there, singing and waving his hand, he stood, leading the pigs with unction and fervour in Handel's Hallelujah Chorus!¹³²

The importation of foreign tunes and lyrics did not discourage local talent from emerging. Some Christian songs were written by the Lisu themselves and set to tunes they composed themselves as well.¹³³ The Bible schools provided the venue for these songs to be taught to others who would in turn pass them on to all the churches as the students returned to their homes or evangelistic activities after the schools had ended.

It was necessary for the Christian leaders from the various villages to come to the Bible schools for a month or two each year in order to have material to teach in the village for the rest of the year. There was also the need for spiritual transformations in the lives of these young leaders. The letters that Leila Cooke and Isobel Kuhn wrote give deep insights into the lives and even the hearts of the Lisu believers. Their husbands might have been teaching the Bible, but the wives were studying the students and through their regular prayer letters making them the objects of specific prayers. They themselves had been directed by J. O. Fraser to share their prayer letters with his prayer circle in England, where he had built up a large constituency of partners through his own regular and insightful letters. The prayer partners were thus not praying for the faceless masses but praying for numerous individuals who could become the leaders in a mass movement or become the cause of stumbling for many if their lives were not Spirit led.

Some missionaries noted that when local Christians get written about by missionaries in prayer letters or books, some negative things either happened to those native believers or became evident in their lives. This caused some missionaries to be reluctant to write about their converts. Leila Cooke had a different perspective. "Mr. Cooke and I do not feel that it necessarily harms the people to write about them. We feel that they will be a target of the enemy whether you tell their story or not because they are doing the Lord's work."¹³⁴

Isobel Kuhn's policy was not to write in detail about someone until at least one of her prayer partners wrote to tell her that he or she would pray for

---

132 Isobel Kuhn, "Prayer Trust," February 1938, 4. Microfilm from Billy Graham Archives, Wheaton, IL.

133 Isobel Kuhn, "Prayer Trust," February 1938, 3. Microfilm from Billy Graham Archives, Wheaton, IL.

134 Leila Cooke, handwritten note [1931?]. Microfilm from Billy Graham Archives, Wheaton, IL.

that individual. In one letter she mentions receiving some mail from a Lisu fellow who was serving as a carrier for a missionary traveling to Paoshan.

> These letters are worth translating, but as none of you have ever mentioned this boy in your letters to us, and so we have no guarantee that he is being regularly prayed for, I think I had better not advertise him. Shy as the wild deer on his own mountains, quaintly frank and naive as an unspoiled child, true and steadfast as the great peaks which look down on the roof of his shanty home, this laddie is worthy of your prayers.
>
> Some of our newest friends may not know that we like to get prayer partners for the Lisu . . . that is, a promise from someone in America that they will pray every day for the spiritual and physical well being of one of our Lisu Christians. In return we try to send you a snapshot of your prayer protege and any news of him from time to time.[135]

One result of this emphasis on prayer for numerous individual Lisu believers was that the evangelical Christian world came to know, love, and earnestly intercede on behalf of these young Christians in a way that has rarely been equaled in the annals of missionary history.[136] Heaven alone knows the specific results of those prayers, but history records the spiritual triumphs that these Lisu men and women experienced over pride, ignorance, hardheartedness, immorality, and sloth. Here is one example of what happened during a Short Term Bible School when prayer partners were upholding the students by name in their prayers.

> Again [Pade-] John was touched . . . He confessed to doing business on Sunday, etc. He said that Ne-do-me-pa had exhorted him privately, and so in front of them all he thanked that dear deacon for being faithful to his duty. And by the way we offered a prize for the best hymn, music and words to be composed by the Lisu. We had four aspirants. And the judges gave it to Pade-John.
>
> Then there was a young lad, Junia, who was so moved he broke down after confession of sin and wept. At the end of School he offered himself for teaching work and the church accepted him (we have always more calls for teachers than men to send). Junia has been sent to Horse-Grass-Level, but as he was leaving here to go John [Kuhn] met him going down the mountainside. "Ma-pa" the lad said, "I'm not taking a thing with me, neither blanket or any cover for my head. I'm going to trust the Lord." We do not encourage "extremes" like that, but it showed the lad's deep desire to be wholly God's.[137]

---

135 Isobel Kuhn, "Prayer Trust," October 1938, 2. Microfilm from Billy Graham Archives, Wheaton, IL.

136 The other examples are almost always connected with women missionaries endowed with a powerful gift of writing.

137 Isobel Kuhn, "Prayer Trust," March 1938, 3. Microfilm from Billy Graham Archives, Wheaton, IL.

Indigenous Principles

J. O. Fraser was a practitioner and promoter of indigenous principles in establishing churches on the mission field. He did not merely practice them but showed them to be effective, and not only for him, but also for his co-workers who followed his example. It was impossible for him to overemphasize the role of prayer in revival and the building up of a cadre of spiritually minded leaders in the Lisu church. When it came to the practice of indigenous principles, the foundational supposition was that prayer would be the grand human means of realizing the objective of establishing a vibrant, indigenous church that would carry the gospel, not merely to all the Lisu villages, but to neighboring tribes as well. The following quote is found both in *Behind the Ranges* and *Mountain Rain*, but bears repeating here as well:

> I want to tell you all about my plans for self support of the work—a subject on which I feel very strongly indeed. But I want to distinguish between temporal self-support and spiritual self-support. The former is eminently desirable and practicable, the latter is almost impossible, perhaps for generations to come.
>
> The Lisu and Kachin converts would be easily able to support their own pastors, teachers, and evangelists by well advised cultivation of their own ample hillsides, and it is fitting that the hillsides should bring forth supplies for the needs of those whose feet are beautiful upon them. But spiritually they are babes, and are as dependent upon us as a child upon her mother. They look to us out here for instruction, guidance, and organization; but they are dependent on the home churches in England in a deeper sense for spiritual life and power. I really believe that if every prayer by the home churches on behalf of the mission field were removed, the latter would be swamped by an incoming flood of the powers of darkness. This seems to have happened in church history—churches losing all their power and life, becoming a mere empty name, or else flickering out altogether. Just as a plant may die for lack of watering, so may a genuine work of God die and rot for lack of prayer.[138]

New believers could be and must be taught to take responsibility for the support of that which would develop within and proceed out of their congregations. However, they could not be expected to comprehend and engage in the spiritual battle that raged around them without the

---

138 Taylor, *Behind the Ranges*, 257–58. Was Fraser correct? If so, what are the implications for mission organizations which begin a work and then move on to new fields and draw their prayer supporters with them to those new fields of service? How many Christians in the West even know of the places and peoples their missionaries pioneered among forty years ago, let alone intercede regularly for them?

continual, fervent prayers of the saints in places where the church was more established. Fraser could be so committed to indigenous methods as the means of establishing strong churches precisely because he was totally dependent on the ministry of prayer. There was one aspect of the work that man could only pray for God to accomplish. There was another inextricably connected dimension of the work that would only bear fruit if Christian workers in obedience to God's direction used proper (indigenous) methods to carry out. They would do so through the enlightening and empowering of the Holy Spirit in answer to prayer. Fraser and those he influenced set the standard first for western Yunnan, then for all of the province, and finally for the Mission as a whole after the exodus from China.

When John Nevius wrote about "New Methods" in the 1880s, his writings stirred up interest but did little to change the way missions were carried out in most of China. The CIM aimed for churches which were locally led, supported by the freewill offerings of the members, and cooperating with other churches and missionaries in outreach to new towns and villages. This was the aim but it was not the method. The method in many cases was to support qualified Chinese workers to assist the missionaries in outreach to new places. As noted previously, Taylor on several occasions made mention of the fact that suitable Chinese workers were in short supply and that harm was done when less-than-suitable workers were hired for the work, but it does not appear that he made serious efforts to revise the method by which the CIM operated. It was not until the time that J. O. Fraser had come to China and begun his ministry in western Yunnan that the issue needed to be addressed by the China Council of the CIM in their quarterly meetings in Shanghai.

In December 1913 the subject came up peripherally to a discussion about the rising cost of living in China.

> Support of Chinese Workers. Renewed consideration was given to this subject. From the facts before the Council, it became evident that, in view of the increased cost of living and other circumstances, the salaries of Chinese workers in the employment of the Mission, especially those with families, were in many instances insufficient to meet their needs, and careful thought was given to the question as to how they might best be supplemented without delaying the realization of the ideal of self-support. It was agreed that a practical solution would, in many cases, be found by the Chinese Churches contributing funds for the increase of the salaries already provided by the Mission. It was also agreed that further relief should, in the cases of workers with families, be afforded by making a grant for the education

of their children, or, where more convenient, by receiving them into the Mission boarding schools free of charge, the principle being recognized that the size of a worker's family might rightly be taken into account in fixing his allowance.[139]

Self-support was seen as the ideal toward which the Mission and the local congregations should work. Financial considerations reminded the Mission to make more of an effort to get the churches to take on more support of local church workers, but the issue was not a pressing one at that time. The assumption was that CIM-administered schools and boarding houses would be available in the places where the workers operated. It was taken for granted that schools for the education of the children of Chinese believers would advance hand in hand with the gathering of new congregations of believers. These schools could not be immediately self-supporting, and this meant that it was considered normal that the Mission would be employing a large number of teachers and staff as long as the gospel was spreading into new locations. The objective in 1913 was not so much to avoid supporting national workers as to make sure they had enough to live on, and to encourage the churches to increasingly contribute toward their support.

In 1915 the issue came up again, and this time more attention was given to the issues that needed addressing regarding the support of large numbers of Chinese helpers. The first concern was with those placed in outstations.

> In reference to the employment of Evangelists supported by foreign funds, the opinion was expressed that the practice of placing such men permanently at outstations was, as a rule, open to objection. It was not good for them themselves; moreover it tended to hinder the development of ministry and self-effort on the part of the local congregations. It was felt that, generally speaking, the better plan was for these men to reside at the Central Station, visiting the outstations as might be arranged. In this way, the workers themselves would have the benefit of more constant and direct influence and oversight on the part of the Missionary, and would be preserved from the temptations, to which residence in outstations exposed them. It was also felt that the whole system of paid evangelists had been extended more than was helpful. Further, it was to be feared that a good many men were thus employed, whose zeal and gifts scarcely warranted it.[140]

---

139 China Inland Mission, "Support of Chinese Workers," in Minutes of [China] Council Meeting, December 13, 1913, 21–22. Microfilm from Billy Graham Archives, Wheaton, IL.

140 China Inland Mission, "Support of Chinese Workers," in Minutes of [China] Council Meeting, December 9, 1915, 19. Microfilm from Billy Graham Archives, Wheaton, IL. It is possible that Roland Allen's book *Missionary Methods: Saint Paul's or Ours*, which was first

The more the leadership of the CIM sought to deal with the issue of national workers, the more complex it became. For one thing, they had fifty years of history to deal with. Moreover, they had a rapidly changing situation in China and the West, which meant that maintaining the status quo was not an option. The first priority of the CIM was to evangelize China's millions, and that required establishing churches wherever they did not yet exist so that there would be a congregation of Chinese believers faithfully witnessing for Christ in the community round about them. The CIM was not a denomination and did not consider that it was a church, but rather was a representative of the churches in the West who sought to establish the church in China. As many of the members were not ordained pastors themselves, they did not consider it necessary to be ordained in order to baptize, serve Communion, or establish churches with locally elected leaders. In line with that view, those that they hired were not ordained pastors with formal theological training, but were evangelists and helpers who in a very real sense became extensions of the missionaries themselves. They, like the majority of the converts in the churches that the CIM established, were generally not highly educated. It became increasingly apparent as the leaders of the Mission tried to hand the responsibility for the financial support of these workers over to the Chinese church that the Chinese Christians expressed strong reluctance to take on the responsibility. The national workers were likewise reluctant to be placed under (or be made responsible for) the care and direction of a local congregation.

There were various factors involved in creating this state of affairs. First of all, gifted and proven Chinese pastors were already supported by local congregations. From the first years of the CIM, the Chinese believers in Chekiang Province had shown themselves willing and able to support their own workers when they found them to be suited for the ministry of caring for a church. Hence, quite a few congregations had already become self-supporting, self-propagating, and self-governing long before the issue had to be addressed by the CIM leadership. Where it had not happened, several causes might be considered. For one example, some missionaries had become too entrenched in a particular place for local leadership to develop. In such cases it appeared that the missionaries were going to remain in one district until they retired. The

---

published in 1912, contributed to the discussion, but it is also possible that others were noting the problems that he wrote about simultaneously, but were more reluctant than he to recommend radical solutions. Allen wanted a clean break from the methods then currently in use.

evangelists and helpers appeared to be working for the missionaries and were apparently chosen primarily because they met the needs of the missionaries and not necessarily the needs of the church members. In such cases it should not be surprising that the church members saw no reason to take the responsibility of supporting such workers themselves.

As these realities were becoming apparent to the leaders of the CIM, a new issue emerged. By 1918, with a rising cost of living in China and lower income from the West due to World War I, there was a lack of funds for national workers. This meant that there was a greater incentive to deal with the problems. It was decided to reapply an old rule (which had been long ignored) that superintendents of the various provinces would need to approve of any new Chinese workers before they began to receive support through mission channels. Apparently, inexperienced (new?) field workers were hiring helpers who were quite unsuited for the work, and thus burdening the Mission financially while creating stumbling blocks for the Chinese churches themselves. This reapplication of an old policy then led to a new discovery. Some of the missionaries had written to their supporters back in their home countries and claimed that they needed funds to support national workers. So they were getting personal gifts to support *their* Chinese helpers. This, combined with the fact that many of these privately supported, unsuitable workers were being sent to outstations (smaller cities or towns some distance from the main cities where the missionaries were generally based), meant that they had little or no supervision or opportunity to improve their limited skills.

As D. E. Hoste and the superintendents of the various provinces worked to deal with these issues in the years immediately following World War I, new challenges emerged which were in some ways positive. Japanese encroachment on Chinese territory had been going on for years, but at last it led to a great backlash after the German concessions in China were handed over to the Japanese at the end of World War I. Since the Chinese had actually sent laborers to help the French fight the Germans in Europe, the Chinese had every right to be furious not only with the Japanese but with the other foreign powers who supported the Japanese claim. Thus from 1919 onward the Chinese became increasingly nationalistic and antiforeign. Missionaries running mission stations and mission schools were one visible face of foreign domination of China, and Christians in the pay of foreign missionaries naturally attracted the condemnation of the Chinese. Even Chinese Christians began to criticize foreigners for dominating the churches by their use of foreign funds. The positive side of this was that the Chinese Christians made amazing progress in increasing financial giving and taking responsibility not only for supporting pastors but even for some Christian institutions as well.[141]

By the mid-1920s a new generation of Chinese leaders in Eastern China, such as Wang Ming-tao and Leland and Wilson Wang, emerged. They took the evangelical gospel message wholeheartedly from the missionaries who had brought it to China, but saw no need to work under their ecclesiastical structures. At the same time the churches which had emerged through the major denominational missions were coming of age. A generation of theologically trained Chinese leaders arose and took up the mandate which had come from the 1910 Edinburgh Missionary Conference to establish a united, nationally led Chinese church. At first the CIM was warmly supportive of this move. Then two issues emerged which caused the CIM to reluctantly draw back. The first and greatest issue of concern was that some of the leading Chinese advocates of church unity were also wholly committed to modernist unbelief. As was happening to the Presbyterian and American Baptist churches in the U.S., so also in China, the mass of those in the pews were conservative, but the influential leaders in the denominations and seminaries were modernists. The CIM could not be party to a movement which rejected the fundamentals of the Christian faith, so with regret it pulled out of the Chinese Christian Council. The other issue only became an issue after the split occurred. The modernists wished to portray their opponents as uneducated and ignorant. They pointed to the fact that few Chinese pastors, evangelists, or helpers in CIM-founded congregations had any formal theological training, and even among the missionaries few had ever been ordained. The claim was correct and might have been painful for some Chinese Christians connected to the CIM to hear, but the Mission considered it to be irrelevant. Those with the high theological education were not evangelizing the masses of China's interior, and that was what the CIM was called to do.

The independent Chinese churches created pressure on the CIM to release its grip on the churches it had started. The effect of the modernists within the mainline denominations was to make the CIM very cautious about relaxing its grip over churches and church-related schools for fear that modernist teaching might enter and wreck havoc among the believers. To help guard against this danger, a "Doctrinal Basis of the Mission" was

---

141 Kenneth Scott Latourette, *A History of Christian Missions in China* (London: Society for the Propagation of Christian Knowledge, 1929), 806–7.

reaffirmed by the China Council shortly before the National Christian Conference met in 1922, and was done in anticipation of the event:

Doctrinal Position of the Mission

It was stated that the regrettable spread in China of Modernist views had increased a sense of uneasiness in the minds of many. It was agreed in the interests of the Mission, that the Council should take this opportunity of reaffirming their adherence to the statement of the Doctrinal basis of the Mission and meaning attached to its language as contained in the letter of Mr. Hudson Taylor to Mr. Theodore Howard of January 1, 1903, at the time of his retirement from the office of General Director. The said statement is appended as follows:

Doctrinal Basis of the Mission

1. The Divine Inspiration and consequent authority of the whole canonical Scriptures.
2. The Doctrine of the Trinity.
3. The Fall of Man, his consequent moral depravity and his need of regeneration.
4. The Atonement, through the substitutionary death of Christ.
5. The Doctrine of the Justification by Faith.
6. The Resurrection of the body both in the case of the just and the unjust.
7. The Eternal life of the saved and the Eternal punishment of the lost.

The Council, in placing on record their continued adherence to the above statement by the Founder of the Mission, expressed the hope that their colleagues in the Home countries will agree with them in taking the same action.[142]

While the statement in many ways reflects the Modernist/Fundamentalist battles that rocked the mainline denominations in America in the late 1920s and 1930s, it had some very distinct CIM features. First of all, it was based on a letter of Hudson Taylor, which while certainly orthodox, lacked some key elements of what was under attack in the 1920s, namely the resurrection of Jesus Christ and his personal return to judge the living and the dead. These truths were certainly implied but left unstated. In CIM circles it served its purpose because it was written by the founder himself. Secondly, it came from the Mission's leaders in China and was sent to the home councils with the hope that they would

---

142 China Inland Mission, "Doctrinal Position of the Mission," in Minutes of the [China] Council Meeting, April 18, 1922, 2–3. Microfilm from Billy Graham Archives, Wheaton, IL. See also: Alvyn Austin, *China's Millions: the China Inland Mission and late Qing society, 1832–1905* (Grand Rapids: Eerdmans, 2007). The author investigates in great depth the development of CIM's theological stance in the late nineteenth and early twentieth century, and proposes that British evangelicalism was gradually replaced by American Fundamentalism as the years went by.

affirm it as well. By mid-1923 all the home countries had expressed their reaffirmation of Taylor's statement.[143] The subject did not need to be raised again by the China Council. The theological stance of the Mission was not going to be downgraded.

At the same time there were concerted efforts on the part of the Mission to promote the development of ecclesiastical structures for congregations to interact with each other at the district, provincial, and regional level. The idea was that local congregations could not effectively operate at a strictly congregational level, and therefore should be encouraged to cooperate with other like-minded congregations in order to lessen their dependence on the Mission and encourage their mutual interdependence. Here progress was slow in some instances. Where local congregations had nothing else in common than the fact that they were established by missionaries who were sent out by the same mission society, they would have little reason to relate to each other, except in order to please the missionaries who told them that they ought to do so. In those places where new congregations were formed through the evangelistic activities of older congregations, such intercongregational ties would naturally exist from the very beginning.

As much as the CIM might wish to avoid the implications of their work, they were in effect creating a denomination without being willing to admit to themselves or to the Chinese believers that they were doing so. It must have been confusing to the Chinese believers, just as it is confusing to someone in the twenty-first century reading the minutes of the discussions on the subject that occurred in the council meetings. Perhaps the best explanation is that as an interdenominational mission the CIM could not very well tell its supporters that they were promoting a particular sort of church structure in China. But to any observer, impartial or otherwise, it must have looked like they were doing just that. Certainly the fact that Chinese Christians connected to the CIM referred to themselves as Nui Ti Hui, the China Inland Church, showed that to their minds they were a distinct body. This issue was to continually resurface for as long as the CIM was in China. The problem could not be solved easily. On one hand, they were recruiting workers from diverse denominations in the West. These new workers might not have had fixed views on how churches should be governed in China, and they might not have fixed views on what doctrines should be taught in those churches (beyond the broad framework of

---

143 China Inland Mission, "Doctrinal Position of the Mission," in Minutes of the [China] Council Meeting, November 9, 1923, 11. Microfilm from Billy Graham Archives, Wheaton, IL.

late nineteenth-century evangelical theology or early twentieth-century fundamentalist teaching). But the churches that sent them often did have strong views on such things and wanted the missionaries whom they sent out to propagate a variety of Christianity that shared at least some of the distinctive features of the sending body.

In China there were Bible-believing Chinese Christians who wanted the missionaries to bring only the gospel and not any of the cultural accretions that had taken hold of it in the West. One gifted communicator who expressed this view quite effectively in both Chinese and English was Nee To-sheng, better known as Watchman Nee. He was strongly antidenominational and believed that there should only be one church in one location and that church must not be denominational. Therefore his disciples would never try to compete with CIM-related congregations in a town or city, but rather they would try to get the entire existing congregation to come under the care of his nondenominational Christian structure. Leslie Lyall, had a good personal relationship with Watchman Nee, and could write positively about him in *God Reigns in China*, years after the CIM left China and Nee himself had died. However there can be no doubt that Nee's work created challenges for the CIM missionaries, especially for those who could not find his version of perfectionism or church ecclesiology spelled out in their own Bibles. One of the biggest problems was that in many ways Nee's theology, which owes everything to the English Brethren and the Keswick Movement, was in many points similar to that which many CIM missionaries held. He could not be labeled an opponent of the gospel, because he clearly was a proponent of the gospel, but he and his disciples did not appear as friends to those missionaries and churches which happened to be in their own line of advance.[144]

It must be noted that what I have just been covering was taking place in Eastern China, not Southwest China. The coastal churches were one or two generations older than those in the Southwest and thus set the tone for the rest of the country with regard to the development of the "Chinese church."

---

144 Robert Finley, *Reformation in Foreign Missions* (Maitland, FL: Xulon Press, 2005), 43–59. In this delightful diatribe against the way other agencies carry out their mission, Mr. Finley quotes a letter of Nee to a member of the CIM in England at great length. In it Nee chides the CIM for creating a denomination, which was the very thing they had been unwilling to do. Had they done so, they would have been in a much better position to keep their congregations from joining up with Nee's nondenominational denomination.

A Restatement of Policy

It was at the very time when "political and ecclesiastical changes"[145] were crashing down upon the Mission that D. E. Hoste applied the lessons he had learned over the decades and began something new.

> With a view to the more speedy carrying out of the Mission's policy of establishing self-supporting, self-governing and self-propagating Churches, we urge where Churches have not already been duly organized, the importance of proceeding without delay to the election and appointment of Chinese Church officers, including, where practicable, the setting apart of pastors.
>
> That when a Church has been organized the oversight of all Church matters should be handed over to it, including responsibility for (a) the arrangements for public worship, (b) the reception, discipline and spiritual oversight of Church members, (c) the conducting of baptisms, the Lord's Supper, as well as marriages and funerals, (d) the selection and appointment of Church officers and workers, (e) and the administration of all funds used in connection with its work.
>
> Further it should be recognized that the appointment of missionaries to the stations does not entitle them to any office in the Chinese Church. Care should, therefore, be exercised by them to avoid assuming any office or any authority that would weaken the independence of the Church or retard its progress in self-government and self-support.
>
> We would strongly recommend that the Churches in each provincial district adopt some means for promoting intercourse and fellowship between them, so as to afford opportunities for united devotional gatherings and mutual conference on common problems and difficulties. We suggest that arrangements for the periodic convening of such conferences be in the hands of a standing committee elected by the conference.[146]

Hoste and the others on the China Council knew that such a radical change was necessary, but that it would not be easy. Some missionaries would be incapable of handing over responsibilities to the Chinese Christians, and some of the Chinese Christians would be reluctant to take up the responsibilities that were being handed to them. Therefore there would be a need to instruct both groups in how to go about making such a change. The best instructor would naturally be someone who actually helped to establish indigenous churches in the past. J. O. Fraser, who established the model of an

---

145 China Inland Mission, "Acceptance for Training of Candidates in London," in Minutes of the [China] Council Meeting, July 8[?], 1927, 6–7. Microfilm from Billy Graham Archives, Wheaton, IL.

146 China Inland Mission, "Church Organization," in Minutes of the [China] Council Meeting, November 23, 1927, 10–11. Microfilm from Billy Graham Archives, Wheaton, IL.

indigenous church planting movement and spoke fluent Chinese, would be a natural choice to help in this time of transition. On November 14, 1927, the council discussed the need for a new superintendent for Yunnan Province and Fraser was mentioned as being suitable.

> In the ensuing conversation it was suggested that Mr. J. O. Fraser was well qualified for the post: the importance of adequate oversight and help for the work, both Chinese and tribal, being emphasized. Mr. Hoste said that this was recognized by the Executive, but that there were reasons in favour of Mr. Fraser taking up work in one of the more central provinces, where it was essential that adequate oversight should be provided. With this in view, the Executive had Mr. Fraser in mind as Superintendent of Chinkiang and the Stations on the Grand Canal, combining with that office the work of Bible teaching of Chinese Christians in the Stations of Anhwei. There was, however, reason to think that Mr. Fraser might feel that he should now return to Yunnan, and might therefore, decline the appointment to Kiangsu. It was finally agreed that Mr. Hoste should put before Mr. Fraser the latter proposal, and if this were declined, Mr. Fraser should be asked to become Superintendent of Yunnan.[147]

The result was that Fraser chose to return to Yunnan in the role of superintendent. While that was good for the work in the province, it was to mean that his influence on the Mission as a whole was to be limited. Much time each year was spent visiting the various stations in the province. This was exceptionally time consuming due to poor or nonexistent roads and the continual threat from bandits and local armies. Eventually he was to recommend that Yunnan be divided up between two superintendents, which thus reduced the individual responsibility to almost human proportions. It is evident from the minutes of the council in the 1930s that Fraser often was absent from these meetings. Fraser could have exercised an influence over CIM policy throughout China had he been present, and it is likely that part of the reason that Hoste had wished to have him in Kiangsu Province was precisely so that he would have an impact on how the CIM operated throughout the country. As it was, the progress in terms of indigenizing the work throughout China was not uniformly successful.

The other new venture that Hoste set out to do was to regain the initiative in evangelizing the unreached portions of China. He saw that churches and missionaries were stagnating because the missionaries

---

147 China Inland Mission, "Superintendentship of Yunnan and Kiangsu," in Minutes of [China] Council Meeting, November 14, 1927, 2–3. Microfilm from Billy Graham Archives, Wheaton, IL.

were too much engaged in caring for the existing churches, rather than working with the Chinese Christians to enter new areas that had no Christian witness. As part of this effort, there was the Re-statement of Policy in November1928 which appeared in the *China's Millions* for January 1929.[148] Hoste showed clearly that the Mission leaders had to take the initiative to end the domination over the Chinese churches by some (many?) CIM missionaries so that the churches themselves could grow mature and so that the missionaries could do what they had in theory come to China to accomplish. The expectation was that workers and funds would be freed up by actively working toward self-supporting, self-governing Chinese churches. These funds and personnel could then become redirected to outreach in new areas. Hoste did not mention the third "self"—namely, self-propagating—because he believed that evangelism was to be done cooperatively.

> In this forward evangelism, experience has shown that the missionaries need the co-operation of like-minded Chinese colleagues, whose knowledge of their own countrymen and their ways is necessarily better than most foreigners can attain to. We expect that the number of Chinese hitherto working in settled districts, but who under the new order will no longer be needed there, will thus take an important share in the forward movement; while, no doubt, new ones will also be required.[149]

The Forward Movement, sometimes referred to as the Forward Evangelistic Movement, was a major half step forward. The Chinese Christians were recognized as an essential part of the Forward Movement, but it was the "professional" ones who previously worked (for pay) in the settled districts who were to make the move to new districts which did not yet have churches. In fact, while it is to be recognized that the gifts of the pastor and the gifts of the evangelists do differ, those with pastoral gifts would generally be kept by the existing Chinese congregations, and those without those gifts would work with (or for) the missionaries. The problem was that the CIM would be creating a whole new generation of dependent congregations which would then need to be taught to stop being dependent on the Mission after they had been established. This harmful cycle had been prevented from developing among the Western Lisu by Fraser's strict policy of not paying evangelists, but putting the burden on the emerging Lisu congregations themselves to send out their own workers to unreached villages. Perhaps Hoste himself recognized

---

148 See the Appendix for complete document.
149 D. E. Hoste, "A Re-statement of Policy," *China's Millions*, January 1929 (written in Shanghai, November 3, 1928).

this tension but felt that this was as far as he could go to get the Mission on to the right track. It is hard, however, to see how Fraser would have been effective in promoting this "two-self" model when he had already shown that the "three-self model" was the most effective approach. Many years later, after Fraser had died and the CIM had withdrawn from China, John Kuhn was to write about Fraser's principles in this manner:

> One of the wisest principles Fraser ever laid down was that of the spearhead in native evangelism being native. Missionaries supplied the fuel. And where this principle was followed through the years there was blessing.[150]

Hoste's Forward Movement, with the recruitment of two hundred new workers and the attempt to refocus the CIM's efforts on the unevangelized fields, made the foreign missionary, not the native Christians, to be the spearhead. Its effectiveness was limited, as the future years were to show.

The 1930s: Triumphing in Adversity

The 1930s taught the Chinese and the missionaries in China that however bad things might seem to be today they would get worse tomorrow. Warlords and bandits remained, along with the attendant famines and oppression that followed in their wake, but they were gradually forced to follow agendas set for them by the Nationalists, the Communists, and the Japanese. Tens of millions of Chinese became refugees, and oftentimes the missionaries shared in their trials and sorrows. At the same time the 1930s taught anyone with eyes to see that the church in China had come of age and would be an active force for good in the country, no matter how desperate the situation would become.

Among the tribes in the Southwest the church continued to expand. Among the Miao there were no longer great turnings like those seen in the first two decades of the century, but there was evidence of spiritual life. Some would see the end of the mass movement as evidence that Miao were primarily responding to social pressure when they earlier turned to Christianity in the hopes of material benefits.[151] Other factors were at work as well. One major factor was that the province of Kweichow was always poor. In times of political unrest banditry became rampant. For those who were already living on the margins, as the Miao were, staying alive required all of their energies. Missionary work itself was

---

150 John Kuhn to Arnold Lea, February 9, 1953, 2. OMF International Headquarters Archives, Singapore: AR5.1.5, DOM: North Thailand Box 2.5; Correspondence 1953.

151 W. G. Windsor, *Through Fire: The Story of 1938* "The Aboriginal Tribes" (London: China Inland Mission 1939), 65–66.

often hindered by robbers and Reds. For example, in March 1930 the following note appeared in the China Inland Mission *Monthly Notes*.

> Mr. Windsor writes that whole districts are under arms. Every little area is controlled by a different leader and all the suitable caves and hilltops have been transformed into forts. Where these are not available two and three-storied towers are built. At one place the party was ambushed, but the leader was known by Mr. Windsor and it was soon explained that the party was mistaken for a hostile force and hence the ambush.[152]

Missionaries were rarely killed, but it seems that most had some experiences of being captured or robbed at some point in their ministries. The Chinese and tribal believers themselves suffered greatly, but it was clear at this time that the foreigners in the interior had no special privileges and for the most part shared in the sufferings of the local populations. For those who were based in Kweichow or Yunnan, any evacuation to Burma or the coast would have taken many weeks, if not months, and was not considered as an option. Generally it was thought best to leave cities when brigands or rebel armies approached and hide out in the hills with the tribal believers.

All of this unrest meant that some tribal churches were not visited for years at a time. With the social breakdown, temptations to compromise and sin increased. One particular temptation was the growing of opium. In Fraser's earlier years he spent much time helping the Lisu to find new crops to plant, but no crop was as easily carried to market or sold for as high a price as opium. The fact that many Christians refused to succumb to this temptation was a sign of the quality of their faith. Where they did succumb it was evidence that prayer for revival was needed. In 1932 Allyn and Leila Cooke wrote about this situation realistically.

> The fact is the Lisu have been Christian for about ten years, and the glamour of the Christian religion has worn off. They have tested it out, and the fleshly-eyed folks have found no earthly gain in being Christians. They still get sick and die just as the heathen do and they are still poor and suffering. So some are saying, "What's the use? Let's plant opium and drink wine as we used to do."

> Very few want to go back to demon worship. They laugh at the suggestion, and boil up angrily when their neighbors call them heathen. But they want to live for self instead of for God. I visited a village of "selfers" a couple of weeks ago, and exhorted them to be either downright heathen or else out-and-out Christians. But that did not suit their fancy. They wanted to stand

---

152 "Keihkow—Difficult Conditions," China Inland Mission, *Monthly Notes*, March 1930, 3.

on the fence ... So a few whole villages are as lifeless as some professing Christians at home.[153]

So, with all the best practices of Christian missionary theory of that day, the workers among the Lisu sometimes found themselves in exactly the same place as missionaries who had used older methods. And what was the solution? The same one as was tried and proved in places as distant as Kiangsu and Shantung:

> We cried to God in helpless darkness. We had a day of fasting and prayer. The very next day a village which had been quarreling for a year ended their quarrel by a real Christlike sacrifice on the part of one young man. And this village which had not taken the Lord's supper for many months because of the quarrel, once more met together in His communion.
>
> Then every few days since, sunshine has been bursting through the dark cloud. First one then another has come expressing his desire to come back to the Lord.[154]

The 1930s, even more than the 1920s, were a time of spiritual renewal for Christians throughout China. There are two points to mention here. One is that revival is what the leadership and most of the rank-and-file missionaries sought for themselves and their churches. *The China's Millions* printed numerous articles about the revivals which occurred throughout China during that decade. New methods and new evangelistic forward movements could not succeed without a new infusion of the Holy Spirit in the lives of Christians in China.

The second point is that while missionaries were in some cases mightily used as instruments for bringing new life to Chinese Christians, the Chinese Christians themselves were the main force in spreading revival. The danger of the church in China succumbing to the forces of modernism that were evident in the National Christian Council was averted. A generation of Chinese evangelicals who were born in the first years of the twentieth century emerged, and it was these men who helped to shape the character of the church down to the present day. Andrew Gih, Wang Ming-dao, John Sung, Leland and Wilson Wang, Nee To-sheng, and others arose in Eastern China. In some cases they grew up in churches that were founded and built up along Western models by missionaries from the main denominations. They borrowed some Western elements of Christian practice but proclaimed it in such a way that it

---

153 Allyn Cooke and Leila Cooke, "The Clouds of Lisu-land," *China's Millions*, August 1932, 119.

154 Ibid.

represented the gospel as truly good news for the Chinese. One group that had a very positive reception from the CIM was the Bethel Mission. This was a Chinese mission founded by an American-educated Chinese medical doctor named Shi Meiyu, whose English name was Mary Stone, and an American, Miss Jennie Hughes. The work included a hospital, a Bible school, a church, and numerous evangelistic teams. While based in Shanghai, its influence extended throughout China. Through their work bands of young, often Western-educated and Western-dressed evangelists traversed the country preaching a very clear gospel message of personal salvation through personal faith in Jesus Christ.[155]

When a Bethel Band came to Kweichow and Yunnan, it was warmly received by the churches in the larger cities. They were not particularly suited for reaching the tribal communities but could and did have a major impact on the ethic Chinese populations, which had for the most part been quite unreceptive to the gospel when they heard it through the medium of foreign missionaries. In the CIM report for 1935, which was appropriately entitled *New Life the Dead Receive*, details where shared regarding the influence of the Bethel Bands on the churches in the Southwest. Sister Welzel from Pichieh in Kweichow reported:

> Early in November we had the great joy of having the visit of a Bethel Band for eight days. These were never-to-be-forgotten days of blessing. Christians were quickened, backsliders restored, converts won. A number of our Christians attended in both places, three of our helpers have followed the Band since to get more help and experience, for the Band desires six from here to form an evangelistic band for tent evangelism in different parts of the province. This new movement needs much prayer and these helpers will be missed in the work here. May the Lord raise up others. One has given up his position in the city Middle School (as well as official positions which were offered to him) to be a whole-time evangelist.[156]

Miss Embery showed the impact of a Bethel Band on the city of Paoshan, where Fraser had first served as a new missionary twenty-five years earlier.

> Paoshan city is an educational centre, and as such, is strangely opposed to the Gospel as being brought by the hated foreigner. Many who know the truth of the Gospel, and would like to believe, dare not do so because it would mean excommunication from recognized society. The common saying formerly was that only ignorant country women believed the "JESUS" religion; no

---

155 R. G. Tiedemann, "Bethel Mission," Ricci Roundtable, http://ricci.rt.usfca.edu/institution/view.aspx?institutionID=195.

156 China Inland Mission, *New Life the Dead Receive: The Story of 1935* (London: China Inland Misson, 1936), 12.

city person of any standing ever had or ever would. And at the close of last year there were indeed only five city people who came to worship; two were men from another city, and three were uneducated women. "But with God nothing is impossible." Towards the end of January a Bethel Band of three evangelists preached here for a week, and about twenty were won for the LORD, who have remained true until now. They are all city people and many of them educated and of good social standing.[157]

The success of the Bethel Bands was evidence of what was possible when the Chinese Christians took the initiative in evangelism and the missionaries supported and followed up on their efforts. It should have clearly revealed the wisdom of having Chinese doing the evangelism among the Chinese populations of the larger towns and cities rather than having missionaries engage in pioneer work on their own. However, there does not seem to have been an immediate recognition of this concept, or perhaps once again, as fifty years earlier, it appeared that there were still not enough suitable Chinese evangelists to do the work, either on their own or alongside the missionaries.

Reaching More of the Tribes

While the missionaries to the tribes in the Southwest were primarily engaged in work among the Miao and the Lisu, inroads into other groups were also occurring. It was very much anticipated that the Forward Evangelistic Movement would include starting new efforts among unreached tribes. The Nosu *lairds* had often persecuted the Miao believers, but this had given them a chance to see Christianity firsthand. Eventually the gospel began to spread among the Nosu as well. The ruling Nosu were known as Black Nosu, while the ones who were often themselves landless peasants were called White Nosu. While converts came from both groups, there was a greater response from the lower-class White Nosu. Across the Kweichow border to the north in Szechwan Province were the Independent Nosu. Efforts to reach them were also made. In the early 1930s they were targeted as one group that should be reached as part of the Forward Evangelistic Movement. It was recognized however that they were not only independent but also isolationists. Foreigners, whether Chinese or Western, were not welcome in their territory, so the most that could be done at that time was to try to establish mission stations in the key cities on the border of the Independent Nosu territory and seek to build relationships that would be of use in gaining access to the interior in the future.

---

157 Ibid., 12–13.

Other groups that the CIM sought to reach were the Chiarung (later spelled Kiarung) in western Szechwan Province, and the Chiang, who were tribal people on the border of Tibet. Tali was the base from which they could be reached. The Tibetans were a prize that the missionaries also sought to gain for Christ, but in the 1930s the door into Tibet was sealed and the hearts of most Tibetans in Chinese ruled territory were tightly closed as well. There were a few encouraging signs like the case of a Buddhist *lama* who sent a request for the Old Testament because he had finished reading a New Testament and had been very impressed with its teaching. Then, after reading the Psalms of David he sent in a request for more Scriptures. Still, only the eye of faith could see to a day when the lands and the hearts of the Tibetans would be open to the gospel.[158]

Other groups were coming to faith through the passive or active witness of the Christian churches that had been established among the Miao and the Lisu. Allyn Cooke wrote a list in the late 1930s of the groups that had yet to be reached. He estimated there were at least fifty such groups. A partial list of those who had been partially reached would include:

- The Miao (the Flowery, the Great Flowery, and the Black).
- The Lisu who had been reached in eastern Yunnan through the Miao and later follow-up efforts by Mr. Metcalf, and in the West through Ba Thaw and J. O. Fraser and those who followed him.
- The Lakka (Lakkia) through the instrumentality of the Miao.
- The Tongchia (formerly they were lumped together as Chung-chía and later they would be known as Dong). A small number became believers.
- The Tai Ya south of Kunming who were reached by Presbyterians who had come up from Chiang Mai in cooperation with members of an associate mission of the CIM.
- The Lahu who were reached by the Lisu in the area of Gengma in China just north of the Wa State in Burma. Allyn Cooke learned to speak the main Lahu Na (Black Lahu) dialect and gave considerable time to follow-up.
- The Atsi Kachin (Zaiwa), whom Fraser had a special burden for. His wife, Roxie, was one of the missionaries who worked with this group.
- The Wa were primarily the responsibility of the American Baptists, but J. Harold Casto of the CIM learned one of their dialects and carried out a ministry among them not far from Gengma.
- Near Ta-li a small movement occurred among the Min-chia (Bai).

---

158 China Inland Mission, "A Head Lama Asks for Scriptures," *Monthly Notes*, January 1930, 3.

- The A Kau (Akha) were said by Vincent Young of the American Baptist Mission to be reachable, but he was unable to do so because the Baptists did not want him to expand the work; and according to Cooke, Vincent Young "has not the faith to start out independently."[159]

While this was certainly a good beginning, there was a clear recognition that much more needed to be done, and that in many cases new workers would need to not only learn Chinese but also learn tribal languages as well. This created tensions, and the question of how much language study a new worker needed was an issue that regularly needed to be discussed at the China Council. There was no easy solution. Good Chinese was essential as missionaries needed to be able to speak with government officials, shop and inn managers, and bandit leaders on a regular basis. To start a work among the tribes would also require knowing enough Chinese to find an educated, multilingual member of that tribe who could serve as a language helper. At the same time, if most of one's time and energy would be spent in tribal villages, there was a natural desire to give primary attention to learning the tribal language. It went without saying that those who worked in a province like Yunnan needed to pick up the local dialect of Chinese, as most of the local people would not speak or even understand much of the Putonghua (standard Mandarin Chinese) that the missionaries would have learned at language school in Anking. A good language learner might make progress in these various languages and dialects within four or five years, but marriages, diseases, bandits, and the inability to find good language helpers would all delay the process. Though the Forward Evangelistic Movement gave special attention to the needs of the tribes in Southwest China, and some of the two hundred were designated to help meet this need, there could be few visible results expected before the end of the decade.

Meanwhile the Forward Movement itself was meeting obstacles. Perhaps Mr. Hoste was too understanding, and perhaps field workers in some locations always had good reasons to delay handing responsibilities over to the local churches and moving on to new unreached locations. When he retired in 1935, Mr. George Watt Gibb, who had long years of experience at the Shanghai headquarters, replaced him. He took the responsibility reluctantly, and it was given to him reluctantly as well. Clearly the Mission would have preferred to choose a general director who had proved himself as a superintendent with plenty of field experience

---

159 [Mrs. Howard Taylor?], "Conversations with Cooke," Los Angeles, 1938. Microfilm from Billy Graham Archives, Wheaton, IL.

to build upon. No such candidate existed. A partial solution was to ask J. O. Fraser to leave Yunnan and come to join the Executive Committee of the CIM as a China Director where he could help advise Mr. Gibb on policies that affected how the ministry on the field was to be carried out. For some reason Fraser did not get the invitation, or did not accept it if he did receive it. This does seem unfortunate, for it was evident that Mr. Gibb during his short (five-year) tenure really made a sincere effort to put the policy agreed upon in 1928 into practice. A recorded interview of Mrs. Jenny Fitzwilliams in 1984 throws some light on subject of Fraser and the leadership of CIM.

> ... as I understood ... Mr Hoste who was the ... general director at that time, wanted Mr. Fraser to succeed him but Mr. Fraser felt that there were so many ... in the mission that didn't agree with his strong stand on ... the indigenous policies of church planting that it just wouldn't work. So he wouldn't consider it. And shortly after that the Lord took him home. And I've always felt (maybe this is a thought I shouldn't even express) but I always felt that the mission ... because they couldn't see his policies, missed out on a very wonderful leadership. 'Cause I think he would have taken the mission earlier into indigenous policies, which they later adopted wholeheartedly. But at that time there were a lot of the older missionaries that just didn't go along with that. And I know that some of the senior missionaries in the province of Yunnan didn't always agree with his strong stand, but all the younger missionaries were 100 percent for him.[160]

Jenny and her husband, Francis "Fitz" Fitzwilliams worked with the Atsi Kachin and actually shared a bamboo house with the Frasers so Jennie was in a good position to know some of the more confidential matters regarding what the directors had offered to Fraser. But there might be an element of speculation in what she said nearly fifty years after the actual events.

By the mid-1930s some CIM-related churches had made rapid strides forward in self-government and self-support. Others had made little or no progress at all. As is common in all institutions, the top leadership rarely gives time and attention to those aspects of the work which are flourishing. The successes were written up in the *China's Millions*. The failures come to light in the dreary pages of the minutes of the China Council.

Gibb sought to clarify what churches were expected to do and what missionaries were expected to do and not to do. They were specifically not to baptize, perform Communion, or conduct weddings. Their role was to

---

160 Collection 272-*Jennie Kingston Fitzwilliam*. T3 Transcript Billy Graham Center Archives (http://www2.wheaton.edu/bgc/archives/trans/272t03.htm).

evangelize and instruct, and especially to instruct the Chinese evangelists and encourage them in their work. Without creating a denomination they were to encourage interchurch cooperation. Their work, if done right, was a temporary one, and they should not assume that they would spend their lives in one district. The example of Hudson Taylor and the early pioneers had to be reapplied even though the new workers might only move from one district to the next in a single prefecture and not pass through whole provinces in a single journey.

To a considerable extent Mr. Gibb was able to push the Mission forward in this direction, even as the Communists were pushing their bases forward in Northern China and the Japanese were pushing their empire southward from Manchuko (Manchuria) to Shantung and Peking, until at last in 1937 they were at the gates of the foreign settlement in Shanghai.

A Director's Conference and Special Session of the China Council was held in Shanghai from December 22, 1938, to January 9, 1939, This meeting was held at a time when the Japanese army had encircled Shanghai and travel was quite uncertain. However, most of the superintendents as well as the home directors from Great Britain and America were in attendance. The result of their discussions was published in the *Report of Director's Conference and Special Session of the China Council*. It was a carefully laid-out document which dealt with both the objectives and the organizational structure of the Mission. Knowing that a plan on paper did not always result in practice on the field, the introduction closed with the following request.

> The purpose in view, the plans for giving effect to it, the compiling of the agenda were all steeped in prayer, both during the preparatory stages as well as during the days of Conference, and now that this is over there is more need than ever to continue in intercession, for we are all aware that there is often some hiatus between resolved determination and the actual working out of them in fact.[161]

The report provides a glimpse of where the Mission was after over seventy years in China with scarcely a dozen left before all foreign workers had to leave. Attention was given to education and medical work. In Taylor's day educational work was considered essential for the sake of the children of the Christians. In many cases there was no alternative to having the missionaries start and run schools. In Hoste's era there was still the need in some locations for Mission-run schools, but it was hoped that the direction

---

161 China Inland Mission, *Report of Director's Conference and Special Session of the China Council*, December 22, 1938, to January 9, 1939, 1. Microfilm from Billy Graham Archives, Wheaton, IL.

of the school would become the responsibility of the local Christians. In some places there was a concern that if the CIM did not run its own schools then the children of the local Christians would send their children to the schools of other missionary societies. Then the children, when they grew up, would not retain ties to the CIM-founded churches. They would also be at risk in some cases of imbibing modernist teaching. Furthermore, there was the fact that by the early twentieth century many of the Christian schools in China were not operated with the objective of leading the students into developing a personal relationship with Jesus Christ.

By the time Gibb became the general director, the Nationalist government had implemented a program of public education. Government regulations made it increasingly difficult to run private Christian schools, and in many ways made them redundant. While there was a clear recognition that efforts needed to be made to reach children and youth with the gospel, it was felt that in most cases Mission-run schools were no longer essential.

In the area of medical work it was plainly stated:

"The medical work of the China Inland Mission was instituted in obedience to our Lord's command to heal the sick as well as to preach the Gospel." Its purpose could be summarized as evangelizing, healing and disseminating the knowledge of hygiene.[162]

While medical work certainly contributed to evangelism, it was not to be judged as to its value based on that single criteria. In tribal work many missionaries helped to provide basic medical assistance in the communities where they lived. Dr. Stuart and Sally Harverson were connected with Lisu work during the 1930s. From his autobiography, *Doctor in the Orient*, it would appear that learning Chinese and Lisu, extensive traveling in difficult environments, and a lack of medicines or medical equipment meant that the impact of medical work among the Lisu was somewhat limited. They did however experience some positive results in helping Lisu who had become Christians to break free from their opium addictions.[163]

For our purposes the statements of the China Council with regard to evangelism demand special attention.

Consideration was given to the conditions under which Junior missionaries can develop ere they attain Senior status. It was suggested that greater advantages might accrue from concentration in comparatively large centres

---

162 Ibid., 9.
163 Harverson, *Doctor in the Orient*, 32.

rather than distribution over wider areas in isolated stations. The question as to the best methods of work in any given district was raised. In this connection it was felt that, instead of emphasizing station responsibility, workers should, from their earliest contact with the Mission right throughout their training at home, and on the field, be preparing themselves for an itinerant ministry. The aim before all workers should be the evangelization of the districts to which they are appointed. Whilst the importance of a systematic study of the language was not overlooked, nor the need ignored of a faithful witness being given in the larger cities, especially where our Mission centres exist, missionaries should seek to familiarize themselves with the entire district in which they reside. The preparation and constant use of a fairly detailed map was regarded as indispensable. The realization that there has been a failure on the part of some workers within our Mission adequately to evangelize the districts for which they are responsible had a very humbling effect. It was determined that every effort should be made to rectify the situation where failure was found to exist.[164]

The objective to evangelize China's millions had not changed, but there was a recognition that the methods needed to be revised.

Evangelism

This is the prime reason for the Mission's existence and therefore needs no re-emphasis. The following is set forth by way of reminder of lines of evangelism which need to be followed as circumstances and varying conditions permit.

Generally speaking, there are three fields for evangelistic effort, namely:

a. Unevangelized areas.

b. Partly evangelized areas.

c. Church areas.

The evangelization of an unevangelized area should be undertaken, whenever possible, from an adjacent centre already occupied, rather than by the opening of a new centre for permanent residence.

This will mean that certain strategic centres will need to be strongly reinforced, local conditions determining the form the work should take: it is essential, however, that all such work should be carried out systematically.

We would call attention to the advantages of team work, such as tent groups, preaching bands etc., in addition to the older methods of colportage and itineration. The Assistant Director of a given region should seek to stimulate evangelistic effort, especially where it is weak; and where Chinese workers cannot be found locally, should seriously consider bringing them in from other provinces.

---

164 China Inland Mission, *Report of Director's Conference*, 10.

All evangelistic work must be done with the definite objective of founding indigenous Churches. Where the field is already partly evangelized, every effort should be made to work in association with the existing Church.

Missionaries in Church areas should do all in their power to inspire the Churches to evangelistic zeal and effort, and where desired, to co-operate with them in their work. Realizing the impossibility of weak Churches fully evangelizing large cities, the Mission should be prepared to open strong evangelistic centres, where work would be carried on in close co-operation with the local Church. Amongst the specialized forms of work which might be inaugurated in these centres would be newspaper, prison and radio evangelism, as well as efforts to reach such classes as the police, postal officials, etc.[165]

Looking at the plan from a twenty-first-century perspective, this concept of teams seems both far advanced for its time and slightly unrealistic. There was a need for pioneering work, but the lone pioneer worker was no longer going to be the norm. Whether the implications of creating multinational teams, which might include new workers in their midtwenties being overseen by senior workers in their sixties, had been fully thought out is unknown. There was a recognition that, at age seventy, senior workers should relinquish their leadership responsibilities over mission stations so that they could get a well-earned rest, and younger workers would have a chance to develop their gifts. Teams would work closely with Chinese churches and even bring in suitable Chinese workers from other provinces if they were not locally available. But how would the interaction between the Mission and the Chinese churches be arranged? How would work be turned over to the Chinese in the future? It would be several war-torn years later before these issues could be addressed.

Little mention was made of the tribal work directly, except with regard to the need for more workers to reach the Lolo (Nosu) of Szechwan Province, but this reference is more of an afterthought appended to a call to develop a work among the Tibetans on the Szechwan border. In a sense the problems that Mr. Gibb and the council were trying to solve did not directly affect the *successful* work in the Southwest. It also did not affect many of the healthier churches in the East which had long ago become self-governing, self-supporting bodies which were active in evangelism both near and far. The Chinese work in the Southwest was in general fairly weak, and many of the topics that Mr. Gibb tried to address were relevant to those churches and mission stations.

---

165 Ibid., 17–18.

It may be a tautology to say that a slow work is a weak work, but this is what the CIM was discovering. It would appear that where churches grew fairly rapidly from the very beginning, as was the case with the Lisu and Miao, as well as among the Chinese in some of the eastern provinces, the missionaries were naturally busy making sure that new leaders were continually being trained to help oversee the work. As believers went out witnessing in villages where they had friends and relations, the missionary would naturally go out with them and devote his attention to how to do effective follow-up. In such a situation he was not in a position to fall into the role of being the priest or pastor of a single congregation. Of necessity he learned to delegate responsibility and do only what no one else was truly capable of doing. Where the work was slow and converts were few, the opposite tendency applied. Unless the missionary had strong willpower that would drive him out day by day to share the gospel in unreached and often unresponsive villages, he was likely to be drawn into dealing with the smallest issues in the life of a congregation, and thus would fall into the role of becoming the chief teacher and ruling elder of a small, weak church. The result was that local believers would not have their faith tested and their gifts applied. As long as they did not grow, they confirmed the missionary in his mindset that they would not grow.

To bring an end to the lethargy that was plaguing some districts, Gibb attempted to increase the authority of the superintendents. Now this may have been a wise decision, but no matter how lethargic someone is, he will almost always find the energy to stand up and protest when one of his brethren is raised up to lord it over him. Once again we find that those who were actively pursuing their calling had no complaints about giving superintendents more authority. They were not the ones who needed much oversight from a superintendent in the first place.

In order to keep the missionaries from ruling over the churches, there was a renewed effort to get the churches to support their own pastors. Often superintendents found that church workers had been placed over churches by the local missionaries. Then they needed to determine if the church leaders would gradually take on the support of the pastor as the Mission gradually reduced its level of support to zero. Where local churches did not want to take on the support of these workers, they were to be retired with some sort of a stipend or parting gift.

Some of these individuals might be suited to evangelism and not pastoral duties. In such a case it was to be determined whether they should work with a church association to start new congregations in nearby towns or city neighborhoods, or to work with the Mission in starting a new work in an unreached district.

Meanwhile, J. O. Fraser died of malarial fever in Paoshan, Yunnan, on September 25, 1938. This would help explain why so little attention was given to the tribes at the Director's Conference a few months later. In July 1939 John Kuhn was appointed as (acting) superintendent of western Yunnan in his place. He followed the methods and practices that he had learned from J. O. Fraser. Relatively speaking, western Yunnan was as peaceful as any place in China at that time. This does not mean the work was easy, but it did mean that the missionaries were able to visit churches and hold Short Term Bible Schools with a fair degree of regularity. This needs to be borne in mind whenever comparisons are made between the Miao work in Kweichow and eastern Yunnan with the Lisu work further west. There were cases of villages relapsing back to heathenism among both groups. With the Lisu it was possible for their own evangelists, alone or with a missionary, to visit such communities and bring them back; but in war-torn, bandit-infested Kweichow some villages were inaccessible for years.

Chapter 5
The 1940s and the Houghton Era

On October 22–23, 1940, George Gibb retired and was replaced by Bishop Frank Houghton. Gibb was sick at the time and died at the age of seventy-one only three weeks later. A tribute was written of him after his death:

> Born in 1869 in Inverurie, Aberdeenshire, a part of Scotland where nature is cold but blood is warm, and men look impassive when they are most moved, Mr. Gibb came to China in his twenty-sixth year . . .
>
> By correspondence and visits he maintained personal contact with every part of the Mission's far flung field, thus acquainting himself with the needs and claims of the work and workers. This detailed knowledge of the Mission's personnel, with his nature and finely balanced judgment, was of great help to him in making appointments or designation of workers—always a delicate matter . . .
>
> He also had a large share in formulating the Mission's "Statement of Policy." His own loyal adherence to the principles underlying that policy strengthened the hands of the Superintendents as they sought to apply them in their respective fields. It was largely owing to his wise leadership that in the recent years of strain the work of the Mission was so well maintained.[166]

It might have been that Gibb saw the writing on the wall. In the years following his death, communications in China became increasingly disrupted by war. If the hands of the superintendents had not been strengthened, it is hard to imagine how the work could have continued at all.

Frank Houghton apparently neither hailed from Inverurie nor shared those qualities which were so evident in his predecessor. Still, to borrow a phrase from bygone days, he was a man "not without parts." He was a skillful writer and a hymnist, and he had a good grasp of the missiological issues of the day. He was bold and had an optimism that was the fruit of deep faith in Jesus Christ. In a tribute to him written after his death in 1972, A. J. Broomhall wrote of Houghton's days as a field worker.

---

166 China Inland Mission, "Special Minute of the China Council at the One Hundred and Ninety-Seventh Session," January 1941, in *Minutes of China Council Session 157 to 205*, September 10, 1930, to April 9, 1945. OMF International Headquarters Archives, Singapore.

When he went out in 1920, he was posted to West China. Those were days of upheaval, misery and suffering in the young Republic. At one time in Szechwan no fewer than four armies were in conflict, and while the Houghtons were there Suiting changed hands and was looted in the most shameful manner. Crowds of women and girls rushed into the Mission Compound for refuge, while soldiers invaded the premises, helping themselves to whatever they wanted.

But it was in such circumstances that Frank Houghton wrote these lines which remained appropriate to every phase of his missionary life.

>   Ringed around by Satan's power,
>   Ceaselessly at grips with sin,
>   Battle-stained and faint within—
>   "Father save me from this hour!"
>
>   Nay—it was for this I came!
>   Heard afar God's trumpet-call,
>   Heard and answered, rose, left all—
>   "Father, glorify Thy Name!"
>
>   Thou to whom this cry ascends
>   From the death-strewn battle line,
>   On whose energy divine
>   All our burning hope depends,
>
>   Hear, O Lord, Thy warrior's plea
>   Not that we should tamely cease
>   Not for some inglorious peace,
>   Bringing shame to us—and Thee—
>
>   But for faith Thine aid to claim,
>   Grace to struggle on, nor tire,
>   Deathless life and quenchless fire—
>   "Father, glorify Thy Name!"[167]

After one term Frank Houghton became the editor of *China's Millions* and was thus influential through this medium in recruiting the

---

167 Overseas Missionary Fellowship, "Bishop Frank Houghton: A Tribute," *O.M.F. Bulletin*, July 1972, 64–5.

two hundred new workers for the Forward Movement. Then he returned to Szechwan, but this time to be ordained as bishop. As a bishop over the CIM-established churches in Szechwan, he had firsthand knowledge of what it meant to be "facing the task unfinished." He had a high esteem for the Chinese church. Both out of theological considerations and from personal experience, he was convinced that the key to evangelizing China was to work with the Chinese church to establish strong churches throughout the country.

In some ways he tried to follow the policy laid down under Gibb's tenure. His own distinct emphasis was on the role of the Chinese church in the evangelization of China. Here he had some valuable contributions to make. The problem was that he did not have much time to build a consensus or implement his new ideas. Most of the world was at war, with China being one of the main theaters. As a general director he was not simply responsible for China, but also for maintaining good relations with the home countries. As such he was away from China for considerable periods of time. When he became general director he spent only a few months in Shanghai before making a tour of the world, which was greatly complicated by Japan's attack on Pearl Harbor and the events that followed. When he returned it was to the temporary headquarters in Chungking in Western China. After the war ended and the headquarters staff returned to Shanghai, he made another trip to the home countries; then he was forced to relocate for an extended period to Australia due to ill health. The result was that he sought to develop new policies, but he left the headquarters staff to implement them without fully recognizing the real situation that the field workers were facing. The reason for bringing up these points is that Houghton had some very advanced views on how the Mission should operate, but the times were not conducive to considering his proposals in depth, let alone to applying them throughout China.

Among the first topics of discussion that he raised was one that had first been considered during the last months of Mr. Gibb's tenure. Could Chinese seminary graduates who felt called to work with the CIM be allowed to do so? The need for such workers was plainly evident, but the mechanism for sending them out and supporting them did not exist. Discussions were begun in November 1940 and were continued in January 1941. There were concerns that by bringing in these seminary graduates they would be going back on the indigenous church policy. A subcommittee considered the issue and reported back to the council with a list of difficulties and suggestions.

Difficulty: The use of such workers would appear to conflict with the Mission policy of encouraging the development of indigenous churches.

Suggestion: The Statement of Policy still envisages the use of Chinese workers in certain circumstances. The use of such workers will not militate against the development of indigenous churches if it be clearly understood that they are not church workers, and that their ministry in any one place is temporary and supplementary.

Furthermore, although such workers might be supported by Mission funds, this need be no deterrent to local church giving, for if they exercise an effective ministry, leading to spiritual growth in the churches, there should be an increased willingness and ability for voluntary works and also a greater readiness to meet financial obligations ...

Difficulty: Conditions of Service—support, traveling expenses, family, health, duration.

Suggestions: Whenever candidates offer for service, the Superintendent (or, if in Shanghai, a member of the Directorate) should confer with others, including responsible spiritually minded Chinese, concerning their suitability and conditions (financial and otherwise) under which they would work. Where their support is found in whole or in part by the Mission they will be expected to stand with us in looking to the Lord and not to the Mission for their support, sharing with our fellowship the responsibility of praying for funds and accepting whatever proportion of allowance the Mission may be able to send without question.[168]

Here we see an early stage of the development in the concept of Chinese Christians working at least temporarily alongside CIM missionaries in a missionary rather than a church worker role. In the same council session, there were renewed discussions about the need to increase the support of national workers due to the high cost of living, which was due to the war. During the discussion it was also noted that, despite a policy of pooling all the funds for national workers, some donors still insisted on designating their gifts for specific native workers. It was further noted that some Chinese churches were increasing their support for their workers. In other words, while there may have been progress occurring slowly but surely, the slowly was very sure. In that context, there may have been some on the council who, while welcoming the idea of seeing Chinese Christians commit themselves to home missions, might have been hesitant about becoming entangled in relationships that could lead to further dependency.

---

168 China Inland Mission, "Minutes of Council Meeting," January 20, 1941, in *Minutes of China Council Session 157 to 205*, 488–89.

In the spring of 1941 Bishop Houghton made a visit to the western provinces and met many of the missionaries at their annual conferences. The reports he received convinced him that some corrective measures were definitely needed.

"C.I.M." Churches. As a result of his visit to West China and consequent upon the convening of two full provincial conferences, at Kweiyang and Kaolan, and also a smaller conference at Chengtu, Bishop Houghton felt he should bring to the Council a report of the condition of the churches in the fields visited, as far as he had been able to judge it. Whilst there was much that was commendable and a cause of thanksgiving, the General Director felt he was not misstating the character of the churches when he judged them to be, for the most part, both very small and very needy.

They were small numerically and Bishop Houghton pointed out that out of a total of 6,923 reported church members in Kweichow at the end of 1940, only 363 of these were Chinese church members, the remainder being tribal Christians, and this in spite of the fact that by far the greater proportion of missionaries was engaged in Chinese work, compared with the few devoting their time to tribal work. Again, with regard to Kansu, Tsinghai and Ningsia, existing work in these fields was represented by only 1,222 Chinese church members.

The need of the churches in these areas was great, from the point of view of Chinese leadership, the church in Kansu being without a single pastor, although among those assuming leadership, particularly in South Kansu, there were a number of earnest laymen. There appeared to be an almost uniform barrenness in Chinese churches of Kansu, and spiritual life, it had to be confessed, was at a low ebb. Young missionaries had been thrust out into new districts to stand or fall in the face of real difficulties, with the result that some had been unequal to the strain placed upon them and the work begun showed little life or vitality. The policy of concentrating missionaries in one centre appeared to have greater prospects of success than scattering comparatively inexperienced workers over a wide area.[169]

It was the moment of truth and bore considerable resemblance to the report Nehemiah received concerning the condition of Jerusalem. Balancing these negative points, the bishop brought up the positive side of the matter.

Over against these lamentable weaknesses there were factors of potential strength to be taken into consideration. The General Director had been impressed by the fine body of missionaries whom he had met and with whom he had conferred in the centres visited. In a spirit of frankness and

---

169 China Inland Mission, "Minutes of Council Meeting," June 2, 1941, in *Minutes of China Council Session 157 to 205*, 502.

cooperation, they had not shirked facing the facts, but had prayerfully set themselves to explore the causes for the apparent little success of the work. Bishop Houghton recalled the presence, in many of the churches in the West, of Chinese Christians who migrated to West China as a result of the war. In a large number of cases their presence was a help and stimulus to the local churches.[170]

Bishop Houghton thought that he perceived both a major cause of the problem, as well as some means of obtaining a solution.

Referring again to the need of the churches, Bishop Houghton spoke of the relationship between the missionary and the local church and its leaders. In an endeavor to carry out the Mission's policy to establish autonomous churches, it was evident that some workers had tended to place an exaggerated emphasis on some aspects of it. In their earnest desire to see the church shouldering its own responsibilities, they had adopted a policy of isolationism, a detachment which was being misinterpreted by some Chinese who failed to grasp the real motives behind this extreme attitude as one which deprived the church of the practical and spiritual contribution which each worker should be expected to make.

Houghton asked a subcommittee to make a table showing the problems and means to rectify them. It was shown that the problems stemmed from an improper emphasis on having the missionaries try to do pioneer evangelism in unreached areas when they should have been working with existing churches and Christians to expand the church into adjacent areas. While the conclusions were far reaching, they could not be immediately acted upon throughout China, for Bishop Houghton was due to make his round-the-world tour. Before he returned, the Japanese attack on the Americans and English in the Pacific and China meant that the CIM headquarters staff had to join in the mass migration to the west of China. By mid-December 1941 they were established in Chungking in Szechan Province, and with difficulty kept hundreds of missionaries supplied with sufficient funds and direction to continue spreading the gospel throughout free China and even in war-torn areas.[171]

One example of Houghton's new emphasis on how missionaries should operate can be found in Leslie Lyall's *God Reigns in China*. Lyall, a Cambridge graduate who was in his midthirties when the war began, had already spent over a decade in North China. In 1940 he

---

170 Ibid.

171 A book well worth reading is Margaret Rice Elliot Crossett, *Harvest at the Front* (Philadelphia: China Inland Mission, 1946). It shows how missionaries supported and encouraged Chinese Christians as they (the Chinese) reached out to those suffering around them to win them for Christ and establish new congregations of believers.

was reassigned to Anshun, Kweichow Province, where J. R. Adam had once worked among the Chinese and Miao. The Chinese church had ceased to function, and the Miao had been left for many years without any missionary supervision or assistance. It was Lyall's gift for working with the Chinese believers that enabled them together to reestablish the church in that city and lead both local Chinese and displaced Chinese from the East to faith. During those years, he made occasional visits to Miao villages to encourage the leaders of the churches there. While he could not speak their language, his visits apparently helped to strengthen the congregations. Some Chinese Christians were able to join in this ministry and brought spiritual renewal to the believers whom they visited. In the particular area they visited, there were to be no other missionaries to the Miao before the Communist takeover.[172]

In October 1943 Bishop Houghton was at last able to convene a council in Chungking, and much of the time and attention were given to the concerns expressed in 1941. The result was that a revision of principles was determined necessary to correct some of the failings that he considered were in part a result of the misapplication of the policies that had been promoted since 1928.

> While the findings of the Council are, for the most part in accord with the "Principles and Practice" of the Mission, the Statement of Policy (1928) and the "Report of the Directors' Conference and Special Session of the China Council" (1938–39), it will be found that in certain particulars they imply a modification of the "Statement" and the "Report," and it will also be necessary to undertake a careful revision of the "Principles and Practice," in order that our main objective may be stated more clearly and passages which envisage circumstances wholly different from those which exist today may be altered to conform to present conditions.[173]

The report was perhaps the most revolutionary statement ever to come out of a CIM council up until that time. The Statement of Policy of 1928 was an attempt to get the CIM back on track in terms of evangelizing China, but this Report of 1943 was an effort to set the CIM on a new track. The keynote of the session was Ephesians 3:8–11:

---

172   Leslie T. Lyall, *God Reigns in China* (London: Hodder & Stoughton, and Overseas Missionary Fellowship, 1985), 84–85. In his later years Lyall wrote some letters in the *China Bulletin* which showed a critical attitude to some of OMF's methodology in the area of pioneer evangelism. It does seem that he was more inclined to have missionaries work with the existing Christians than to have them try to start new work on their own.

173   China Inland Mission, foreword to the "Private Report of the Two Hundred and Second Session of the China Council Held at Chungking," October 13–30, 1943. Microfilm from Billy Graham Archives, Wheaton, IL.

> Unto me, who am less than the least of all saints, is this grace given, that I should preach among the Gentiles the unsearchable riches of Christ; And to make all men see what is the fellowship of the mystery, which from the beginning of the world hath been hid in God, who created all things by Jesus Christ: To the intent that now unto the principalities and powers in heavenly places might be known by the church the manifold wisdom of God, According to the eternal purpose which he purposed in Christ Jesus our Lord. (KJV)

The new emphasis was based on the new reality that there were now 120,000 Christians in China who were members of congregations formed through the ministry of the CIM. The first missionaries (outside of Chekiang Province) could not work through the native churches because there were no churches to work with. Now that churches had emerged in all the provinces, it was incumbent on the CIM missionaries to work with these churches to evangelize the rest of China. It was recognized that the churches in various places had not all developed to the same degree, so the level and nature of cooperation with them would vary, but the aim would ever be to help the churches mature to the point where full cooperation was possible. While the goal of the CIM was still the evangelization of China's millions, the Mission was to work humbly with the churches and not be aloof or isolated from them. There was a reference to the steps made in 1928 to speed up the process of establishing church associations or federations in districts where congregations had already emerged.

> In districts where the churches are linked together in some sort of federation (Lien Moh Hwei), such associations of churches are the natural focal point of cooperation. The Mission is to be regarded as a Foreign Legion, working with the Church, and wherever possible under its direction. The Council Minute on this subject reads as follows:
>
> "Where groups of churches are linked together . . . their representative conference, or its standing committee, should be recognized as the focal point for our cooperation with the Church."[174]

It was readily acknowledged that in some places federations had not developed to the point where full cooperation was possible, but where it was possible the superintendents would work closely with them.

The superintendents were to work with these associations in order to determine where missionaries were to be placed and what sort of work they were to do.

---

174 China Inland Mission, "Private Report," 2.

It was agreed that when a missionary leaves China for furlough, the Superintendent should, from Chinese leaders and the Provincial Council, privately seek to ascertain whether the worker was acceptable to the Church. It was the duty of the Superintendent to report accordingly to the Mission Directorate.[175]

From this it became obvious that in the new paradigm the church was the primary instrument for the evangelization of China.

As soon as a Church has been brought into being in any country, evangelism is the task of the Church, and not merely of individuals within it, still less of Christians from other lands through whose ministry the Church has been established. The evangelization of the whole of China is the task of the whole Christian Church in China.[176]

In all of this there was a clear call for missionaries to relate closely to the Chinese churches. Membership in them was made a possibility, and even membership on committees was possible in cases where the missionary would not be in a position of dominance over the Chinese. Houghton was trying to develop a biblical model that recognized the potential of the Chinese church and the growing sensitivities that emerged with the development of Chinese nationalism and love of country. When it came to the non-Chinese races, it was recognized that the CIM was called to evangelize not just the Chinese but all the inhabitants of the Republic of China. Regarding the work among the tribes it was noted:

The commission of the C.I.M. is co-extensive with the bounds of the Chinese Republic. Thus the Council recognized that work among Moslems, Tibetans and aboriginal tribes is an integral part of the Mission programme, and not merely a burden on the heart of individuals.

Roughly speaking, there are two distinct problems. The first is that of large tribal churches in the southwest, where hundreds of families have turned from superstition to God, and thousands more are accessible. A number of well-qualified workers are required immediately to reinforce the small group in Kweichow and Yunnan. In this field, owing to racial antipathies, missionaries are at present more acceptable than Chinese workers would be. In Sheicheng (of Kweichow) alone there are no less than 2000 baptized Christians needing teaching and shepherding. No missionary currently speaks the Black Miao language. Several married couples are needed urgently in West Yunnan. Medical work and a printing establishment would be of great value there. The danger is that the tribes will be "sinicized" before they are evangelized.[177]

---

175 Ibid.
176 Ibid., 3.
177 Ibid., 10.

The comment about racial antipathies showed that the leaders of the Mission recognized that ethnic identity was a key element in reaching communities for Christ. While a general commitment was being made to work with provincial associations, there was also a commitment to continue to reach the tribes as tribes, and not simply see them as Chinese simply because they lived in China.

After the session, Bishop Houghton wrote a document called the "The Pattern Shewn," in which he sought to present the new emphasis to supporters in the West. Some members of the British Council took exception to some of the points raised, and apparently feared that there was a loss of focus on reaching the unreached. This provided Houghton with a chance to explain himself further on the subject of how the building up of the body of believers was in fact the most effective method of evangelizing unreached Chinese.

> Yet the great majority of truly converted church members trace their conversion to the witness of other Chinese and not that of the missionary. A deeper and fuller apprehension of truth increases the urge to evangelize. In other words, if Christians grow in grace the Church grows in numbers. Acts 9:31 and other passages show that "edifying" and a "multiplying" are indissolubly connected. It is a spurious edification which does not lead to evangelization; but unless our babes in Christ are to be handed over to others for nurture (and this has never been the CIM practice, from Hudson Taylor's pre-CIM days onward!) their growth as well as their birth is our concern. What is there that is "misleading" about this? How can it "lead the Mission away from its original commission" when in actual fact this is what we have been doing (though often feebly and inadequately) for these eighty years?[178]

Bishop Houghton was right, both theologically and historically. He knew it and he knew how to express his views forcefully. However, he might not always have known the best way to convince others to share in those views, or to convince others that he had carefully listened to and considered their views. There were numerous implications to the new emphasis, which in many cases were obvious to Houghton and the council from the very beginning, or became evident soon after.

One point was that the sort of worker who could contribute to an existing church would usually have been one who already had church experience before arriving in China. This would mean workers would often be older and thus find language learning more difficult. Connected

---

178 Ibid., Memorandum on the New Emphasis.

with this is the fact that older workers would either come out married or want to rush to the altar as soon as possible after they arrived. Policies regarding language learning and rules regarding marriage were a perennial favorite at China Councils. There was no "solution." Married couples tended to make less progress in language than singles did. When it came to tribal work where two or more languages were required, the challenge was greater still.

Another issue was that the role of the superintendent must develop. Superintendents would be nominated by the senior CIM workers of a province, but they would increasingly be required to work closely with the Chinese church councils, and they would have a much stronger say in what the other workers in the province were to do. Half a generation of missionaries had been focusing on starting new churches in lonely outposts of China, so there would be a dearth of individuals with the qualities or prerequisite experience necessary to become superintendents. There were always provinces in need of new superintendents, and especially with the war raging, it was very hard for directors to interact with field workers in order to find out whom they would be willing to have as a superintendent over them.

CIM's Last Years in China

While missionaries on the field were able to continue their ministries to some extent in Kweichow and Yunnan during the war, they were seriously handicapped in their efforts.

The Cookes, for instance, were able to get back from their furlough to the base in Luda in western Yunnan in January 1941, but in 1942 both the husband and wife were laid low with typhoid. In May 1943 Leila had a relapse and died. She had personally struggled in her early years with whether or not women should be Bible teachers of men, but it would seem that she received a special dispensation to do so in a place where so many needed to be taught and few other teachers were available.[179] Clearly she had a good grasp of the Lisu language as she helped to translate many hymns into their language. Allyn was left to mourn alone. One son was in the army and the other interred by the Japanese with the rest of the Chefoo School students in Northeast China.

---

179 According to Dr. Ted Hope, who worked with the Lisu after the CIM left China, it was said that Leila would only teach the women in the building, but as buildings had thin walls or no walls, men who were outside could still hear everything that was said.

John Kuhn, with his duties as superintendent, was able to give reports of the progress of the work at the various stations, but in 1943, as the Japanese advanced through Northern Burma into Yunnan, the only thing Mr. Kuhn could report for several stations was that he had no communication with them for several months. The best news was that in the midst of the trials of war the Christians were standing firm in their faith, and the gospel was spreading to such an extent that there was a need to find ways to bring in more Christian literature for the new believers.[180]

Isobel reported new districts near the Japanese lines that were responding to the gospel as well.

> Other churches in that area, when their American leaders fled have seemed to melt into nothing, but the Kuma church, self-supporting and self-governing, still goes on, and even increases. At Christmas a group returned with Lucius and pled for more teachers to take back with them. There is a whole new district turning to Christ they say, and one man could not handle all that work.[181]

It was experiences like this which showed clearly the value of the indigenous methods that Fraser had promoted and the later Lisu workers built upon. They did not pay workers to serve God, but they did share their lives with them wholeheartedly. There was no aloofness or isolationism in their work. In the same letter, Isobel shared their own special trial of not having seen their daughter Kathryn for five years, as she, like so many of the students, was interned by the Japanese while studying at Chefoo School. While the trials that the missionaries faced might be different from those of the local believers, it was evident to them that the missionaries were willing to pay a price for bringing the gospel to them.

Farther east in Yunnan a CIM associate mission, the Vandsburger Mission, was experiencing responsiveness among the Lahu. But not all tribes were equally responsive. The Dai-Chia in the same area had shown interest several decades earlier but were now quite indifferent to the gospel. The work had been begun by the American Presbyterians, but apparently the more committed Christians had migrated to North Thailand (where they are known as Tai Ya) at the invitation of the Presbyterian Mission, and those who remained were turned over to this same German Vandsburger Mission that was seeing results with the Lahu.

---

180 China Inland Mission, *Field Bulletin of the China Inland Mission* 5, no. 9 (September 1943): 10.

181 Isobel Kuhn, "Prayer Trust," February 27, 1943. Microfilm from Billy Graham Archives, Wheaton, IL.

Speaking of work among the tribes, Dai-Chia, at Yuankiang and Mosha, we are praying for a new revival. A good many families have moved back to Siam, where they have come from, and the rest are not very eager for the Bread of Life, but rather seek worldly things. Formerly there was a Christian school at Yuankiang for the Dai children, so they have been well educated in the Christian way, but not much fruit is to be seen now. At Mosha the school is still going on, and some more result is to be noticed. There is also more life in the Dai church.[182]

There were and are reasons why one group is responsive and another one is not, or one group is responsive for a certain period of time and then ceases to be so. However, we often do not know what those reasons are, and those who speculate are simply speculating.

With the end of World War II, it took many months for missionaries who had been "trapped" on the field for many years to be able to leave for long-delayed furloughs. Missionaries who had been on furlough likewise took a long time getting back. There simply were not enough ships, trains, or trucks to carry all the millions of people who were in motion at that time.

By August 1946, however, John Kuhn was ready to initiate a new advance among the tribes by both surveying the unreached tribes in Yunnan and stimulating the Christians to share in the work to reach out to the other tribes around them. The team consisted of John himself, two Lisu evangelists, and two Lisu carriers. In some cases congregations had gone years without any spiritual care.

There were wide-open doors on every hand, especially in the church areas. It was most heartwarming and heartrending too, at times, as we entered various districts where Christian work had been begun. For instance, there was the Atsi Kachin tribe who have had no missionary since their pioneer, Mr. Francis Fitzwilliam, died in 1939. But at news of our approach the Christians built a flower arch-of-welcome and stood behind it with their hands outstretched pleadingly toward us while they sang the song of welcome. To remember that they had had no missionary for eight years, and that we could only stay a day or so, stirred our souls to the point of tears.[183]

Some of those they visited had fallen into sin, but the small team's ministry was effective, and with repentance these believers were restored to active fellowship with their churches.

---

182 China Inland Mission, *Field Bulletin*, 11.

183 John Kuhn, *We Found One Hundred Tribes* (Philadelphia: China Inland Mission, [1947?]), 6.

We engaged in Bible conferences at many points over the hills, ministering to thousands of souls. There were times of refreshing; God honored His Word and visited His flock with new life and power. Sins, failures and pitfalls were humbly acknowledged; new vision was given, fresh dedication was covenanted before the Lord. In a word, we had revival down there in that remote corner of Yunnan. Those were precious days! God used His Word by conviction, and people came out clear and clean for Christ. The Kachin, the Lisu, the Chinese—God blessed them.[184]

It was when the revival was fresh that the call to look farther afield was given.

At services such as this we introduced to them the present tribal survey. "You already enjoy salvation, but what of the tribes who have never heard the gospel?" we asked them. "Where do they live? What language do they speak? What part shall the Lisu church have in the future evangelistic work of sister tribes?"

These and kindred inquiries were brought forward and these loveable Lisu Christians were kindled. They began to pray, to consider and to sense the new responsibility. *In the coming forward march the church will move hand-in-hand with the missionary, sharing every phase of evangelizing new tribes and establishing churches in the unreached areas, and only thus can we hope to accomplish our goal—the gospel available to every tribe in this generation.* Having sown these seed thoughts, we had to leave them and push on.[185]

This was what the "new emphasis" of Bishop Houghton was all about. The duty to reach the unevangelized tribes belonged to the church that already existed in the mountains and valleys of Yunnan. The church was to share every phase of the process of making the gospel available to every tribe. The fact that John conducted the survey with four Lisu believers as his co-workers was a sign of what was envisioned for the future.

The result of the four-month and three-week journey was that one hundred distinct ethnic groups had been identified. "One hundred tribes in Yunnan! And two-thirds of these have never had a gospel witness. Among the one-third who have, four tribes have been fairly well evangelized, having witnessed mass movements toward Christianity break out in their midst. These are the Miao, Nosu, Lisu, and Lahu tribes."[186] Other groups like the Shan in Yunnan were virtually unreached. (John Kuhn and his team led one Shan to faith, but as this man called himself

---

184 John Kuhn, *We Found One Hundred Tribes* (Philadelphia: China Inland Mission, [1947?]), 6.

185 Ibid., 7–8.

186 Ibid., 9.

a Kang, which is normally the Shan word for Kachin, perhaps this man might have been a Kachin who had grown up in a Shan community, which was not at all uncommon.) The task was great, but the successes among some of the tribes in the past were a pledge of victories among the remaining groups in the future.

It was obvious that John Kuhn during this long journey had plenty of opportunity to think about the implications of the work. The need to find appropriate scripts for translating Scriptures and providing literature in the local languages was one concern. The simple rule of thumb for determining who needed their own written language was whether or not Chinese was spoken in the home.

> The opinion of the writer is that, where Chinese is understood in the home, we should by all means evangelize in that language; but where Chinese is understood by only a few educated men of the tribe, which applies to most in our generation, then the most potent weapon in evangelization (with the working of the Holy Spirit, of course) is to bring the message to them in their own mother tongue.[187]

From here John Kuhn went on to give examples of why close observation of how a member of a tribe speaks and acts in a variety of contexts is necessary before a judgment can be made on what language is the best one for evangelism. There was a need for urgency but not for haste. For example the Min-chia who lived near Tali could speak Chinese, but only used Min-chia in their homes. Some Shan would claim to be Chinese, but in other places he saw it was unlikely that they would be sinicized for many years to come. On the other end of the spectrum were places where the Chinese became assimilated to the tribes.

> Now let us go to the remote mountain tribes, especially those along the Salween gorge of the far west. Here high rugged mountains and difficult passes have cut the tribespeople off from modern communications, and Chinese influence is not very strong. In fact, in some areas Chinese penetration means that after a generation or two the Chinese will themselves become tribal, rather than the tribes become Chinese. It is not extraordinary to come across people whose ancestors came from Nanking, but who today have lost the Chinese tongue and tell you all this in the tribal tongue! To evangelize such tribes, a knowledge of their own tongue is indispensable.[188]

He concluded his views on methodology with the following summary:
1. By all means employ the Chinese language where feasible.

---

187 Ibid., 14.
188 Ibid., 16–17.

2. Where tribes are bi-lingual, encourage the use of the tribal tongue for worship, even where there is no written language.
3. Stick to the principle of taking the gospel message to each tribe in the language used in their homes. You will then have a good chance of winning the entire family.
4. Make use of the most humble home, if necessary, for initiating Christian testimony. Much of the spadework of existing tribal churches was done in the home.
5. Missionary and tribal Christian workers should together carry out this work.[189]

As for the CIM in this work, Mr. Kuhn suggested that twenty-five to fifty workers would suffice, especially if some were already experienced workers who could make inroads while new recruits got their basic training. Finally he made this plea.

> The tribal door is open as never before. There are very few from the Chinese churches who are called to this work, therefore our responsibility is the greater. The tribes welcome us. They absolutely need our association, cooperation, inspiration and fellowship. The native church aroused to the new sense of responsibility toward sister tribes, together with the hand-in-hand, heart-to-heart fellowship of the foreign missionary group, is the answer to the present startling need. Let us bear our share in facing the challenge of the Unfinished Task in Yunnan, taking heed that an all-out effort is made for the spread of the gospel of Christ among all the remaining unreached tribes throughout Yunnan in this our own generation.[190]

The call was heeded and some senior and new workers did volunteer for the tribes. By the end of the decade there were workers making a beginning among the Shan, the Black Miao, and the Nosu.

The "hand-in-hand and heart-to-heart with the native church" concept was easier said than done. In A. J. Broomhall's account of his own work among the Nosu, it is evident that he made efforts to relate well with Chinese believers from the East as well as local believers, but the working relations did not always prove satisfactory. The work among the Lisu had an advantage in that those who would work hand in hand with the CIM missionaries had been their own converts and had practiced their methods already. In the case of the Nosu work, one native agency was operating near the area where Dr. Broomhall was heading. Bishop Houghton warned him to exercise caution in his relations with

---

189 Ibid., 17.
190 Ibid., 20.

this group "since its published aims are very inadequate and its methods very different from our own."¹⁹¹

In the area of medical work, there were Chinese Christian doctors who were invited to work with CIM doctors in several hospitals. Here it became evident that working hand in hand would not be easy. In a period of hyperinflation, when salaries were paid in sacks of rice because Chinese currency was almost worthless, there were many opportunities for faith to be tested. In some cases Chinese co-workers felt that they were not being treated as equals when it came to pooling resources. Many cultural misunderstandings emerged, partly because of the fact that the CIM had a culture all its own. Chinese who came to work alongside of foreign doctors as co-laborers (rather than as employees) never shared in the CIM inculturation process, either as candidates or as language students. The experience was painful for all parties involved and showed that cooperation would not yield its rich potential harvest without a long, conscious effort.¹⁹²

Another issue emerged at the same time, namely that of comity agreements. When the CIM had first entered Southwest China, they were all alone as far as Protestant missionary societies were concerned. After choosing for themselves where to focus their attention, they chose where to invite other groups to work. In many cases these other groups, at least originally, came out as associate missions of the CIM. In the 1920s there was one case of a Pentecostal group claiming a right to an area pioneered by J. O. Fraser because another CIM missionary spoke too fast and let them do some work in the main city of the district. On the other hand, the American Baptists and CIM along the Yunnan-Burma border needed to deal with the fact that they were both very overextended and needed to transfer certain districts to each other so that the believers would at least get occasional visits from a missionary or evangelist.

In the late 1940s, with this new emphasis on the tribes, it was necessary to reconsider where CIM wished to work. Other groups had filled in most of the map, at least theoretically, and needed to be consulted before the CIM sent their own workers in to begin a new work. There

---

191   Frank Houghton, "Conversation with Dr. A. J. Broomhall," February 3, 1944. OMF International Headquarters Archives, Singapore: AR5.1.4 Box 1.15; Correspondence, etc.; Yunnan, China, 1944–51.

192   Dr. Paul Adolph "Letter to Rev. C. J. Glittenberg January 21, 1949." OMF International Headquarters Archives, Singapore: AR5.1.4, Box 1.15; Correspondence, etc.; Yunnan, China, 1944–51. This letter is one of several which show how susceptible all parties were to miscommunication, misunderstanding, and mistrust during the first tentative efforts to draw Chinese nationals into the CIM.

was still considerable ground to cover and few workers to cover it, so the negotiations were fairly amicable. When Dr. Broomhall prepared to reach the Nosu, it was necessary to come to an agreement on territorial divisions with the Methodists and the newly formed Conservative Baptists from the U.S., but the areas that were discussed were so vast that there was a large no man's land in between that each group knew they were not yet ready to fill.

The fact was the doors would soon be closed to new workers, and even those who were on the field would need to depart. In 1949 the Communists seized power over all of mainland China. Their policy toward the missionaries showed that they were as wise as serpents and equally as innocent. There are numerous reports of the experiences of those missionaries who departed from China after "liberation," as it was known when the Communists established their rule in all parts of the country. The experience of Ernie and Mertie Heimbach, the last CIM missionaries to the Black Miao, provides a sample of many varied experiences that confirmed a common policy that the Communists carried out in their efforts to bring disgrace to the missionaries and their message while at the same time effecting their expulsion from the country at the hands of the Christians themselves.

> We had seen the new government go through three stages in their taking control of the country. At first they said, "Carry on as usual. We are not restricting anyone." The communist [sic] soldiers were very polite and well disciplined. When they came to borrow our church benches they returned them promptly. The second stage was restrictions and indoctrination. Everyone was required to attend indoctrination classes . . . People were encouraged to report on neighbors who offended them. The third stage was the beginning of imprisonments and executions. These three stages were called, "Dee Tow, Dien Tow, Da Tow," meaning "Nod the head, shake the head, and chop the head." We had entered the third stage. We couldn't travel. When one of our missionaries was very ill and in a coma, our mission nurse was not allowed to go and tend her. She could only advise by phone. If we talked to any of the Christians, he would be called by the police and asked, "What did you talk about?" Executions were frequent outside the city wall. The situation was dangerous. So early in 1951 our mission asked each missionary to apply for permission to leave the country.[193]

The Communists had their agenda, which does not concern us here except insofar as it affected how the CIM was forced to revise its mode of operations during the missionaries' final years in China. In decades

---

193 Mertis Byram Heimbach, "Byram Heritage" (unpublished book), 83–84.

past, individual missionaries had experienced opposition and were unable to work in certain provinces. But never before had a single, somewhat uniform policy been imposed on the entire country. Not only were missionaries increasingly restricted in what they could do and where they could go, but they also saw their teaching directly attacked by Communist cadres who had been trained to refute Christian teaching, mock Christian beliefs and practices, and to threaten those who persisted in following the foreign religion. While some missionaries had relatively more freedom than others and some were treated more respectfully than others, it gradually became evident that Christians throughout the country were being pressured to break off ties with the missionaries and to encourage their departure.

It appears in hindsight that it would have been better for the missionaries to have departed sooner. By mid-1950 there was little in terms of ministry that most of them were allowed to do. The presence and interaction with national believers became a ground for accusations to be made against the believers for associating with foreign imperialists. There are several reasons why the call for departure was delayed. One was that Bishop Houghton was worn down from the excessive pressures of the job and had required a long period of house rest in Australia. He was thus greatly limited in his understanding of the situation in China. His responsibilities had been taken up by the headquarters staff in Shanghai. These were capable and experienced men, but their experience from the past was perhaps a hindrance to interpreting the present trials. Communists are nothing if they are not gifted in the art of dissimulation. In Wuting, Yunnan, one particularly honest Communist boasted of this fact. W. T. Simpkin recorded the following disclosure:

> A Communist lecturer was speaking at an open air meeting on market day at Wuting. He said, "America's weakness is they tell the truth, so you know where they are and all about them. We never tell the truth so no one knows anything about us. That is our strong point (or our strength)."[194]

Travel was greatly restricted. Letters were censored. Missionaries in distant locations often did not know what was happening outside their own local station. They did know that they must be cautious about what they wrote to the Shanghai staff. So the staff could only get part of the picture. These members of the staff remembered the great evacuation in 1927, had lived with warlords, and had recently passed through the

---

194 W. T. Simpkin, "'Exodus' report 1951," 5. OMF International Headquarters Archives, Singapore: AR5.1.4, Box 1.15; Correspondence, etc.; Yunnan, China, 1944–51.

war with the Japanese and the final years of the Civil War between the Nationalists and the Communists. They saw that the situation was difficult, but actual danger to the missionaries in the field appeared no greater than it had on several occasions in the past. The CIM was called to China and therefore there was a commitment to stay put unless they were forced to leave. Bishop Houghton himself seems to have had a Victorian-era view of honor which could not easily accept a "strategic redeployment" of the Mission as being in keeping with the victory of the Cross. Finally there was the simple question of where the missionaries could go if they left China. It was only when it became apparent that there was no longer any place on mainland China where the CIM could operate, or even be present without causing grave difficulties for the local believers, that the call to depart was issued.

For the headquarters staff, even in the first half of 1950, it was not so clear that time was running out. Even when in Kunming a missionary was shot dead at his office desk in April, the Mission was still discussing the pay of district evangelists in Northwest China and the purchase of a jeep for Kweiyang in Kweichow. Only during the second half of 1950 did it become increasingly apparent that the work of missionaries was being restricted to the point that their presence in the country could no longer be of any benefit to the church. Finally the minute of the headquarters staff meeting of Monday, December 10, 1950, recorded the acceptance of the new situation.

> During several recent sessions of the Headquarters Staff, prayerful consideration has been given to the serious complications that are developing in many churches, due to the presence of missionaries. In some cases church leaders have advised the missionaries to leave, because they are causing embarrassment to the churches vis-a-vis their relationships with the authorities. This turn of events has come about largely through the circularization of the manifesto which has been issued by a group of national church leaders, setting forth to free themselves from associations with foreign missionaries. The fact has been mentioned more than once that Christians are called upon to suffer, not only because of their faith but because of the presence of foreign missionaries in their midst.
>
> The activities of many in the Mission fellowship are becoming increasingly restricted, and the basic purpose of continuing in "humble cooperation with the churches" is generally no longer possible of realization. Attempts have been made in the past to transfer workers from one district to another, but recent experience has shown that such applications now meet with categorical refusal.[195]

---

195 China Inland Mission, "Minutes of a Meeting of the Headquarters Staff Held in

So for those who remained in China a final evacuation was announced. Many workers had already left the country on their own as they found it impossible to remain at their stations or move to other districts. Those who had been on furlough could not return to their stations. Most workers departed through Hong Kong, and the trials that they faced were clearly designed by the Communists to break their spirits. To some degree they succeeded, but it is one of the evidences of the truth of the gospel that missionaries who had such difficulties during their final months in China, in many cases became the vanguard of new pioneering efforts in other parts of Southeast Asia.

Those last months in China were of value in a variety of ways. First of all, the Chinese believers could see the missionaries were willing to be threatened, disgraced, and impoverished for the sake of the gospel. Secondly, they were able though, to a continually decreasing degree as time went on, to privately teach those who would be the leaders of the church in the years to come. Perhaps most importantly, they were able to observe how the Communists would treat the Christians and see which Christians showed the qualities of spiritual vitality in time of greatest trial. Those last glimpses would help the church in the West to pray with confidence during the next several decades of silence, that the believers who were left behind would stand for Christ, even to death if necessary.

When the missionaries did depart, they were required to write a debriefing report, and it was these reports which show clearly both the methods of the Communists and the quality of the churches that were called to face them. A few quotes from these "exodus" reports help to illustrate the state of the church in Kweichow and Yunnan at the time of their departure.

W. A. Allen of Mitu, Yunnan, wrote:

> As foreign missionaries we have felt during the past few years that our greatest contribution to the work has been one of "teaching the teachers."— "The same commit thou to faithful men who will be able to teach others also." To this end from 1945 until the beginning of 1951 there has been a programme of monthly conferences (sometimes bi-monthly) when systematic teaching could be given and when the needs of the church were discussed. Twice a year there have been Bible schools for two weeks, to which we have often had an attendance of over 100 persons. Naturally these longer periods of study have proved the greatest benefit to those who gathered, but some said until they attended either one of the monthly conferences or one

---

Shanghai," December 11, 1950, 3. Microfilm from Billy Graham Archives, Wheaton, IL.

of the Bible Schools, that their faith in Christ was not stable. It was not until they had come under the prolonged study of the Scriptures that each knew what salvation and sanctification really meant.[196]

Other reports confirmed the view that the Christians who stood strong were the ones who had received concentrated Bible teaching. In this regard the new emphasis that Bishop Houghton had placed on the need for missionaries to work with existing churches to strengthen them for outreach was validated. Even though he did not believe at that time (the early 1940s) that the day of the missionary was soon to end, the course he chose for the Mission was in fact the right one for that time.

The report of Mr. Simpkin of Wuting and neighboring Miao, Lisu, and Nosu areas shows another aspect of the fruit of the Mission's efforts.

6. The response to the Gospel was greater during the first year after liberation than before in quite a few districts. In 1949 (before liberation) 319 Miao were baptized into the Church. In 1950 (after liberation) the number was 332. Perhaps the most outstanding case was in a district near Taku, controlled by a Nosu, T'u Si. Some thirty years ago, some of his tenants wished to become Christians, but he forbade them joining the Church. In 1950 he was liquidated by the Communists as a rich landlord. At once many of these tenants renewed their request for Christian teaching. Some Nosu and Lisu evangelists went to them with the Gospel and in a few months 150 families had burned their idols. This was only the beginning however, and they were not grounded in the truth. The latest news we heard was that many of them had already grown cold or gone back again to their old lives ...

8. Our presence was extremely welcome to the Miao right up until the time came for us to leave (February 1951) ... I had asked the Miao leaders on several occasions to be quite frank in telling me whether our presence was a help or an embarrassment, and they invariably showed extreme reluctance to let us go. However, in January 1951, an Enquiry Commission was sent from Mao in Peking to enquire into tribal affairs. This Commission told the Miao that they must break off all relations with the foreigners at once. The Sapushan Church leaders immediately informed all the outstations and invited all the Miao leaders in to give us a farewell. Somewhere about 80 elders, evangelists and teachers came. They gave us a farewell feast. Then at the evening service I was asked to give them a farewell talk. Then one representative from each group (one teacher, one evangelist, one deacon, one elder, etc.) stood up and spoke on behalf of the others. In most cases they thanked the missionaries for coming and bringing the Gospel to them, and for teaching, preaching and healing the sick in their midst. One specially outspoken said, "No matter what 'they' say, we will always remember where

---

196 China Inland Mission, "'Exodus' report 1951," 11.

we were lifted from. I am a teacher, and I shall always remember there would never have been anyone to teach if the Missionaries had not come." ('They' of course, referred to the Communists.) After the close of the service the leaders said they wanted to say another final farewell in private, so we repaired to the schoolroom. Then it was in private that they told us they had been ordered to break off relations with us. After saying how loth [loath] they were to let us go, they asked if I had any further words of counsel. One very earnest Christian caused a laugh by saying he would be glad to see us go—and then added how concerned he was for our safety, and would not feel relieved until we were safely home with our children. The following Sunday about 600 ordinary Christians came to the Service to say Goodbye. I gave a farewell message. I gave two or three more "farewell" messages before we actually left, as our pass to Kunming was delayed. After we left, the break was almost complete. One of them wrote a letter saying that all their mail was being censored, and requesting me not to write as it would get them into trouble. On three occasions groups of Miao came to see me at Kunming. Then such visits stopped, but a note came saying they were being watched too closely and could not come, so would I forgive them and make every allowance for them.[197]

The Communists could force the Miao to ask the missionaries to depart, but they could not make the Miao want them to depart.

There was a group of Miao Christians who had long before organized an Independent Miao movement and had caused much difficulty for the CIM missionaries and the Miao believers who were loyal to them. Just how Christian this group actually was is not our concern at the present, but they did render a single service to the missionaries as the time of their departure drew near by showing just what sort of reputation they had obtained in the wider community.

A young Miao teacher named Chang had been under conviction of sin for some time. One Sunday in September 1950 while I was preaching, his experience reached a climax. That night he came to me for prayer and advice, and very definitely accepted the Lord. From then on he was very eager to witness for the Lord. Then he was appointed to be one of the village representatives at the Communist meetings. At one meeting an Independent Miao named Wang who had long been the enemy of the Sapushan Church, stood up and made a lot of wild accusations against the Church, the Mission, and the Missionaries. The young teacher, Chang, asked the Communist Chairman if it were right to allow such charges which could not be substantiated. Then a Moslem representative from a nearby village stood up and said that the Mission and Church at Sapushan

---

197 Ibid., 2–3.

had a record of nearly fifty years of doing good to the people, whereupon the Chairman strongly rebuked Wang for making untrue charges. Teacher Chang told me all about it a few days later.[198]

Ernie Heimbach and his wife Mertis were the last CIM workers to have the opportunity to visit the Black Miao before the withdrawal. His report clearly highlights the strengths and weaknesses of the churches which the CIM left behind in Kweichow Province.

> While in Tuyün we had the opportunity in Sept. 1949 to make a two week survey of the Black Miao field visiting almost every center where Christians, + professing Christians remained after the long absence of resident missionaries (since 1936 or thereabouts). Naturally after such a long period without help the work as a whole was in a terribly decadent state with Christians backslidden, chapels unused, children growing up uninstructed, Bibles and hymn books unused etc. Nevertheless the encouraging thing was that we did find a nucleus of true believers, a faithful remnant still carrying on worship and witness and with whom we could have the deepest of soul fellowship. Due to a Mission Conference and other matters it was not possible for us to move into tribes land immediately and just as we were ready to do so the "liberation" overtook us in Tuyün in Nov. 1949.[199]

The Heimbachs then went to Panghai in December 1949 and began studying Black Miao while meeting on a daily basis with local believers. Even though they avoided market evangelism in order not to attract undue attention, their presence was noted, and in February they were forced to leave. After meeting with robbers they went first to Tuyün and then on to Kweiyang in June 1950, where they remained until October 1951 and were thus able to provide a valuable report on the situation in Kweichow in the early days of Communist rule.

> After arrival in Kweiyang I was asked to help in the speaking at some young peoples meetings and then in October when the STBS [Short Term Bible School] opened I was invited to teach the course in the four gospels. At that time the work in Kweiyang was going ahead with real blessing, church meetings were crowded, souls being saved, open air meetings were held and a city wide evangelistic campaign in progress. The church and ourselves were pretty much left alone. This continued until December when about the middle of the month evidence was plain that attention was being increasingly focused on the church. Eric Norgate and myself felt best voluntarily to cease teaching at the STBS which we did. The church leaders continued for a time

---

198 Ibid., 1.

199 Ernie Heimbach, "'Exodus' report 1951," *S.S. Ile De France*, Mid-Atlantic, December 18, 1951, 1. OMF International Headquarters Archives, Singapore: AR5.1.4, Box 1.8; Correspondence, etc.; Guizhou, China, 1947–48.

to come to the CIM compound for the accustomed weekly prayer meeting but soon that dwindled out and then we all voluntarily ceased attending Chinese church services. All was done voluntarily for the best interests of all concerned. Little was said about the change but everyone understood it. The church people we really believe held us in the same place in their hearts as we did them but they seldom came to see us and we were glad in a way that it was so. Such in general was the situation until we left. Those ten months from Jan. 1951 to Oct. 1951 we had no active connection with the local Chinese Church in Kweiyang which had been really independent for some years previously.[200]

After giving other details about the situation which prevailed in Kweiyang and surrounding locations during that period, he wrote:

> The Kweiyang church and other city churches are still holding services as far as we know. We know of at least one country tribal station where services are forbidden and presumably this may also be the case in other small places, especially during the period of land reform. *Most* of the difficulties come from without but the *most serious* came from within! Strife, division, accusation etc.[201]

The Mission had succeeded in enabling many if not most of the larger churches to become independent, but obviously had not succeeded in perfecting all the saints in these congregations. However, there is no evidence to suggest that Paul had been able to plant any perfect churches in the "golden era" of the apostles either. In fact, the troubles that the churches faced at the hands of the Communists, when the missionaries were no longer in a position to help as mediators, may well have been the very tool that God saw fit to use to continue the perfecting process far beyond what any missionary might accomplish on his own.

---

200 Ibid., 2.
201 Ibid., 3.

Chapter 6
In Summary

The missionary work of the CIM in mainland China effectively ended in 1951. While a few members of the Mission were not allowed by the Communist authorities to leave until 1952, their actual missionary functions had been curtailed long before their departure. The CIM went through a name change and became the Overseas Missionary Fellowship of the China Inland Mission. In years to come many regretted the change of name and the attendant loss of name recognition that resulted from the change. But the subject had been long and thoroughly considered by the directors of the Mission. While alternative names had been considered which maintained the same initials, it was felt that a completely new name was needed for the sake of the Chinese Christians. The Chinese propaganda machine had made strenuous efforts to connect the work of the CIM with foreign imperialism. Having left mainland China and begun anew in Japan (China's old enemy) and Taiwan (Communist China's new enemy), it would not be advisable to provide more propaganda fodder for the Communist regime by using the old name. Whether the threat was more real or imagined is hardly relevant now. The point was that the Mission did not wish to create any unnecessary difficulties for the Chinese church, and hence the new label.

The newly reorganized Overseas Missionary Fellowship of the China Inland Mission did not lose its concern for the work in China. In the development of a prayer ministry for China, encouraging radio broadcasts into China, and the production of evangelistic and teaching materials in Chinese, the Mission showed its commitment to the work that it had begun over eighty years before. But compared to what had been done before, the OMF was a new Mission with a new mission. For this reason we have come to a good place to summarize how the CIM's ministry to the peoples of Southwest China developed and expanded, what manner of church they left behind when they departed, and what lessons they took with them when they entered into the new fields.

The Expansion of the Work

The CIM first sought to enter Yunnan through Burma. In 1875 the first workers reached Bhamo in Upper Burma with the wholehearted support and assistance of the American Baptist missionaries who had long worked in Burma. Cooperation with the Baptists along the border was to continue for the next seventy-five years. The first obstacle to entering Yunnan from Upper Burma was neither the Chinese nor the Burmese government but rather the British government, which had its own designs in the area and did not wish to have the missionaries somehow complicate their plans. It was not until 1881 that the border was fully opened. By that time CIM missionaries had already learned to make the several-months-long journey up the Yangtze River and then overland to Kweiyang and Yunnan-fu (Kunming). The first missionaries gave their attention to establishing Chinese congregations in the major cities of both provinces. Their knowledge of the surrounding tribes was extremely limited during the first decade in the region, and it was not until the 1890s that serious efforts to reach the tribes actually began. The Chinese work itself developed very slowly. Whether the Chinese in the West were just harder to reach than those in the East, or whether the Chinese helpers from the East were not highly effective in the West for cultural reasons is open for debate. What is clear is that no real responsiveness on the part of the Chinese was evident in Yunnan and Kweichow until the 1930s, and only in the 1940s was indigenous church growth and expansion evident.

Tribal work for all intents and purposes began with the Miao in the late 1890s, and they began to respond in large numbers within a few years. By 1907 a movement was in progress, which was in many ways biblical and indigenous, with Miao believers sharing their faith in distant villages, and communities becoming transformed by the impact of the gospel message. The movements among the Miao led to openings among the Lisu in eastern Yunnan as well as the Nosu. These initial bridgeheads led to smaller movements among these two groups over the next few decades. The movement among the Miao tapered off by about 1920, in part due to the fact that two key missionaries, J. R. Adam and Samuel Pollard, both died in 1915. While several veteran missionaries remained to carry on, they were overstretched to the extreme. Banditry, famines, and open warfare in the areas where the Miao predominated during the next several decades meant that the development of strong Miao leadership was greatly hindered.

Meanwhile, the work among the Lisu in western Yunnan and Upper Burma was commenced in the 1910s. Within a few years thousands had responded. J. O. Fraser was blessed with seven years of uninterrupted work among the Lisu with no competing missionary groups or missionary methods to deal with. Then he was further blessed to have the Cookes and Kuhns follow in his footsteps with long years of ministry and a commitment to following methods very similar to his own. While banditry and warfare were not absent from western Yunnan, they did not interfere with the work to the degree that they did in Kweichow, where the bulk of the Miao work was occurring. For these reasons it is very difficult to compare the methods and results of the work among these two groups.

From the 1930s onward the primary role of the missionaries among the tribes was in the areas of grassroots Bible teaching through Short Term (or "Rainy Season") Bible Schools, seeking the spiritual uplift of the tribal churches through personal discipleship and preaching on the spiritual life, and not least, by stirring the Christians in the Western world to pray constantly for the tribes and especially the Lisu.

While there were efforts on the part of the Mission to give more attention to the tribes, both with the recruitment of the two hundred in the early 1930s and with the call to reach the one hundred tribes in Yunnan in the late 1940s, these thrusts did not lead to major new movements among unreached tribes. Some workers were absorbed into the Lisu and Miao work. Without their help these movements might have been stifled. Daniel Smith was instrumental in new advances among the Nosu who lived under Chinese rule, while Dr. A. J. Broomhall made a good beginning among the "Independent" Nosu in Szechwan Province. A few other tribes had workers assigned to them, but the results did not start to compare with the breakthroughs previously seen among the Lisu, Miao, and Lahu in earlier decades. During this time the large number of CIM workers among the Chinese population in Southwest China were seeing limited response to their message.

Methodologically, the CIM went through several stages in their work in Southwest China. The first was to focus on population centers and to work alongside Chinese evangelists and helpers. In the 1890s workers were first assigned specifically to do tribal work, generally after having been thoroughly trained in Chinese ministry. Sinicized tribal workers often assisted them in getting entrance into the tribal communities.

With the coming of Fraser, there was a greater emphasis on the Chinese or tribal believers being co-laborers who would be supported, often on a short-term basis, by fellow believers rather than by the Mission itself. There was much emphasis in the widely circulated prayer letters regarding individual tribal believers as subjects for continual prayer by prayer partners in the West. In this sense the connections between the national workers and the foreign supporters of the Mission might actually be said to have become more intimate than in the cases where the primary link was financial support. During the last days, as the Communist government began to apply their control over Southwest China, their direct impact on the missionaries' ministry was not generally significant at the first stages. The missionaries had already chosen the model of being in the background as they sought to train leaders. However, in those places where the missionaries were necessarily the pioneers and there was not a church to work with, their work was curtailed immediately. By 1951, with the Chinese and Americans at war in Korea, and the Chinese Christian Council issuing its Christian Manifesto calling for a Patriotic Church free from all foreign control, it became evident that the Communist agenda left no room for even a limited missionary presence in China. So after eighty-five years in China and seventy-five years in the southwest provinces, the remaining missionaries could do nothing more than pack a few bags and depart, in many cases forever.

The Conclusion of the Whole Matter

Now we come to the conclusion. This may be divided into two parts: (1) What vast horizons are still available for further research, and (2) What lessons we have learned that can be applied to our work in the twenty-first century.

New horizons for research

Having laid out a framework for understanding what the CIM was attempting to accomplish at various stages of its work in China, it will now be most helpful to produce local histories for various mission stations and various tribal ministries. It is important that both are done simultaneously as the relationship between tribal and Chinese work needs to be explored in greater depth. There is also the sad reality that work among some of the less responsive minority groups, such as the Lakka and the Min-chia, will be overlooked unless it is studied in the context of the stations from whence the work originated.

Another major area for investigation is how the work of the OMF among the tribes and Shan in North Thailand grew out of the work of the CIM in China. The dissertation by Dr. David Huntley on "The Withdrawal of the CIM from China; and the Redeployment as OMF to New Fields in East Asia" will prove valuable to any who wish to investigate this topic in greater detail.

The other great need is for multiple histories of the various ethnic churches that emerged in the Upper Mekong Region. At this point the greatest need is for skilled researchers to interview the older generation of Christian leaders and carefully store the data digitally and in hard copy form in suitable libraries worldwide. Interviews are best carried out with the living. Histories are best written about the dead. (It is hard to write objectively about a subject when that subject has his own ideas about how he would like to be remembered.) Still, without the interviews and the careful storage of the transcripts, the "histories," when they do get written, will be nothing more than myths and legends. Westerners are as good at creating myths and legends as anyone. So where it is still possible to obtain interviews with older Christians about the earlier days of the church among the tribes, the effort needs to be made.

Lessons learned

All who have read this far will have long ago noticed that much of this tale does not take place in Southwest China, nor is it directly concerned with mission efforts among tribal people. Missionary work does not take place in a vacuum. Without undervaluing the importance of the individual, it is necessary to recognize that the parameters of what he or she could potentially accomplish is determined, under providence, by forces utterly beyond the control of that individual. It should be obvious that the elementary question of whether or not a white foreigner could even travel to and live in Yunnan or Kweichow was determined in such places as London, Mandalay, and Peking. With the exception of the visit of John Stevenson and Henry Soltau to the court of the king of Burma in 1875 in order to seek permission to establish a base in Bhamo, all the key national or international decisions on which all ministry in the region hinged were determined primarily by people who had little or no knowledge of the CIM and no particular positive interest in the missionary movement in general.

Even in the realm of the worldwide Christian community, the missionaries in the Upper Mekong Region were very much at the receiving end of theological, ecclesiastical, and missiological controversies that generally began in the Western world and stirred up the older churches in Eastern China before ever being felt in the southwestern provinces.

These human phenomena, no less than the mountainous terrain of Southwest China, determined to a large extent the nature and shape of the missionary effort in the region. The missionaries were at the mercy of forces which they had no influence over. That this did not lead to a sense of fatalism or despair can only be ascribed to their faith. As Bishop Houghton worded it in the middle of World War II, "Economic difficulties in free China, restrictions, privations, possible danger in the occupied zone—all may be attributable to the power of the Enemy and yet play a predetermined part in the accomplishment of the FATHER'S plan."[202]

There was one area where individual missionaries might potentially have had more opportunity to maintain control of some of their affairs. This was in the area of mission policy. It has been seen that at various times when the directors in Shanghai sought to promote innovations, such as decreasing dependence on Mission-supported national workers, some missionaries still found various ways to work around those directives which they received. With a large mission force spread out across such a great expanse of territory, the overall impression given is that the directors could and did make policies which they thought would help promote the spread of the gospel in China, but their power to turn their directives into practice on the field was always slow, and often limited at best. The men and women who joined the CIM did so because they shared the objectives of the Mission which had been implanted in it by its founder. The members agreed to work together under the leadership of the Mission directors. Those directors, for the most part, recognized the limits of their authority.

While some freedom of operation might have been sacrificed by those who worked under the direction of a mission agency, the obvious gain was that continuity was maintained over the decades. Missionaries like Adam, Pollard, Fraser, and the Cookes and Kuhns made noteworthy contributions to the spread of the gospel among certain segments of their people groups, but no individual or couple ever did or ever could claim that they laid the foundation and their native converts were able to complete the edifice. Foreign missions was the work of decades and

---

202 China Inland Mission, *According to Plan: "I Will Build My Church"* (London: China Inland Mission, 1944), 14.

of several generations of missionaries in those places and among those people groups where there was an extraordinary response. Adam, Pollard, and Fraser all were struck down by diseases while they were still heartily engaged in their respective works. Those of the later generation were forced to leave the country following "liberation" with the knowledge that the majority of the work among the majority of the tribes was scarcely begun, if begun at all.

One cannot prove a missiological axiom through historical research in the way one might prove a geometric theorem using the rules of logic. There are simply too many variables and too many facts that we are ignorant of. That being admitted, all the evidence does seem to reinforce the contention of Robert Morrison in the early years of the Protestant missionary movement. For the benefit of those who do not as a rule read prefaces, I will repeat it here:

> It is true, that, since health is uncertain, and life is short, the efforts of an individual being soon intermitted, produce but little effect, and therefore it becomes desirable in our plans of usefulness to unite many persons who shall assist each other, and gradually attach more friends to succeed them, when they shall be required, by the great Sovereign of the universe, to remove to other worlds.[203]

One personal motivation for doing the research for this book was to determine whether there is historical evidence to support a cyclical view of the history of missions or a progressive one. It would be possible by carefully choosing which facts to present to show that the CIM as a corporate body learned over time from its successes and failures in the past so that it was a more effective mission in the 1940s than it had been in the 1870s. First the missionaries were the primary evangelists, working with Chinese helpers. Then they became the trainers and motivators of the native believers. Finally they were partners with the Chinese and tribal Christians in the work of evangelizing new tribes, towns, and villages, with much of the initiative coming from the local believers themselves. This certainly is progress. However, the data could also be arranged to show that failures were often responded to with new methods which did not achieve much better results than the old methods. Moreover, successes among the Miao and Lisu, and to a lesser extent among Nosu and Lahu, were not reproducible to any large extent among rural or urban Chinese in the Southwest, nor were they applied effectively to Tai animists, let alone to Tai (Shan) Buddhists. With the

---

203 Morrison, *Memoirs*, 188.

Chinese populations especially, it is hard to prove that breakthroughs in the late 1930s and 1940s were as much a result of improved missionary methods as they were evidence of the great upheaval that all of China was going through in those years where all the old foundations of the society were being overthrown. It is equally possible that old methods actually did work but simply took several decades to begin to take effect. For if the Chinese in the East were showing more response to the gospel than those in the West, it must be acknowledged that the gospel had been proclaimed in the East for several decades before the first few pioneers went out to the West with the gospel.

The realist may quote the Preacher:

> The thing that has been, it is that which shall be; and that which is done is that which shall be done: and there is no new thing under the sun. Is there any thing whereof it may be said, See, this is new? it has been already of old time, which was before us. There is no remembrance of former things; neither shall there be any remembrance of things that are to come with those that shall come after. (Eccl 1:9–11 AKJV)

Or to paraphrase these verses: much of what is claimed to be new mission methodology is simply so old and long discarded as to have been forgotten.

The alternate view is found in Paul's words to the church in Ephesus:

> And he gave some, apostles; and some, prophets; and some, evangelists; and some, pastors and teachers; For the perfecting of the saints, for the work of the ministry, for the edifying of the body of Christ: Till we all come in the unity of the faith, and of the knowledge of the Son of God, to a perfect man, to the measure of the stature of the fullness of Christ. (Eph 4:11–13 AKJV)

Here we see real progress being described. It is progress in terms of the quality of Christlikeness that is evident in the church. This passage sees the church growing to perfection. This may not be totally fulfilled in the present age, but progress is to be expected nonetheless. A mission organization is not the church, but missionaries are members of the church. Individually they are expected to grow in grace and in usefulness over the years. Where they are formed into a mission, they may, and in fact ought to be, expected to transfer some of what they have learned through hard experience to the next generation. Human limitations and mortality inevitably mean that some lessons are lost in transmission. Furthermore, as situations change, new opportunities and challenges present themselves. The cooperation with church associations that Bishop Houghton promoted in the 1940s was not possible outside of Chekiang Province when Hudson Taylor first founded the Mission. On the other hand, the danger of missionaries remaining in a district long after their useful work was finished was not a temptation for the first generation of missionaries, nor an option for the last of them.

It would thus appear that the Mission leaders were cognizant of the chief obstacles to the progress of the work that they were responsible for; sooner or later they responded to the challenges in ways that enabled the work to develop and advance. Moreover, they made adjustments to methods and policies based on their own decades of experience with the Chinese and the Chinese church. In their discussions they often turned to their personal and corporate experience for insights into what needed to be done differently in the future. At times they may have misread those experiences, and possibly they misinterpreted the lessons taught from experience. Be that as it may, their intimate knowledge of China made them much better able to respond to the specific challenges which beset them than would have been possible for anyone who lacked their decades of experience in the country.

Perhaps the biggest issue that was not fully resolved until the withdrawal of the CIM from China in 1951 was with regard to establishing indigenous churches. The Lisu churches in western Yunnan were established using indigenous methods, in the sense that Lisu Christians were not paid by the Mission to preach or teach. They did, however, need missionaries to train their teachers. Missionaries also served in the role of peacemakers, both within the churches when feuds erupted and with the Chinese when persecution occurred. On various occasions the comments of the missionaries suggested that the Lisu Christians on their own did not always seek the noblest of biblical principles in dealing with those who opposed them. When the missionaries departed they were confident that the Lisu church as a whole would withstand the trials that were coming its way, but none would go so far as to say that they would not have benefited from a few more years of Rainy Season Bible Schools.

In cases of churches which had been established through more traditional methods, including the use of Mission funds for purchase of land and support of Chinese workers, there were reports of uniform progress towards self-support, locally initiated evangelistic efforts, and development of local leadership. Now that sixty years have elapsed since the last missionaries left those churches, their continued existence proves that churches which were started with nonindigenous methods, not only were able to become indigenous, but actually were able to endure and triumph over extended persecution. Here quantitative studies of statistics for the Lisu and the Miao might be beneficial. Yet, as noted previously, the state of anarchy that reigned for so long over Kweichow would make meaningful comparison of data difficult if not impossible. What does seem fairly evident is that the Lisu churches in southwest Yunnan were established using indigenous methods, and they for the most part were able to maintain old congregations, train leaders, and even establish new churches for many decades following the departure of the missionaries. So while one cannot prove from Miao church history that traditional methods do not work, a case *might* be made that they would have endured the decades of unsettled conditions much better had those indigenous methods been applied from the first.

The final conclusion of the matter

While it is possible that the Bible provides an invariable, universal methodology for successful cross-cultural missions, the Holy Spirit never revealed that method to the leaders of the CIM. Instead he led them to wrestle with the challenges of their day and to lay plans for the future without always revealing to them just what that future would be. They learned through trial and error as well as trial and success. When they were forced to leave China, long before they would have thought their work was done, they left behind the seeds of countless churches which grew and bore much fruit during the following half a century. Thus they confirmed the truth of two verses that are not often quoted in unison:

> In the morning sow your seed, and in the evening withhold not your hand: for you know not whether shall prosper, either this or that, or whether they both shall be alike good. (Eccl 11:6 AKJV)
>
> Therefore, my beloved brothers, be you steadfast, unmovable, always abounding in the work of the Lord, for as much as you know that your labor is not in vain in the Lord. (1 Cor 15:58 AKJV)

Appendix
A Re-statement of Policy[204]

By the General Director of the China Inland Mission
China Inland Mission, Shanghai, November 3, 1928
To the Friends and Supporters of the Mission in North America

Dear Friends:

Now that so many of our friends have returned to the field and there is good prospect of the remainder doing so shortly, it is felt by my colleagues, both in China and in the home countries, that some words should be addressed to you. We realize with gratitude how much, under God, we owe to your prayers, your gifts, and your fellowship with us; and we specially appreciate your continued sympathy and support during the past period of enforced separation from our work. It is fitting therefore that, without burdening you with details, we should take you into our confidence regarding our aims and plans of work at this important juncture.

Previous to the withdrawal from the field, considerable progress had been made in the establishment and building up of self-governing, self-supporting, and self-propagating churches, which has always been one of our main objectives. After much prayer and also consultation with fellow missionaries, we are convinced that a vigorous advance with a view to the full realization of this objective, must now be made. In other words, there must be a full transfer of the oversight of the churches from the missionaries to the Chinese leaders. That this will in many cases be difficult and will call for self-sacrifice on the part of both missionaries and Chinese is certain. It is, perhaps, inevitable that the continued presence of gifted and devoted missionaries in a center should tend to stunt the development of leadership among the Chinese, not withstanding the sincere desire of the former to avoid it. The Chinese may be given office; but so long as those to whom they have grown accustomed to look for

---

204   D. E. Hoste, "A Re-statement of Policy," *China's Millions*, January 1929.

counsel and guidance are at their side, the force of habit will, as a rule, assert itself. Hence the carrying out of these plans will largely depend upon the location of the missionaries; and we ask your special prayers that grace and guidance may be granted to all concerned with this problem. The severance of ties resulting from years of fellowship in Christian love and labor, is no light or easy matter; but unless there is willingness for the sacrifice on both sides, it is to be feared that our efforts to realize the objective of Chinese self-government will largely be in vain. People will not learn to exercise full responsibility and initiative by having others, in whole or in part, do these things for them. It must be made clear, however, that moving of missionaries from their former stations will not in all cases be called for. There will be need that a number, who in the past have not had much share in church affairs, give themselves to Bible teaching and devotional meetings, while avoiding participation in the oversight of the church.

An essential part of these arrangements will be the appointment of church councils and setting apart of church officers, where this has not already been done; this, too, will need the guidance and power of the Holy Spirit, for the granting of which we beg your co-operation in earnest prayer. While in a number of districts, where considerable progress has already been made in self-government and self-support, these plans will be perfected with comparative ease and quickness, in districts where the progress has been less, the difficulty and time required will tend to be proportionally greater. Similarly, the time required for gaining full financial self-support will vary; and so long as the money contributed from Western countries is thus used, we feel a responsibility to see that it is not misused. That greater liberty and independence will open the door to new dangers is evident. We are persuaded, however that the worst evil is the stunting and even paralysis of Chinese leadership by undue continuance of the missionary's oversight. The risk of unworthy men, on the withdrawal of the missionary, usurping authority in the church, cannot be ignored; this consideration may, in some instances, render necessary a gradual rather than an abrupt change; a process rather than an act.

From the foregoing it will be clear that our plans will result in a number of missionaries and also a considerable sum of money being released from past service and uses. This brings us to what is the most urgent and the most important fact of our program. We believe that God is calling us as a Mission to enter upon a widespread forward movement for the evangelization of unreached areas; thus realizing in fuller measure than ever before the original purpose and aim which pressed so heavily on the heart of our beloved Founder, and which inspired him and his companions in the earlier years of the Mission to lives of such devoted toil, self-sacrifice, and steadfast endurance of loneliness, privation, and danger. Pray for us, dear friends, that we now may be actuated by a like spirit, thus being enabled to fulfill the aspirations of our honored predecessors, and to maintain the high tradition and example we have inherited from them.

In this forward evangelism, experience has shown that the missionaries need the co-operation of like-minded Chinese colleagues, whose knowledge of their own countrymen and their ways is necessarily better than most foreigners can attain to. We expect that the number of Chinese hitherto working in settled districts, but who under the new order will no longer be needed there, will thus take an important share in the forward movement; while, no doubt, new ones will also be required. It will be clear that the prosecution of this great enterprise will include renting of houses, to be used as resting places by the missionaries between their journeys, for the systematic evangelization of the surrounding country. That the Chinese will need financial support as well as the missionaries, also traveling expenses, and a place for rest between their journeys, will be recognized. It would, therefore, be a mistake to suppose that the new plans imply that the gifts contributed for the support of Chinese workers will no longer be required. After a few years, perhaps not more than two or three, it is intended that the evangelists, both Chinese and foreign, will move on to another district leaving the converts to continue their corporate life, with an occasional visit from a missionary or Chinese worker.

With regard to hospitals and schools, we propose that advisory committees, composed of Chinese and foreigners, shall assist in their management; the ultimate control remaining with the Mission. The experience of others in recent years has shown that this is the plan best adapted to present conditions. At present it remains uncertain whether we can open our schools or not. We have decided not to do so unless the continued teaching of the Bible and its truths is permitted as part of the curriculum. Will you, dear friends, join us in special prayer that, if it be God's will, the present government regulations may be modified so as to admit of this? The object of our schools is the instruction of the children of the Christians in Christian truth, while also teaching the subjects required by the government.

History has shown that an organization like ours is exposed, as time goes on, to various dangers, such as the letting slip of sound doctrine and a gradual sinking down from the life of devotion and willingness for self-sacrifice and contempt of hardship and danger, which an intense belief in the teaching of the Bible regarding the spiritual need and claims of those without Christ, wrought in Mr. Hudson Taylor and his companions. We count upon your prayers, dear friends, that we may ever be preserved from these insidious influences, and that, at this time of renewed opportunity in inland China, we may, as a Mission, be granted grace to respond to the call of God to further advance, and also a willingness to pay in full the price required for its fulfillment.

With our united gratitude and greetings,

Believe me, yours faithfully in Christ,

D. E. Hoste

Bibliography

Beauchamp, Montague. *Days of Blessing in Inland China: Being an Account of Meetings Held in the Province of Shan-si*. London: Morgan & Scott, 1877. http://docs.google.com/View?docid=dd42sgj3_3dn2bsdb.

Broomhall, A. J. *Hudson Taylor and China's Open Century*. Vol. 3, *If I Had a Thousand Lives*. London: Hodder & Stoughton, and Overseas Missionary Fellowship, 1982.

Broomhall, Marshall. *The Jubilee Story of the China Inland Mission*. London: China Inland Mission, 1929. First published 1915.

———. *Some a Hundredfold: The Life and Work of James R. Adam among the Tribes of South-West China*. London: China Inland Mission, [1915?].

Broumton, J. F. "Work in Kwei-yang." *China's Millions*, January 1878.

China Inland Mission. "Acceptance for Training of Candidates in London." In Minutes of the [China] Council Meeting, July 8[?], 1927, 6–7. Microfilm from Billy Graham Archives, Wheaton, IL.

———. *According to Plan: "I Will Build My Church."* London: China Inland Mission, 1944.

———. "China Council 1914-09-09." Microfilm from Billy Graham Archives, Wheaton, IL.

———. "China Council 1915-04-15." Microfilm from Billy Graham Archives, Wheaton, IL.

———. *China's Millions*, December 1875.

———. *China's Millions*, October 1876.

———. *China's Millions*, July–August 1878.

———. *China's Millions*, U.S. ed., 1907.

———. "Church Organization." In Minutes of the [China] Council Meeting, November 23, 1927, 10–11. Microfilm from Billy Graham Archives, Wheaton, IL.

———. "Conversation with Dr. A. J. Broomhall," February 3, 1944. OMF International Headquarters Archives, Singapore: AR5.1.4, Box 1.15, Correspondence, etc.; Yunnan, China, 1944–51.

———. "Correspondence of Dr. Paul Adolph from 1947–1949." OMF International Headquarters Archives, Singapore: AR5.1.4, Box 1.15; Correspondence, etc.; Yunnan, China, 1944–51.

———. "Doctrinal Position of the Mission." In Minutes of the [China] Council Meeting, April 18, 1922, 2–3. Microfilm from Billy Graham Archives, Wheaton, IL.

———. "Doctrinal Position of the Mission." In Minutes of the [China] Council Meeting, November 9, 1923, 11. Microfilm from Billy Graham Archives, Wheaton, IL.

———. "'Exodus' report 1951." OMF International Headquarters Archives, Singapore: AR5.1.4, Box 1.15; Correspondence, etc.; Yunnan, China, 1944–51.

———. *Field Bulletin of the China Inland Mission* 5, no. 9 (September 1943).

———. "Good News from Burma." *China's Millions*, May 1877.

———. "A Head Lama Asks for Scriptures." *Monthly Notes*, January 1930.

———. "History of the Bhamo Branch of the China Inland Mission." *China's Millions*, May 1879.

———. "Itineration Near and Far as an Evangelizing Agency: Delivered by the Editor at Shanghai before the Missionary Conference," May 12, 1877. *China's Millions*, September 1877.

———. "Keihkow—Difficult Conditions." *Monthly Notes*, March 1930.

———. "Kweichow." *Monthly Notes*, July 1926.

———. "Kweichow." *Monthly Notes*, February 1929.

———. "Letter from Burma." *China's Millions*, July 1877.

———. "Letter from Mr. Judd." *China's Millions*, August 1877.

———. "Minutes of a Meeting of the Headquarters Staff Held in Shanghai," December 11, 1950, 3. Microfilm from Billy Graham Archives, Wheaton, IL.

———. *Minutes of China Council Session 157 to 205*, September 10, 1930, to April 9, 1945. OMF International Headquarters Archives, Singapore.

———. "Minutes of Council Meeting," January 20, 1941. In *Minutes of China Council Session 157 to 205*, 488–89.

———. "Minutes of Council Meeting," June 2, 1941. In *Minutes of China Council Session 157 to 205*, 502–3.

———. "Missionary Correspondence." *China's Millions*, September 1877.

———. *Monthly Notes*, March 1908.

———. *New Life the Dead Receive: The Story of 1935*. London: China Inland Misson, 1936.

———. "Plan of Operations of the China Inland Mission." *China's Millions*, September 1875.

———. "Private Report of the Two Hundred and Second Session of the China Council Held at Chungking," October 13–30, 1943. Microfilm from Billy Graham Archives, Wheaton, IL.

———. "Reginald Radcliffe." *China's Millions*, July–August 1878.

———. *Report of Director's Conference and Special Session of the China Council*, December 22, 1938, to January 9, 1939. Microfilm from Billy Graham Archives, Wheaton, IL.

———. "Special Minute of the China Council at the One Hundred and Ninety-Seventh Session," January 1941. In *Minutes of China Council Session 157 to 205*.

———. "Superintendentship of Yunnan and Kiangsu." In Minutes of [China] Council Meeting, November 14, 1927, 2–3. Microfilm from Billy Graham Archives, Wheaton, IL.

———. "Support of Chinese Workers." In Minutes of [China] Council Meeting, December 13, 1913, 21–22. Microfilm from Billy Graham Archives, Wheaton, IL.

———. "Support of Chinese Workers." In Minutes of [China] Council Meeting, December 9, 1915, 19. Microfilm from Billy Graham Archives, Wheaton, IL.

———. "The Work in Kin-chau: Native Preachers." *China's Millions*, November 1878.

———. "The Work of the China Inland Mission." *China's Millions*, April 1877.

———. "Yunnan." *Monthly Notes*, July 1926.

The Christian Guardian and Church of England Magazine. London: Seeleys, 1849.

Christianity in China: State and Progress of the Work of the Native Evangelists Contained in a Series of Tracts. London: Partridge & Oakey, 1850.

Clarke, Samuel R. *Among the Tribes of South-West China*. London: China Inland Mission, 1911.

Colquhoun, Archibald R. *Overland to China*. New York: Harper & Brothers, 1900.

Conference on Missions Held in Liverpool. London: Nisbet, 1860.

Cooke, Allyn, and Leila Cooke. "The Clouds of Lisu-land." *China's Millions*, August 1932.

———. Correspondence: Cooke, Allyn and Leila; 1919–1932. Microfilm from Billy Graham Archives, Wheaton, IL: Collection 215, Box 4, Folder 1.

Cooke, Leila. Handwritten note [1931?]. Microfilm from Billy Graham Archives, Wheaton, IL.

Crossman, Eileen. *Mountain Rain*, joint ed. Robesonia, PA: OMF Books, 1985.

Curtis, Lillian Johnson. *The Laos of North Siam*. Bangkok: White Lotus Books, 1998. First published 1903 by Revell.

Dean, William. *The China Mission*. New York: Sheldon, 1859.

Dowsett, Rose. "Cooperation and the Promotion of Unity: An Evangelical Perspective." Towards 2010. April 2007. http://www.towards2010.org/downloads/t2010paper08dowsett.pdf.

Dyer, Helen S. *Revival in India*. London: Morgan & Scott, 1907.

England, John C. *The Hidden History of Christianity: The Churches of the East before the Year 1500*. Hong Kong: CCA, 1998.

Evangelical Christendom: Its State and Prospects, vol. 3. London: Partridge & Oakey, and Paternoster Row, 1849.

Fairbank, John King, and Merle Goldman. "The Second Coming of the Chinese Communist Party." In *China: A New History*, 2nd enl. ed., 294–311. Cambridge, MA: Belknap Press of Harvard University Press, 2006.

Fife, Eric S. *Against the Clock: The Story of Ray Buker, Sr., Olympic Runner and Missionary Statesman*. Grand Rapids: Zondervan, 1981.

Finley, Robert. *Reformation in Foreign Missions*. Maitland, FL: Xulon Press, 2005.

Fishbourne, Edmund Gardiner. *Impressions of China, and the Present Revolution: Its Progress and Prospects*. London: Seeley, Jackson & Halliday, 1855.

Freiday, Mr. and Mrs. J. A. "Report from Shan Department, Bhamo." In *65th Annual Report*, edited by American Baptist Missionary Union. 1879.

Geraldine Guinness Taylor. *Hudson Taylor and the China Inland Mission*. Vol. 2, *The Growth of a Work of God*. London: China Inland Mission, 1955. First published 1918.

Goforth, Jonathan. *By My Spirit*. Grand Rapids: Zondervan, 1942.

Grist, W. A. *Samuel Pollard: Pioneer Missionary in China*. London: United Methodist Publishing House, [1920?].

Guinness, Geraldine. "The Spiritual Need and Claims of China." In *The Student Missionary Enterprise: Addresses and Discussions of the Second International Convention of the Student Volunteer Movement for Foreign Missions*, edited by Max Wood Moorhead, 54–61. N.p.: T. O. Metcalf, 1894.

Harverson, Stuart. *Doctor in the Orient*. London: Hodder & Stoughton, 1976.

Heimbach, Ernie. "'Exodus' report 1951," *S.S. Ile De France*, Mid-Atlantic, December 18, 1951. OMF International Headquarters Archives, Singapore: AR5.1.4, Box 1.8; Correspondence, etc.; Guizhou, China, 1947–48.

Heimbach, Mertis Byram. "Byram Heritage." Unpublished book.

Hocking, William Ernest. *Re-Thinking Missions: A Laymen's Inquiry after One Hundred Years*. New York: Harper & Brothers, 1932.

Hoste, D. E. "A Re-statement of Policy." *China's Millions*, January 1929.

Kuhn, Isobel. *Ascent to the Tribes: Pioneering in North Thailand*, rev. ed. London: Overseas Missionary Fellowship, 1968. First published 1956.

———. "Prayer Trust," February 1938. Microfilm from Billy Graham Archives, Wheaton, IL.

———. "Prayer Trust," March 1938. Microfilm from Billy Graham Archives, Wheaton, IL.

———. "Prayer Trust," August 1938. Microfilm from Billy Graham Archives, Wheaton, IL.

———. "Prayer Trust," October 1938. Microfilm from Billy Graham Archives, Wheaton, IL.

———. "Prayer Trust," February 27, 1943.

Kuhn, John. John Kuhn to Arnold Lea, February 9, 1952, 2. OMF International Headquarters Archives, Singapore: AR5.1.5, DOM: North Thailand Box 2.5, Correspondence 1952.

———. *We Found One Hundred Tribes*. Philadelphia: China Inland Mission, [1947?].

Latourette, Kenneth Scott. *A History of Christian Missions in China.* London: Society for the Propagation of Christian Knowledge, 1929.

———. *A History of the Expansion of Christianity.* Vol. 6, *The Great Century in Northern Africa and Asia.* New York: Harper & Brothers, 1944.

———. *A History of the Expansion of Christianity.* Vol. 7, *Advance through the Storm.* New York: Harper & Brothers, 1945.

Lauer, Kathrin. "A Communist Always Tells Lies." *Report: Magazine for Arts and Civil Society in Eastern- and Central Europe*, January 2007. http://web.redaktionsbuero.at/output/?e=58&page=rb_ARTIKEL&a=fee95ea1&c=Eastern%20Europe&f=e.

Lyall, Leslie T. *God Reigns in China.* London: Hodder & Stoughton, and Overseas Missionary Fellowship, 1985.

———. *A Passion for the Impossible: The Continuing Story of the China Inland Mission.* London: OMF Books, 1975. First published 1965.

Malasaem, Sawaeng. ประวัติศาสตร์ท้องถิ่น คนยองย้ายแผ่นดิน [Local history: The relocation of the Yong]. Bangkok: Thammasart University Press, 2001.

Meadows, Thomas Taylor. *The Chinese and Their Rebellions.* London: Smith, Elder & Co., 1856.

Morrison, Eliza. *Memoirs of the Life and Labours of Robert Morrison, D.D.*, vol. 2. London: Longman, Orme, Brown, Green, & Longmans, 1839.

Nevius, John Livingston. *Methods of Mission Work.* New York: Foreign Mission Library, 1895. http://www.newchurches.com/mediafiles/MethodsofMission-Nevius.pdf.

Orr, J. Edwin. *The Outpouring of the Spirit in Revival and Awakening and Its Issue in Church Growth.* Pontypridd, UK: British Church Growth Association, 2000. http://www.churchmodel.org.uk/Orr%20HS%20BOOKLET%20A4.pdf.

Overseas Missionary Fellowship. "Bishop Frank Houghton: A Tribute." *O.M.F. Bulletin*, July 1972.

Pierson, A. T. "The Welsh Revival and God's Signals." *The Missionary Review of the World* (March 1905): 163–68.

Report of the Missionary Conference Held in Shanghai, May 1890. Shanghai: Printed at the *North China Herald* office, 1890.

Seagrave, Gordon S. *Waste-Basket Surgery.* Philadelphia: Judson Press, 1930.

Taylor, Howard. *Behind the Ranges: Biography of J. O. Fraser of Lisuland.* Chicago: Moody Press, 1964.

[Taylor, Mrs. Howard?]. "Conversations with Cooke," Los Angeles, 1938. Microfilm from Billy Graham Archives, Wheaton, IL.

Taylor, J. Hudson. *After Thirty Years: Three Decades of the China Inland Mission.* London: Morgan & Scott, 1895.

Tegenfeldt, Herman G. *A Century of Growth: The Kachin Baptist Church of Burma.* Pasadena: William Carey Library, 1974.

Tiedemann, R. G. "Bethel Mission." Ricci Roundtable, http://ricci.rt.usfca.edu/institution/view.aspx?institutionID=195.

Williams, Samuel Wells. *The Middle Kingdom*, vol. 2. New York: Charles Scribner's Sons, 1914. First published 1882.

Windsor, W. G. *Through Fire: The Story of 1938.* London: China Inland Mission, 1939.

Wing-hung, Lam. *Chinese Theology in Construction.* Pasadena: William Carey Library, 1983.

Winter, Ralph, and Steven Hawthorne. *Perspectives on the World Christian Movement: A Reader*, rev. ed. Pasadena: William Carey Library, 1992.

People Index

A
A Kau (Akha) people, 109
Adam, James R., 43, 45, 51–53, 55, 58–59, 64–69, 123, 144, 148–49
Adams, Joseph, 32, 36
Allen, W. A., 137
Anderson, Rufus, 22
Atsi Kachin people, 108, 110, 129

B
Ba Thaw, 80, 108
Barth, Dr., 3
Bishop Ryle, 61, 75
Bolton, Mr., 50, 52
Brainerd, David, 78
Broomhall, Dr. A. J., 2, 11, 41, 69, 117, 132, 134, 145
Broumton, James, 36–40, 42
Buker, Ray, 86–87
Burman people, 30, 57
Burns, W. C., 40

C
Caleb, 40
Carey, William, 13, 27
Casto, J. Harold, 108
Chenery, Charles, 52
Chiang Kai-shek, 73–74
Chiarung people, 108
Chung-chia people, 44, 50, 64, 108
Chung-ngan-kiang people, 51
Ci Xi, 71
Clarke, Samuel R., 43, 45–46, 48–50, 55, 68
Clemens, Samuel, 61
Colquhoun, Archibald R., 6
Cooke, Allyn, 79–80, 87, 89, 104, 108–09, 127, 145, 148
Cooke, Leila, 79–80, 87–89, 104, 127, 145, 148
Cooper, T. T., 40
Crossman, Eileen, 71, 77
Cushing, Josiah, 34–35

D

Dai-Chia people, 128–29
D'Aubigné, Merle, 6
David, 6, 108
Douthwaite, Arthur, 20
Dowager Empress, 46, 53, 71
Dyer, Helen, 63
Dymond, Roxie, 66, 77

E

Embery, Miss, 106

F

Fan, Mr., 37, 39
Fishbourne, Edmund Gardiner, 4
Fitzwilliams, Francis "Fitz", 110, 129
Fitzwilliams, Jenny, 110
Fleming, W. S., 50–52
Fraser, J. O., 71, 76–80, 83–84, 86–89, 91–92, 100–04, 106, 108, 110, 116, 128, 133, 145–46, 148–49
Freiday, Jacob A., 35
Fullerton, Mr., 85

G

Garo people, 63
Gibb, George Watt, 109–12, 114–15, 117, 119
Gih, Andrew, 105
Goforth, Jonathan, 63
Goliath, 6
Grist, W. A., 56, 66
Gutzlaff, Charles, 2–5, 10–11

H

Han people, 5, 28
Harverson, Sally, 76, 112
Harverson, Dr. Stuart, 76, 112
Harvey, Mrs., 32, 35
Harvey, Dr. Thomas, 32–33, 35
Heimbach, Ernie, 134, 140
Heimback, Mertis "Mertie", 134, 140
Hong Siu-chuan, 4–5
Hoste, D. E., 76–77, 95, 100–03, 109–11
Houghton, Bishop Frank, 117–19, 121–23, 125–26, 130, 132, 135–36, 138, 148, 150
Howard, Theodore, 97
Howell, Dean, 62
Hughes, Jennie, 106
Huntley, Dr. David, 147
Huxley, T. H., 61

J

Jones, John, 23
Joshua, 40
Judd, Charles, 36–37

K

Kachin people, 29, 32–37, 91, 108, 110, 129–31
Karen people, 30, 32, 34–37, 80
Kincaid, Eugenio, 32
King George, 60
King Mindon, 29
King William IV, 60
Kuhn, Isobel, 83, 88–89, 145, 148
Kuhn, John, 90, 103, 116, 128–32, 145, 148
Kuo Min-tang, 73–74

L

Lahu people, 63, 86–87, 108, 128, 130, 145, 149
        Na (Black), 108
Lakka people, 64, 68, 108, 146
Lao people, 44
Latourette, Kenneth Scott, 76
Lisu people, 64, 68, 71, 77–80, 83–84, 88–91, 102, 104–05, 107–08, 112, 115–16, 127–30, 132, 138, 144–45, 149, 151–52
Livingstone, David, 27
Lockhart, Dr. William, 7–8
London, Jack, 61
Lyall, Leslie T., 87, 99, 122–23
Lyon, Albert J., 35

M

Manchu people, 5–7, 28, 37, 53–54, 71–72
Mao Zedong, 74
Margary, Augustus, 31, 33–34
McCarthy, John, 39–40
Meadows, James, 23
Meadows, Thomas, 11
Medhurst, Walter, 2, 8
Mesny, General William, 37
Metcalf, George Edgar, 77, 108
Miao people, 5, 37, 42–60, 64–69, 77, 82, 103, 107–08, 115–16, 123, 130, 138–39, 144–45, 149, 151–52
        Black (Heh), 45–46, 48, 50, 52, 58, 108, 125, 132, 134, 140
        Flowery (Hua), 45, 52–53, 58, 64, 108
        Water (Shui), 58
Min-chia people, 80–81, 131, 146
Mingyee people, 29–30
Mizo people, 63

Moody, D. L., 61
Morrison, Robert, 11, 13, 27, 78, 149
Mueller, George, 61

N
Nee To-sheng, 99, 105
Nevius, John Livingston, 21–22, 92
Nicholls, Arthur, 67–68
Norgate, Eric, 140
Nosu (Lolo) people, 44, 59, 68, 107, 114, 130, 132, 134, 138, 144–45, 149

O
Orr, J. Edwin, 62

P
P'an Sheo-shan, 45–46, 51–52
P'an Sï-yin, 51, 54
Pierson, A. T., 61
Pollard, Samuel, 42–43, 56–57, 64–69, 144, 148–49

Q
Queen Victoria, 60–61

R
Radcliffe, Reginald, 40
Rockefeller, John, 75
Rose, A. Taylor, 29–30, 32
Russell, Bertrand, 61

S
Saint Anthony, 79
Shan people, 32, 35, 37, 44, 86, 130–32, 147, 140
Shaw, Bernard, 61
Shi Meiyu (Mary Stone), 106
Siamese people, 44
Simpkin, W. T., 135, 138
Sister Welzel, 106
Smith, Daniel, 145
Soltau, Henry, 29, 32–33, 35–36, 40, 147
Spurgeon, Charles, 61, 75
Stevenson, John, 29, 31–36, 40, 147
Sun Yat-sen, 72–74
Sung, John, 105

T
Tai Ya people, 108, 128
Taylor, Gertrude (Mrs. Howard), 71, 77, 79, 84
Taylor, Gracie, 9

Taylor, J. Hudson, 4–5, 8–11, 13–25, 27–29, 40–41, 43, 76, 92, 97–98, 111, 126, 150, 156
Taylor, Maria, 9
Tegenfeldt, Herman G., 32
Thorne, Samuel Thomas, 41
Ting Li-mei, 80
Tongchia people, 108

V
Vanstone, Thomas Grills, 41
Venn, Henry, 22
von Bismarck, Otto, 55

W
Wa people, 108
Wang, Leland, 96, 105
Wang, Wilson, 96, 105
Wang Ming-dao, 105
Wang Ming-tao, 96
Warren, Mr., 23, 82
Waters, B. Curtis, 59
Webb, F. B., 46–50, 52
Webb, Mrs., 46–49, 52
Wells, H. G., 61
Wesley, John, 14
Winter, Ralph D., 15

Y
Young, Vincent, 109
Yuan Shih-kai, 72

www.ingramcontent.com/pod-product-compliance
Ingram Content Group UK Ltd.
Pitfield, Milton Keynes, MK11 3LW, UK
UKHW022237230426
12048UKWH00018BA/1308